# Behavioural and Supervisory Studies

FOR HOTEL AND CATERING OPERATIONS

*The books are dedicated to Linda and Katy*
*whose tolerance, encouragement and support*
*made the writing of them possible.*

# Behavioural and Supervisory Studies

FOR HOTEL AND CATERING OPERATIONS

**Ken Gale** B.A.(Hons). Cert. Ed.
Lecturer, Plymouth College of
Further Education

STANLEY THORNES (PUBLISHERS) LTD

First published in 1985 by Gale Odgers Publications Ltd
Reprinted 1989

Reprinted in 1990 by:
Stanley Thornes (Publishers) Ltd
Old Station Drive Leckhampton
CHELTENHAM GL53 0DN
England


British Library Cataloguing in Publication Data

Gale, Ken
    Behavioural and supervisory studies for hotel and
    catering operations.
    1.  Food service management — Great Britain
    2.  Hotel management — Great Britain
    I.  Title
    647'.94'068      TX911.3.M27

    ISBN 0 7487 0314 4

Typeset by PICA, Bromley, Kent
Printed and bound in Great Britain by
Courier International, Tiptree, Essex.

# PREFACE

Any study of hotel and catering operations, incorporating both theoretical and practical approaches must, inevitably, take into consideration the human aspects of those operations. The strictly commercial approach to the running of hotel and catering operations will, therefore, need to be blended with an approach that not only pays attention to the needs of customers to the industry but also to the staff working at all levels within it.

Although the emphasis in these study books is toward the supervisory and managerial approach, they are intended to provide students at all levels with an understanding of all that is involved in dealing with the human side of hotel and catering operations. The specific range that the study books are intended to cover may be outlined in the following way.

The material in the books is structured in such a way that they may be relevant and useful for students at BTEC Certificate level, BTEC Diploma level and taking the bridging span of Higher BTEC Diplomas. Considerable attention has been paid, in writing the books, to the structure and content of the new BTEC programmes being introduced in 1985. The books have additional relevance to students taking the HCIMA examinations parts A and B and, in particular, the supervisory studies element which constitutes a part of the recently restructured syllabus for part A.

The study books not only provide students with a relevant and comprehensive set of texts but also with a wide range of learning aids. These take the form of student activites, assessment questions and suggestions for further reading and research. These approaches are intended to assist teachers and students alike. In this context the study books are also designed to be used by students on Open Tech or formal 'top-up' learning schemes and those taking more traditional correspondence type courses. At all stages the study books are structured with the learning objectives of the various units in mind.

Finally the author would like to thank Pete and Jo, Dave and Pam, Dennis, Clive, Dave Farmer, Kim and Jerome for their advice, help and time in assisting with the writing of these books.

KJG

# CONTENTS

**STUDY BOOK ONE**                                                      page
**Introduction** _____1

**Individual  Differences**_____3
Personality, Physique, Intelligence, Formation of Attitudes,
Individual Perception.

**Interpersonal Behaviour**_____16
The Influence of the Environment, Communication in the
Catering Workplace.

**Group Behaviour**_____31
Types of Group, Group Influences.

**Social  Skills**_____42
The Nature of Social Skills, Social Skills and Communication.

**Situational  Skills**_____55
Staff Relations, Customer Relations.

**Conclusion** _____66


**STUDY BOOK TWO**                                                      page
**Introduction** _____70

**Business  Organisations**_____71
The Business, The Supervisor, The Organisation, The
Supervisor and The Staff.

**Work  Supervision**_____87
Planning the Work, Maintenance of Standards.

**People  Supervision**_____103
Behavioural Analysis, A Situational Analysis.

**Performance  Supervision**_____120
Manpower Planning, Levels of Performance

**Conclusion** _____135

**STUDY BOOK THREE**

**Staffing and Staff Development**_____ 139
   Staffing Needs, Organisational and Individual Evaluation.

**Techniques of Supervision**_____ 167
   The Controlling Function, The Supervisor and The Law,
   Interview Techniques.

**Formal Staff Relations**_____ 192
   Policies and Procedures, Representation, Consultation and
   Negotiation

**Conclusion**_____ 208

   **Index** _____

# Behavioural Studies

STUDY BOOK ONE

# INTRODUCTION

Any study of human behaviour will be taken from a number of different perspectives, this approach will not only demonstrate the wide range of differences that exist but also enable us to provide a means of understanding them. This study guide will therefore consider human behaviour in this way, paying particular attention to its significance for the hotel and catering industry.

The first analysis of human behaviour will be in terms of the individual and the various factors which contribute to creating differences between individuals. We will also consider the way in which these differences come about and the effects that they might have on the catering work environment.

This analysis will naturally lead us to consider human behaviour on an inter-personal basis, examining the way in which individuals behave toward one another and the relationships that they enter into. An understanding of inter-personal behaviour in the catering work-place will enable us to consider in detail the way in which communication takes place and examine the factors which affect its successful operation.

Man has been described as a 'social animal' and therefore any analysis of human behaviour would not be complete without a consideration of the relationship between individuals and various forms of social groups that they enter into. In addition we will consider the factors that influence the formation of groups and the kind of human interaction that takes place within them. Most work situations will involve the successful operation of at least one group and usually entails the co-operation of a number of interdependent working groups. This is particularly the case within the catering industry where a great deal of emphasis is placed upon group liaison and teamwork.

Contact with customers provides us with the next area of analysis. It is in this area that the social skills of the individual worker make an important contribution to the success of any catering operation. Careful attention will be paid to the social skills that individuals within the hotel and catering industry employ, because these will pay an important contributory role in developing a friendly and efficient customer service. In this respect we will also examine the various environmental factors which may be of relevance to the development of successful staff-customer relations.

Finally we will assess the role of social skills as they are applied to a variety of situations that may be found in the hotel and catering industry. We will find that in order to apply social skills in a relevant and appropriate manner a careful consideration of a range of situations must first of all be carried out. This represents the final stage in a process which should rationalise and operationalise human behaviour in a range of hotel and catering work situations.

It is hoped that if the various observations that have been made in outlining this process are heeded and the various guidelines that have been suggested are adhered to, then it is likely that a higher degree of efficiency in the catering workplace may be achieved. We will have successfully gained an understanding of the process and features leading to individual differences, we will have become aware of the various factors which influence individual and group behaviour and we will be able to appreciate the importance of social skills as it aids in developing human behaviour appropriate to situations in the hotel and catering industry. By this means we will have obtained a necessary introduction into the field of supervisory studies and manpower management in general.

# Individual Differences

In this section we will consider the various factors which influence the behaviour of individuals; these will be compared and contrasted and the way in which they are distributed will be examined. All individuals are different and the following factors all contribute toward making each individual unique: personality, physique, intelligence, attitudes, motivation and perception.

Each of these will be considered in turn and an assessment of their relative importance carried out.

## A. PERSONALITY

Personality is of fundamental importance in drawing in our analysis of individual differences, in many respects it is seen as providing the key to the person. For example, we sometimes say that a person has a 'strong' personality.

### Student Activity   No. 1
Make a list of different ways of describing someone's personality and discuss the descriptions in your list with others in your group.

There are two basic questions that need to be answered when considering personality: first of all we need to know the origins of personality and secondly, we need to know how to recognise personality.

### The Origins of Personality
It is widely accepted that personality derives from two basic sources; these are *heredity* and *environment*. Considerable debate surrounds how these are balanced in an individual and which is most important in contributing to an individual's personality.

The hereditary factors which influence the personality of an individual derive from the background of that individual. In other words, aspects of an individual's personality can be identified in their parents or their grandparents in a similar way, for example, as certain physical attributes, such as the shape of the nose or the colour of the eyes. It is argued that if we can trace heredity through similar physical characteristics then the same procedure should be possible via mental characteristics.

The environmental factors which influence the personality of an individual are those which surround the individual from the moment of birth. The influence of the environment can be wide ranging; it may be

3

of general significance, such as the political nature of the country in which that individual lives, or it may be of particular significance in terms of the people he meets, the surroundings he lives in or the schools he attends.

We will not engage in the argument surrounding heredity and environment, but will suggest at this stage that personality comprises a number of inherited features that are moulded by personal experiences in the variety of social environments in which an individual finds himself.

### The Recognition of Personality

Behaviour of a certain kind should enable us to recognise personality; if an individual behaves in a certain way then we should be able to say that he is a certain type of personality. The most straightforward approach to an understanding of personality is in terms of what we may call *personality traits.* A personality trait is a recognisable behaviour pattern which indicates elements, or possibly the whole, of an individual's personality. We may also say that any given personality will be recognisable in terms of certain personality traits. Thus we may talk of an individual as having a certain type of personality, for example, *extroversion,* and we will be able to recognise this personality because of certain characteristics or personality traits which it embodies, eg. exaggerated expressions and movements, confidence, gregariousness, aggressive language, wearing of bright clothing etc. In addition, our understanding of this particular type of personality will be further enhanced if we make a comparative analysis, and look at the characteristics or personality traits that make up the personality of *introversion.* These characteristics may include shyness, withdrawal from human contact, nervousness, quiet speech, wearing of non-descript clothes etc.

We may carry out the same process of recognition with other personality types; the individual who has a 'tough' personality or who is perhaps emotionally unstable. In each case we will observe the recognisable characteristics or personality traits and from this assess the existence of a certain personality type.

### Student Activity   No. 2

Make a list of personality traits that may be recognisable in the following personalities.
- (i)   Emotionally stable.
- (ii)  Emotionally unstable.
- (iii) Tough.
- (iv)  Tender.

We will see from the preceding section that personality is a difficult concept to describe and sometimes to clearly recognise. However, the importance of this task cannot be over-emphasised for Behavioural Studies because personality is arguably the most important factor to be considered in attempting to understand the make-up of the individual. Personality is the key to understanding the individual, the person, and will be dealt with further in Section B.

## B. PHYSIQUE

Physical differences between individuals represent perhaps the most obvious and visible means of distinguishing between them. We do not have to know anything about two individuals to recognise the physical differences that exist between them. In contrast, we could only make judgements about personality differences after spending some time with individuals, talking to them and observing their reactions in different situations. We are, however, immediately aware of certain physical differences between people as soon as we meet them. We observe differences in terms of stature, in terms of hair, eye and skin colour; we notice whether they are thin or thick-set and so on. We have to ask, therefore, do these differences in physique bear any relevance to behavioural differences between individuals?

Many studies have been carried out to attempt to ascertain the connections between a person's physique and his patterns of behaviour. Considerable debate continues to surround many of the findings of these studies.

A famous study carried out by an Italian criminologist, Cesare Lombroso, in the 19th century produced results which Lombroso claimed showed a correlation between certain physical characteristics in individuals and forms of criminal behaviour. He concluded that criminals differ from non-criminals in terms of a number of physical characteristics or abnormalities. For example, he noted that criminals possessed excessive arm length in relation to the rest of their build, their ears were much larger, they possessed bushy eyebrows and were much more likely to have unusual eyes, noses etc.

Many criticisms were directed at Lombroso's research and his findings; for our purposes it is sufficient to know that some scientists have argued that a correlation between physical characteristics and forms of human behaviour does exist. The significance of this is small when we consider the range of other factors that contribute to the behavioural differences between individuals.

### Student Activity No. 3.
Look at a range of jobs within the hotel and catering industry which may be more easily carried out by individuals with certain physical characteristics.

### C. INTELLIGENCE
Intelligence is significant to our investigation of individual differences because it is often used as a basis for classifying individuals into different groups or categories. We see this in schools where intelli-

gence tests may be used to place children into different 'bands' or 'streams' for example. Intelligence, like personality, seems to derive partly from heredity and partly from the environment in which the individual grows and develops. Intelligence is a complex combination of a number of important elements. The intellectual capacity of an individual may be represented in a diagrammatic form. See figure 1.

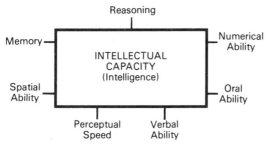

Fig. 1. *Intellectual Capacity*

The balance and composition of these elements will vary from individual to individual; this is demonstrated in such everyday statements as 'she sees things quickly' (perceptual speed) or 'he has a good memory'. We will define each of these elements in turn.

**Reasoning**
Reasoning is the intellectual ability to reach conclusions after having systematically argued or thought through a number of stages, building upon relevant information and eliminating irrelevant information. This power of reasoning may sometimes be described as a 'logical approach'.

**Perceptual Speed**
Perception may be defined as the ability to 'see' things; seeing in this case refers to the use of all our senses, sight, hearing, taste, touch and smell, in helping us to understand the world in which we live. Perceptual speed literally means therefore the speed with which we perceive and understand events and occurrences in the world around us. The quick reactions that perceptual speed may produce can therefore be beneficial in catering operations.

**Memory**
The intellectual ability to recall events, ideas, facts, theories, faces and information is what we call memory. Clearly, a person with a 'good' memory will be able to recall quickly and completely, whereas a person with a 'bad' memory will be one who cannot do this. Memory, as is the case with all elements of intellectual capacity, has its limits and it is therefore common practice to use what we call an aide memoire eg. a chef referring to a cookery book for a recipe, or an assistant manager

looking at health and safety regulations for reference.

Having recognised therefore that it is not possible to memorise all facts and information which may be relevant to us, we must be aware that the value of our memory is that it can be used to recall important and relevant material stored in it for use in certain circumstances.

## Spatial Ability

We may define this element of intelligence as being the means by which an individual is able to visualise the use of space. At first this may not appear to be of great relevance to those involved in catering operations but closer examination will reveal its importance. Graphic designers and architects have the ability to place objects in a functional relationship to one another at the same time as making these objects appear pleasing from a visual point of view. In catering therefore we may see many areas where the application of spatial ability may be of great value. The design of a kitchen area for example, will require that the person carrying out the design will make functional considerations to ensure smooth-running and efficiency but will also require an assessment of the merits of appearance and style in putting together his final design.

Spatial ability is the ability which may be applied to a wide range of activities, from the apparently simple exercise of laying up tables in a functional but attractive manner to the most subtle and difficult task of compiling an advertising brochure.

## Oral-Verbal Ability

We may deal with these two elements of intelligence together although they may be separately defined, as follows. Verbal ability refers to the use of those skills relating to words, and oral ability refers more specifically to the use of the words in a spoken form.

Language is the basis of communication and our use of words, either in a written or spoken form, demonstrates our ability to communicate information, knowledge and skills to others in an effective manner. In an industry whose central concern is to create customer satisfaction the intelligent use of words may be the determining factor in achieving this end. In addition to creating successful customer relations, the careful use of oral and verbal ability may also engender good industrial relations between all levels of staff found within catering operations.

## Numerical Ability

This simply refers to the ability an individual does or does not possess in relation to the use of numbers. Many aids to successful numeracy now exist, such as calculators, adding machines etc, but numerical ability is an attribute of intelligence that cannot be undervalued. It refers not only to the specialised skills of the hotel accountant dealing with the annual budget of a large hotel but also to the quickness and efficiency with which a waitress deals with a customer's bill or a barman calculates the cost of a large round of differently costed drinks.

## Student Activity   No. 4

As a homework or private study exercise write 100 words on each element of intellectual capacity showing its value in relation to a specific individual or task within a hotel and catering operation.

## Intelligence Quotient

Various attempts have been made to measure intelligence which would enable those carrying out the measurement to distinguish between individuals with different intelligence. Intelligence Quotient or IQ refers, in simple terms, to the 'amount' of intelligence that any one individual may possess. The idea of intelligence quotient is, however, more complex than this simple description would suggest and considerable debate centres around the balance between the hereditary and environmental factors which influence it. It has been argued that intelligence, as it is inherited from parents, is less important than the social and economic factors in the environment which influence it.

Intelligence Quotient is seen therefore as being a representation (however accurate or inaccurate) of an individual's mental development. It is calculated in the following way:

Intelligence Quotient (IQ) = mental age ÷ chronological age × 100

The IQ test, based upon a series of questions designed to measure spatial, oral, verbal, numerical, reasoning, perceptual and memory skills, provides an indication of mental age. So we may take the example of a ten year old child sitting the old '11 +' examination, a form of IQ test, whose mental age as revealed by the test is twelve years. Using the above equation his IQ may be calculated in the following way:

$$IQ = 12 \div 10 \times 100 = 120$$

The child in this example can be described as 'above average' because it can be assumed that an average child's IQ would be 100, where the mental and chronological ages would be the same.

## Student Activity   No. 5

Go to the library and find a copy of 'Know Your Own IQ' by H Eysenck and complete a number of timed tests in the back of the book which are intended to demonstrate your IQ scores.

## THE FORMATION OF ATTITUDES

If an individual possesses for example, a particular 'attitude' toward life, this enables us to make a judgement about that individual. Different individuals express different attitudes and this enables us to distinguish between them. Attitudes are therefore very important here in enabling us to deal with all the factors that contribute to the differencs between individuals.

There is no evidence to show that individuals are actually born possessing certain attitudes, therefore we have to look at the environment in which the individual grows up and lives to understand what causes a certain type of attitude to be formed. There are therefore a number of important milestones in the life of an individual which go to affect his attitudes. We will briefly consider each of these in turn.

### The Family
An individual's life within the family normally spans the most formative years of his life. It is for this reason that many argue that the family is the most important agency influencing the formation of attitudes. To this extent it is often the case that a young person's attitudes, or outlook on life closely resembles those of his parents for a certain period of his life.

### The School
It is within the school environment that a child may begin to form attitudes other than those which originated in his family life. Not only is the school designed to bring about formal learning about specific subjects such as geography or domestic science, but also to encourage informal learning and the formation of certain attitudes. So in both the family and the school the young person will be learning from others; parents, brothers and sisters, teachers and so on about religion, politics, morality etc, all of which contribute to the formation of his attitudes.

### The Peer Group
The peer group influence often forms attitudes in a young person which may conflict with those already formed in the home and the school. The peer group is the group of similarly aged young people the individual enters and may represent an environment in which freedom of expression and a degree of independence may first of all be exercised. The peer group may influence a 'rebellious' or 'non-conformist' attitude in the young person and may be represented in dress and behaviour patterns, as well as simply speech patterns.

### The Work Environment
Entry into the work environment imposes a completely new set of restraints upon the individual, all of which influence his behaviour and the attitudes he expresses. For the first time perhaps, he may be in contact with large numbers of peopls who are older than himself, who have a wider range of experience of the specific job at hand and of life in general than he does and who in turn exert a considerable influence upon his attitudes.

## The Mass Media

We may list a variety of other environmental influences which can affect the formation of an individual's attitudes. Membership of a church, attendance at a youth club, going to evening classes, travelling abroad, are all examples of situations which may influence attitude formation. We will finally consider the influence of the mass media, as this is considered by many to be an important influence on attitudes throughout life, affecting our outlook on politics, religion, morality etc.

The major mass media are televison, radio and the newspapers and when we consider how much of our life is spent watching television, listening to the radio and reading newspapers, we can see how potentially influential these may be. There are many ways the mass media may influence our attitudes, we may classify these as follows:

(i)  Propaganda may be used, where the controllers of the media deliberately try to influence people to think in a certain way, irrespective of the truth or falsity of the message that they are attempting to convey.

(ii)  A more common approach used in the media today is what is known as stimulus-response; in other words the media provide a stimulus, perhaps in the form of an advertisement, a fund appeal or a party political broadcast and hope that the public will respond in a certain way, by buying the advertised product, sending a donation to the appeal, or voting for the particular political party.

(iii)  Perhaps the most common way in which our attitudes may be influenced by the mass media is by the most indirect means of all. In any society there will be commonly agreed values, beliefs and attitudes such as: 'It is wrong to kill', 'It is right to help elderly people', 'Democracy is good', 'Oppression is bad', and so on. These attitudes are to be found, though not necessarily openly stated, in much of the media in society. To this extent our popular media figures often represent the good or acceptable outlook on life — 'folk heroes', and conversely, unpopular media figures often represent the bad or unacceptable outlook on life — 'folk devils'. From this representation the popular, or what has been called, the consensual image of society develops.

## Student Activity   No. 6

(i)  Make a list of your attitudes towards the following:
   (a) Strikes.
   (b) Race relations.
   (c) The age of consent.
   (d) The existence of God.
   (e) Euthanasia.

(ii)  Then beside each of your statements indicate which of the influencing agencies were most important in forming your attitude (ie. family, school, peer group, work, the mass media, or others).

10

(iii) In a discussion compare your results with other class mates or friends.

## INDIVIDUAL MOTIVATION

In the last section we considered the environmental influence upon the formation of attitudes. We may extend this analysis further and examine what factors influence an individual's attitude toward work and what motivates different individuals to behave in different ways in the work situation. Motivation is closely related to an individual's attitude toward work and if this attitude toward work is negative and somewhat uncaring then we say that the level of motivation of that individual to work is low.

### Motivation and Needs

It is generally accepted that an individual is motivated to fulfill certain needs. Therefore, if we can analyse human needs then we should be able to understand the factors that motivate human behaviour, ie: those that cause human action.

Needs can normally be classified into two categories, ie: primary needs and secondary needs. *Primary needs* are those needs that are innate and physiological. In other words they are needs which the individual is born with and which are to do with his physical or bodily functioning. We may therefore include in this category the need for air, food, drink, sleep, procreation and bodily elimination. Without the satisfaction of these primary needs, man in any society would not be able to survive. The environment the individual lives in will affect the satisfaction of primary needs, but the needs themselves will not change whatever the environment might be.

*Secondary needs* are less easy to classify because these are affected by the environment in which the individual lives. Secondary needs therefore are needs which are acquired by the individual as he or she develops through life. They may be social and psychological and will be, in whatever form, necessary for the well-being of the individual and the society in which he lives. The social needs an individual may possess might be for love and affection from others, companionship and a recognised position. Psychological needs might include the need for self expression, self respect and confidence. Only careful analysis of the psychological character of the individual and the sociology of the society he lives in, will tell us what his needs might be.

### Motivation to Work

This will be affected by needs and environment. If an individual has a pressing primary need, let us say the need for food, then he will be highly motivated to work to fulfill this need. Similarly, if the environment or social situation in which an individual lives presses upon him a secondary need, let us say for self-expression, then he will be moti-

11

vated to fulfill this need. Therefore, from the point of view of super-visors and managers, it is important to be able to recognise what it is that motivates individuals to work. It is also important that they should be able to recognise that different individuals have different needs and therefore require motivating in different ways. We may demonstrate this by providing two contrasting examples.

In the first case we may describe an individual who has a large family, low pay, high rent and a number of debts or financial commit-ments. He will have an instrumental attitude toward work, in that work will be a means for him to satisfy a particular end, or set of needs. This individual will therefore be motivated by high wages, bonuses, offers of overtime etc.

In the second case, we may describe an individual who has a relatively comfortable social and domestic environment and has satisfied his own and his family's primary needs. Money, in the form of increased wages or bonuses, may not motivate him, so the manager or supervisor might attempt to recognise and satisfy certain secondary needs, eg. giving responsibility in the work place may satisfy the need for self respect or self importance.

Each case may have to be considered on its own merits but the following represent some of the ways in which the individual may be motivated to work:

   (i)   Wages, pay increments, promotional scale.
  (ii)   Working conditions (inc: accommodation).
 (iii)   Demands of the job (eg: shifts, time restraints).
 (iv)   Fringe benefits.
  (v)   Management — worker relations.
 (vi)   Staff relationships (inc. social facilities).
(vii)   Respect for higher level technical skills.
(viii)   Effective communication links, with other levels of the firm.
 (ix)   Job security.
  (x)   Identification with objectives of the firm.


## Student Activity No. 7

Briefly describe the way in which the needs *and* environment of the following list of individuals may affect their motivation to work.

   (i)   An unemployed mine-worker.
  (ii)   A trainee catering manageress.
 (iii)   A Moslem kitchen porter.
 (iv)   A part-time banqueting waiter.
  (v)   A famous, well established artist.
 (vi)   A factory-worker who has just won the pools.

**Student Activity   No. 8**

As a homework or private research exercise look up the following: A.H. Maslow, F. Herzberg, D. McGregor, F.W. Taylor. Briefly describe the contribution of each to an understandiong of the relationship between needs and motivation. (See Activity 21).

## INDIVIDUAL PERCEPTION

We have already seen that perceptual speed is an important component of the intellectual capacity of an individual. It describes how quickly an individual can 'see' through and understand a particular problem or issue. On this level, therefore, perception is an element of our intellectual capacity. Perception in the broader sense, however, needs to embrace the intellectual element and the sensory element. It is in this context that another aspect of individual differences may be developed and explained.

Sensory perception describes the ability of an individual to perceive by means of his senses of sight, sound, taste, touch and smell. The loss of any sense will therefore impede his overall ability to perceive and can be compared to the effect of closing a door and thus restricting entry. Sensory perception is the means by which a range of stimuli, audio, visual etc are experienced by the individual and which are then acted upon by the individual within a given time, dependant upon his perceptual speed.

If we assume that all individuals are capable of sensory perception then the differences between them will relate to the speed with which they achieve understanding and are able to act. This will have different effects in the work situation. We will briefly consider some of these.

The quick reactions that may result from being able to perceive things quickly may prove beneficial to hotel and catering operations in terms of labour, time, money and ingredients. However, the ability of an individual to perceive things on a broad scale may also prove to be beneficial in the above terms. A simple example will illustrate this point. A fire in a hotel kitchen can cause considerable damage to equipment and possible injury to staff and customers. The quick reactions of an individual in detecting the source of the fire, implementing the fire extinguisher to reduce the extent of the fire and of informing the fire prevention services would all be applauded. However, these quick reactions would be to no avail had the telephone, the fire extinguisher and fire alarm not been placed in a position allowing the individual to react as he did. This deployment of fire prevention measures may well have resulted from the perceptive skills of a designer, supervisor or fire prevention officer who was able to see, in advance, the possible dangers of fire and to anticipate the best way of coping with it should it occur. Here perception works in advance of a situation, anticipating its possible effects and making provision for them.

Perception of this kind can be reflected in increased knowledge and experience. As our understanding is based upon perception, our ability to perceive the world increases and so does our understanding of it. The successful preparation of a Hollandaise sauce, for example, illustrates this point. Knowledge of the fact that the sauce will curdle if the butter is added too quickly is obviously important in ensuring that the sauce is produced correctly. However, should the sauce begin to curdle, the experienced chef will perceive this occurring and quickly react to prevent this, by adding the curdled sauce to a teaspoon of boiling water in a clean saucepan and whisking it in.

In both of these examples, the effects of differences in perception can be seen; a wide range of understanding and experience will clearly determine the extent of these effects.

### Student Activity No. 9

Give an example of the way in which different individual perceptions might affect the smooth-running of a catering operation.

The analysis of individual differences on the basis of personality, physique, intelligence, attitudes, motivation and perception should now enable us to understand a little more clearly why different individuals behave in different kinds of ways. Our understanding of these behavioural differences between individuals will be dependant upon a consideration and analysis of all the relevant factors and the interrelationship that exists between each. Without this approach our analysis will be incomplete.

## ASSESSMENT QUESTIONS

1. Explain the differences between hereditary and environmental factors as they affect the personality of the individual.
2. Define personality.
3. State the origins of personality.
4. Define the term 'personality trait'.
5. List the factors that contribute to the intellectual capacity of an individual.
6. Describe by means of a diagram the composition of intellectual capacity.
7. Define the term 'Intelligence Quotient'.
8. Describe some of the problems associated with the measurement of intelligence.
9. Explain how IQ is calculated.
10. List the agencies which influence the formation of attitudes.
11. Explain the importance of attitude in the development of the individual.

12. Explain the role of the following in the formation of attitudes.
    (a) The family.
    (b) The school.
    (c) The peer group.
    (d) The work environment.
    (e) The mass media.
13. Describe
    (a) The relationship between needs and motivation.
    (b) The relationship between environment and motivation.
14. Distinguish between primary needs and secondary needs.
15. List the primary needs of an individual.
16. List the secondary needs of an individual.
17. Explain why the relationship between needs, and a motivation to work, may differ.
18. List 10 ways in which the individual may be motivated to work.
19. Explain how differences in individual perception may affect the work situation.
20. List the effects of differences in individual perception as they affect the work situation.
21. Describe the relationship between perception, understanding, knowledge and experience.

# Interpersonal Behaviour

## THE INFLUENCE OF THE ENVIRONMENT

So far we have discussed the factors which contribute to the differences that exist between individuals, this should enable us to understand why different individuals behave in different ways. This understanding should now be applied to the behaviour of individuals as they come into contact with other individuals. In other words we need to examine the factors which influence behaviour between individuals, that is, interpersonal behaviour.

### The Social Environment

We cannot predict with certainty that any individual will behave in a particular kind of way. We have established that individual differences exist and that these differences are recognisable in terms of different forms of behaviour. The environment that individuals live in will determine their behaviour patterns even though they may have inherited some personal characteristics from their parents. We have seen that the environment is influential in forming personality, attitudes, and intelligence for example, now we will examine the way in which a given environment might influence the relationships and personal contacts an individual might have.

A wide range of environmental circumstances will influence interpersonal behaviour. The home, the school, the college, the work place, the social club, are all examples of environmental circumstances which will influence different forms of interpersonal behaviour. For example, a formal relationship might exist between two individuals in the working environment, they might communicate formally either on the telephone, by means of memoranda or by sending messages through the communication system at the workplace. They may for example discuss detailed aspects of work; duty rotas, health and safety provisions or menus, in a very precise and elaborate manner. One of them may be in a position of authority over the other which may determine certain limits to what they might say to one another. However, the same two individuals in a different environment may behave interpersonally in a totally different manner. In the pub after work, for example, they may converse in a more relaxed informal manner, discussing a range of topics unrelated to the work situation.

## Roles

Here we see therefore, the importance of the environment in the way it influences interpersonal behaviour. We need to explain why the environment influences behaviour in this way. Our explanation may be carried on by referring to the roles that individuals play and these roles to a certain extent will be determined by the environment. An example will illustrate this point. In the home environment individuals will behave in relation to one another according to certain patterns which are determined by the roles of husband, wife, father, mother, son, daughter, brother, sister etc. These roles will carry with them expectations ie. the interpersonal behaviour between father and son will be determined, to an extent, by the roles they are expected to play in the home. The father may have a dominant part in the relationship, giving instructions, advising, offering help and guidance; whereas the son may play a respectful part and may expect paternal advice and look up to his father in a certain way.

Both of these individuals in a different environment, and in contact with different people, will behave in a different way. The father who plays a dominant role in the home environment may well play a rather minor or subservient role in his work situation, carrying out instructions and doing tasks which he has been told to do. The son who might play a rather inferior role in relation to this father in the home, may be a dominant and influential figure in the environment of the youth club or the playground when he is in contact with members of his peer group.

Any individual will therefore carry with him a set of roles which will determine interpersonal behaviour in different environments. The following diagram represents a set of roles that an individual may carry with him and act out in different environments.

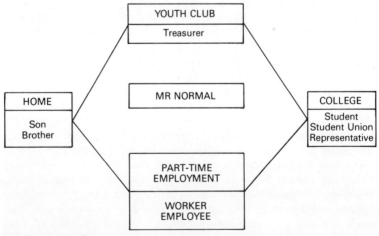

Fig. 2. *A Role Set*

The ability of an individual to carry out a number of different roles and adapt to a number of different environmental influences will be tested throughout life.

An inability to do this can be described as role conflict; where the individual finds difficulty in moving from one role in an environment, to another role in a different environment. For example: a leading member of the church may find it increasingly difficult to be an active member of a political party.

### Student Activity   No. 10

(i)    Draw up a role set for yourself, giving details of the environment and the role/s you play in each.

(ii)   Give an example of role conflict in your own role set or in that of someone you know.

(iii)  Compare the results in (i) and (ii) above with those of your class mates/friends/colleagues.

### The Influence of the Catering Work Environment

We have seen in general terms that the environment influences inter-personal behaviour and the roles that individuals play in those environments. The work environment represents a particularly important element of the individual's life and we will consider the way in which behaviour may be affected by its influence.

There are a wide range of different types of catering operation and within each of these types there are a wide range of different influences upon the behaviour of individuals. For this reason we need to classify the various influences in order to assess the effects they may have.

*The Employer and the Employee*

All individuals as employees of a firm will be placed in a specific situation in relation to their employers. Firstly, their situation will be governed by the restraints of the law of contract, in that both parties, employer and employee will be required to satisfy certain contractual obligations specified by the Contract of Employment Act. This legal framework will provide the basis for the relationship between employer and employee; specifying such details as conditions of employment, length of holiday, form of payment, notice of termination of employment etc.

All employees and employers will be expected to conform to the contractual obligations outlined above, irrespective of the industry that they work in. We will briefly consider the type of employment situation we might find within the catering industry.

The size of the firm and the operational units within it is of major importance here. A large organisation such as a 150 bedroom hotel, or a hospital catering unit, may represent an employment situation whose employers and employees may never meet directly on a face to face basis. If they do have contact it is often via representatives; the employer's representatives being management, the employee's representatives being the trade union. In a small organisation such as, for example, a seaside guest house, the proprietor will exercise managerial functions as well as those of the employer. We will see in a later section the relationships that may develop from such a situation. HCITB surveys show that 31 per cent of the industry's labour force work in operational units employing less than 9 people, so the employment situation most relevant to us here is that which exists in the small-scale operation. The proprietor/manager in a small-scale operation will control, and therefore largely define, the employer/employee relationship. Any discussion of different types of leadership and management styles will demonstrate the wide ranging and different effects of a strict authoritarian approach on the one hand and a more flexible democratic approach on the other. Within the employment situation therefore, the employer's personality, attitude, leadership style and general demeanour may exert a considerable influence upon the employee. In the small-scale operation his influence may be direct, on a daily, face to face basis, during food preparation and service, supervising the cleaning of rooms and the changing of beds and perhaps also during staff meal-times. In a large-scale operation his influence will be indirect and delegated through managerial or supervisory staffs.

**Student Activity   No. 11**
Draw up two lists, one under the heading of 'Direct, Face to Face Employer/Employee Relations', the other under the heading of 'Indirect, Representative Employer/Employee Relations'. Under each heading list what you consider to be the most important behavioural influences on the individuals in the employment situation.

*The Influence of Management and Supervisory Staffs*
We have seen from the previous section that a large-scale organisation's control in the work place is not exerted directly by employers but indirectly through employer representatives. We may classify employer representatives, who themselves are also employees, into the categories of management and supervisory staffs. The specific details of the role of these managerial and supervisory staffs will be dealt with at a later stage but we may describe their role at this stage in the following way. They are appointed by the employer to control the material and human resources within the work situation. The desired effect of their control over the human resources will be to motivate and encourage the work force to be efficient. The degree of skill which they exercise in this function will be recognisable in the attitude and motivation of the employees under their control.

*Organisational Influences*
All catering operations will have a certain form of organisation which will define the relationships that exist between individuals and groups

19

within the organisation. In the previous section we pointed out that a large-scale catering operation such as a 150 bed-room luxury hotel or an industrial or welfare catering operation will require an organisation. Whatever form the organisation takes it will enable communication links to be identified between departments and sections, it will allow a clearly defined chain of command to exist, designating authority relationships, areas of responsibility and ensuring co-ordination between all groups within the organisation. The following is an example of an organisation chart for a small hotel.

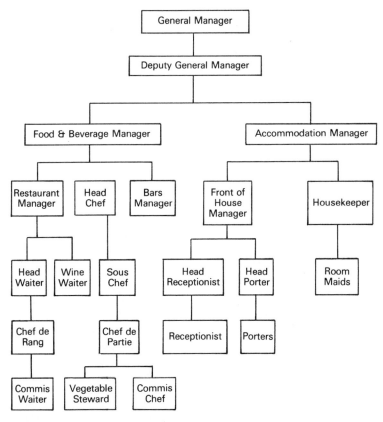

Fig. 3. *Organisation chart for a small hotel*

This type of organisation chart is sometimes referred to as describing *line organisation* which simply means that the organisation of the staff can be traced along the various lines. These not only show the chain of command in the hotel but also the interdepartmental and inter-sectional links. Obviously, this organisation will influence the behaviour of the individual in the work situation.

The organisation will therefore do the following for the individual:

(i)   It will clearly define his role (eg. Head Receptionist, Sous Chef).
(ii)  It will clearly define his relationships with individuals in other departments or sections.
(iii) It will clearly define his position in the chain of command (ie. who are his superiors, and who are his subordinates).

Owners, managers and supervisors use the organisation of any catering operation as a means of control. To this extent the individuals' position and role in the organisation is precisely described and his behaviour is regulated accordingly.

**Student Activity   No. 12**
Using the organisation chart as a reference clearly describe the way in which the behaviour of the following individuals may be influenced by the organisation.

(i)   Sous Chef.
(ii)  Chambermaid.
(iii) Deputy General Manager.
(iv)  Head Waiter.

*Group Influences*
The organisation of any catering operation not only imposes restraints upon individual behaviour but also upon the behaviour of groups that operate within the organisation. Groups such as the kitchen brigade and reception team are all governed by the organisation, but these in turn influence the behaviour of individuals who function within each group. So within each group within the organisation individuals will be placed according to their duties, areas of responsibility etc. The kitchen brigade will be organised in a hierarchy from the Head Chef or Chef de Cuisine through the Sous Chef, the various Chefs de Partie, Commis Chefs and Kitchen Porters. However, for this group to be efficient they will need to operate as a team, particularly in times of intense activity such as at the height of food service. Therefore the group itself imposes special pressures on the individual, sometimes known as *informal social control*. This operates to make the individual feel part of a team, lays down unwritten laws of conduct and places expectations upon the individual which may be quite different from those imposed by the formal organisation.

We will consider the effect of groups on the behaviour of individuals in more detail in Section C.

21

**Student Activity   No. 13**
Informal social control within a group can exert pressure on the individual to behave in certain ways. From your own experience of catering operations, either in college or at work, explain how these might operate in the following groups in certain situations.
  (i)   The Kitchen Brigade during food service.
 (ii)   The Bar Cellar staff after the bar has closed.
(iii)   The Housekeeping team during Saturday changeover in a seaside hotel.

*Task or Job Influence*
So far we have considered the relationships the individual enters into with the employer, management, the organisation and the group and how each of these creates situations which influences the behaviour of individuals. We next need to consider the actual task or job an individual has to do, whether it be the receptionist tabulating a customer's bill or the commis chef preparing vegetables. The situation in which the individual carries out certain tasks will influence his behaviour patterns. It has been argued that some individuals in large-scale organisations work inefficiently and experience discomfort because of what they see as being the routine and monotonous nature of the tasks they have to carry out. Richard Blauner in a study entitled 'Alienation and Freedom' described alienation as being a state of mind which can develop in a person when he feels no sense of purpose in the work that he is doing, when the tasks he is expected to carry out do not allow him any form of creativity or self expression. This can often occur when the individual worker is expected to work in relative isolation from his workmates, perhaps on a production line at a rate of production that may be beyond his control. Alienation may develop further if the demand for his skills in the work place diminishes, his work becomes routine and he sees little point or meaning in what he is doing.
    Alienation is the negative way in which the task or job situation may affect the individual. Conversely the task situation may create a high level of enjoyment in the individual, he may be able to express himself in what he is doing and may gain considerable satisfaction from that which is is creating. This would be the positive effects of the task situation on the individual.

**Student Activity   No. 14.**
Blauner said that Alienation had 4 dimensions. Powerlessness, Meaninglessness, Isolation and Self-Estrangement. With the help of your teacher carry out the following tasks.
  (i)   Try to explain what each of these dimensions of alienation mean *and*
 (ii)   Describe a situation in the hotel and catering industry where a feeling of alienation might develop.

(iii)   Assess whether alienation might affect different individuals in different ways and if so list the factors that might cause these differences to exist.

## The Physical Environment

In the previous sections we have mentioned the importance of the attitude and motivation of the work-force. The attitude and motivation of the work-force will be affected by the supervisor or manager who exercises operational control, the relationships between individuals within the group and the actual job or task that the individual is expected to carry out. In each of these cases individual behaviour will be affected by motivational factors.

Maslow, McGregor and others have given particular attention to these motivational factors ie. those that encourage the worker to 'perform' in the work-place, not only to the benefit of the employer but also to the benefit of the worker himself eg: in obtaining job satisfaction. Herzberg not only considered these motivational factors but also certain *maintenance* or *hygeine* factors ie: those that related to the physical environment of the worker. In this category he included the actual conditions in which the worker is expected to work and dealt with such things as heating, lighting and facilities available, such as staff changing rooms, toilets etc.

Once again we can see that the presence/absence of these physical conditions can affect the behaviour of the individual in the hotel and catering work situation. Therefore careful attention, on the part of employers, managers and supervisors alike, to these conditions will have a bearing on the overall working situation.

## Customer Relations

No analysis of this kind would be meaningful without reference to the situation individuals in the industry are placed in relation to customers. In fact the behaviour of individuals in the work place in all situations dealt with so far is directly or indirectly related to the customer situation. Customer satisfaction is the main prerogative of the catering industry, so the relations that exist between customers and staff at all levels of the industry are of primary importance. Staff treatment of customers is one of the means by which customer satisfaction is achieved, therefore it is often the case that staff may be expected to behave in a certain way simply to satisfy customer demands. For example the impatient customer in the restaurant of a luxury cruise liner who requires rapid service from the steward should receive this, even though the steward may have a number of other customers who themselves require a more prolonged and relaxed form of food service.

We cannot at this stage deal with all aspects of customer satisfaction but it must be realised that it does place special demands upon the workers in the catering industry imposing quite special behavioural demands as the above example illustrates.

**Student Activity   No. 15**

By means of examples illustrate the way in which customer satisfaction imposes special demands on catering staff. Use the following positions as the basis of your example.
- (i)   Hotel Receptionist.
- (ii)  Counter Assistant in a fast food outlet.
- (iii) Cocktail Waiter.
- (iv)  Hotel Management Trainee.

## The Influences of Personality on Staff Interactions

Personality has been described as an important factor which contributes to the existence of differences between individuals. Many different types of personality exist and different individuals display a wide range of personality traits. This leads us to consider the way in which individuals with widely differing personalities behave toward one another. In other words we are considering the influence of personality on staff interactions.

*Personality Types.* One way of carrying out this analysis would be to draw up a list of different types of personality. We may indicate the differences that exist between extroverts and introverts, between tough and tender-minded individuals or between those who are emotionally stable or unstable. A problem does arise here regarding the special character of personality, which is that any personality tends to differ *by degree* from another personality. So for example, an individual may be more or less extroverted than another, or more or less emotionally stable than other.

A further complicating factor is that some individuals only display personality traits for a certain period of time. In certain situations for example, an individual may appear extroverted and in another may appear quite introverted. In certain company an individual may appear emotionally stable and secure and in other company may appear quite unstable and insecure.

It is difficult therefore for us to generalise about the influence of personality upon staff interactions because each set of interactions will be finely tuned to the personalities of the individuals involved and the circumstances in which their interactions are taking place. An example may illustrate this point. The extroverted chef in a large hotel kitchen may dominate interactions between the members of the kitchen brigade. The effects of his personality may be ignored during the relative calm of food preparation but during the frantic activity of food service the effects of his personality might be considerable. The junior trainee on work experience in the kitchen may feel emotionally insecure and nervous in such a situation and become reserved and introverted. In contrast the experienced and mature kitchen porter may be equally extroverted and refuse to be dominated by the chef, in which case, what we sometimes refer to as a clash of personalities may occur.

There are many such examples of the influence of personality on staff interactions; it is important from the managerial and supervisory point of view that these influences do not damage working relationships. Careful analysis of interviewees prior to appointment and continual appraisal of staff relations are two ways which the supervisor can minimise the damaging effects of a personality clash in any work situation. By the same process the good manager or supervisor will be able to recognise certain personality traits in an individual which may encourage him to place this individual in a position of responsibility because his personality is one which fits in well with the personality of others around him.

### Student Activity No. 16
Draw up a list of work situations in which the following personality types would be best suited, bearing in mind not only the different staff involved but also the actual working situation.
 (i)  Emotionally unstable.
 (ii) Extrovert.

## COMMUNICATION IN THE CATERING WORKPLACE

The importance of achieving effective communication in any workplace cannot be over emphasised; without effective communication inefficiency will be an inevitable consequence. We need therefore to examine the process of communication, the different forms of communication that can be most effectively used and the role of communication within the organisation, in terms of different staff interactions that take place within it.

### Communication — A Definition
We say that communication is taking place when an interchange of ideas, information etc occurs between individuals. Effective communication, however, will necessarily entail understanding; without understanding effective communication has not been achieved. It may simply be defined therefore as:
 (i)  Passing on information/ideas to one another.
 (ii) Passing on understanding to one another.
The means we employ to communicate are various, we speak and listen, write and read and use a range of non-verbal expressions to convey our messages eg. pointing, nudging, waving, winking and so on.

When we communicate we *intend* to convey a message to someone and similarly the other participant in this relationship will *intend* to receive a message. Without intention therefore it is unlikely that messages will be conveyed. Therefore communication involves the use of certain skills; we need to employ these skills in order to communi-

25

cate and in a business or industrial situation the kind of skills we might use include: the giving and taking of spoken and written instructions, the production of letters, memoranda and reports and responding to them, passing and receiving information by telephone and a wide range of other skill areas. We next need to explain more clearly what this process of communication entails.

## The Communication Process

We may define the communication process as the stages that exist between the transmission and understanding of information and ideas. This process requires more detailed explanation, and it may therefore be broken down into a number of component parts or stages.

### The Intention of the Sender

Initially there has to exist a 'sender' with a 'message' that he wishes to convey; communication will not begin unless there is a message, in the form of a set of instructions or information of some kind to convey.

### The Language of Communication

Having established an intention to communicate, the 'sender' must next consider the most suitable means of getting the message across to his audience. The 'sender' will therefore need to carefully consider the type of language he is going to use to send the message. He will have to use a form of language that explains his 'message' clearly and which at the same time will be understood by his audience. It is likely, for example, that if the manager of a motorway service station restaurant produced menu cards in culinary French many of his customers could experience difficulty in understanding the language being used and also therefore the contents of the menu. There are many different forms of language suitable for a number of different situations, these may be formal or informal, technical, legal etc and each will be useful in specific contexts.

### The Medium of Communication

When we have formulated the 'message' in the most appropriate type of language, we next have to consider the medium we will use to deliver our message. When we are considering face to face interaction and communication between individuals the medium does not require consideration, but when we have information to pass on to larger numbers we must use the most effective medium or channel of communication. This is particularly important in large scale organisations where large numbers of employees are involved; the medium used might be in the form of a poster, a memorandum, a report or circular, a letter and so on.

### Receiving the Message

This stage in the process of communication changes the initiative from the 'sender' of the 'message' to the receiver of the message. In simple terms the receiver must be in a position to receive. This will involve listening or reading or, more broadly, being aware that a message is being conveyed. Receiving the message is a communication skill that is quite difficult to master; even the most conscientious student will realise how difficult it sometimes is to listen to a lecturer after a very long day in the classroom. This stage of the communication process will be most successfully achieved if intention exists on the part of the receiver.

*Interpretation of the Message*
Although the receiver of the message may have the best intentions to receive the message correctly, it may be the case that he does not and actually misinterprets the meaning which the sender intended to convey. It is at this stage that we realise when a breakdown in communication may have occurred, normally because of an inability to understand the language being used. A hotel receptionist for example, will need to be familiar with the language code of the computer terminal at the reception desk, otherwise she may interpret certain symbols incorrectly and miscalculate a customer's bill.

*Communication and Action*
This is the final stage in the process of communication; it is at this stage that we can demonstrate if communication has been effectively achieved or not. A simple example will demonstrate that the action resulting from the communication process is proof of whether the communication has been effective or not. If the safety officer of a large luxury hotel gives fire drill instructions to all staff and guests telling them, in the event of a fire, to use fire exits and to muster in the hotel forecourt, and in the emergency all the staff and the guests congregate in the hotel foyer causing much confusion and chaos, then clearly a breakdown in the chain of communication has occurred.

Constant appraisal of every stage of the communication process is therefore necessary in order to ensure that it is being effectively carried out. If this is not done some level of inefficiency will inevitably occur.

**Student Activity   No. 17**
  (i)   Define feedback.
 (ii)   Examine the communications process and state at what stage feedback may be most usefully employed.
(iii)   Give three examples of feedback in operation in the communications process.

**Forms of Communication**
Communication can take a variety of forms but for our purposes the most convenient classification is into the verbal and non-verbal categories. We may use these broad categorisations in the following way: Verbal communication employs the use of words in getting the

27

message across, non-verbal communication employs the use of symbols other than words for conveying meaning.

In a highly complex society, which uses an increasing amount of sophisticated technology, intricate verbal descriptions are often required in order to explain the workings of a particular piece of equipment or how a given process is carried out. In contrast, however, non-verbal symbols can often be employed to provide clear unambiguous instructions or directions. Many instruction leaflets contain a series of non-verbal symbols which often are more effective than words in conveying a particular meaning. The symbol is designed to have an immediate effect so that the person viewing the symbol is in no doubt as to its meaning. A series of arrows pointing to a particular destination, a cup of coffee or a knife and fork symbolised in bright neon are all immediate, effective means of communicating information. An additional advantage of non-verbal forms of communication of course is their ability to communicate across language barriers. A range of international motoring signs makes driving through many countries possible without the use of a phrase book to interpret written signs.

Where the message to be conveyed is simple and direct or is one which can be broken down into simple component parts then non-verbal forms of communication can often be very effective. When the message to be conveyed is more complex and contains a number of subtle or complicated elements that are difficult to disentangle, then verbal forms of communications are often more effective.

### Student Activity No. 18
Draw up a range of symbols which would convey information about the following most effectively:
  (i)   Buffet Car.
 (ii)   Restaurant Closed.
(iii)   Open at 6.30.
 (iv)   Men Only.
  (v)   Left Luggage.
 (vi)   Bank.

### The Individual and the Communication Process
The success or failure of any communication is largely dependant upon the individuals who are involved in it. The inability of any one individual to send, receive or understand messages will result in the communication process breaking down at some point. So no matter in what context the communication process takes place and no matter how many aids to effective communication may exist the whole process is dependant upon the skills of the individual involved in the process. Our earlier discussion of individual differences is therefore relevant to the effectiveness of the communication process. A few simple examples will illustrate this point.

If the communication process is based upon the use of words then the individuals involved in it must be competent in terms of their oral and verbal ability. If this element of their intellectual capacity is limited then they may be less effective in this area of communication. Perceptual speed is important in the way it helps the individual to pick up messages quickly and memory is equally important as it enables the individual to retain an important message over a period of time. In fact all the elements of intellectual capacity are closely linked to the individual's ability to participate effectively in the communication process.

Forms of non-verbal communication are also affected by individual differences. An individual does not necessarily have to speak or write a message to communicate, in fact many aspects of the service an individual member of staff may provide to customers in the catering industry are dependant upon effective non-verbal communication. The attitude and personality of the reception team, of waiters and waitresses, and all employees who come into contact with the public should communicate non-verbally an intention to please and to provide a service. Without the right attitude and personality in this context, customer satisfaction may be difficult to achieve.

The careful use of different forms of communication between individuals within the work place will also affect efficiency. The supervisor who communicates with his staff by memoranda rather than by face to face contact may be less able to communicate effectively with them than one who provides a personal contact and makes the effort to establish some rapport between himself and his staff. The effectiveness of the supervisory role is to a large part dependant upon the way in which communication between supervisor and staff is conducted. The successful supervisor may need to employ a range of different techniques to ensure that he communicates effectively with a range of different individuals within the workplace.

**Student Activity   No. 19**
Explain briefly in your own words how a supervisor would communicate most effectively with the following members of staff:
  (i)   The Higher TEC Diploma student employed on work experience as a commis chef.
  (ii)  The part-time banqueting waiter with a low level of motivation.
  (iii) The highly extroverted barman.
In the preceding sections we have considered the position of the individual, both in terms of his own personal make up and in relation to the other individuals he comes into contact with in the workplace. In the next section we will consider the way in which groups influence the individual in the catering workplace.

# ASSESSMENT QUESTIONS

1. Explain the way in which different environments may influence inter-personal behaviour.
2. Explain the relationship between the role an individual plays and the environment he is in.
3. List the situations in hotel and catering which may influence human behaviour.
4. Explain the way in which different situations influence individual behaviour in the hotel and catering workplace.
5. Describe the way in which personality may influence staff inter-actions.
6. Describe the way in which individual differences may influence the customer situation.
7. Explain the importance of communication in an industrial or commercial situation.
8. Define communication.
9. Define the communication process.
10. List and explain each stage of the communication process.
11. Distinguish between verbal and non-verbal forms of communication.
12. Describe, with the use of examples, verbal forms of communication.
13. Describe, with the use of examples, non-verbal forms of communication.
14. Describe the way in which individual differences may influence the effectiveness of the communication process.
15. Identify the influence of individual differences upon the communication process.
16. Explain the role of communication in the relationship between the supervisor and the employee.
17. Identify and explain factors which hinder effective communication.

# Group Behaviour

## TYPES OF GROUP

Group membership is a major determinant of human behaviour; very few individuals in their life can remain isolated from influence by a group of some kind. In a variety of situations and for a variety of purposes we enter into groups to conduct our lives in society. We may define a social group as two or more persons linked in a common purpose, behaviour or interest. All groups we enter may be defined in this way. The use of this definition as it stands does, however, cause us some problems. We may contrast two students meeting after a lecture to discuss a homework question and to exchange relevant notes, with the crowd of football supporters on the terraces at a game, chanting abuse at the opposing team's supporters. The individuals in both of these groups are linked by the defining characteristics of the social group ie. they are linked by a common purpose, behaviour and interest. We would not wish, however, to claim that they resembled each other in many, if any, characteristics. For our purposes, therefore, the above definition is too narrow. We need to distinguish between different types of group and to define each of these types.

### Primary and Secondary Groups

An American sociologist Charles Cooley formulated a distinction between primary and secondary groups. He defined primary groups as 'those characterised by intimate, face to face association and co-operation' and went further by saying that the primary group 'is a certain fusion of individualities in a common whole, so that one's very self, for many purposes at least, is the common purpose of the group'. The most commonly used example of a primary group is the family, where all the individuals in the group have a common identity as members of the family. The members of the primary group will normally be few in number and will live in close physical proximity to one another for an extended period of time. They will share similar aims in life, have mutual respect for one another and place a value on the relationships that exist within the group. The kind of relationships being referred to here are those that might exist between a husband and wife, a parent and child or between two friends. In addition to the family, other examples of primary groups might be a play or friendship group, a neighbourhood or community or a work-team.

The secondary group is most easily defined as everything that the primary group is not. It is not identified by 'intimate face to face association', it does not incorporate a 'fusion of individualities in a common whole, and the individual usually exists within the group as having a separate and recognisable identity. In contrast to the primary group, the secondary group may be large in number, its members may not live in close proximity to one another and may only be members of the group for a short period of time. Where a certain sharing of aims existed within the primary group the secondary group is often identified by its contractual nature ie. members are members by virtue of some form of agreement and their purpose for being a member may be quite different to that of another member. A large business corporation provides us with a good illustration of a secondary group, in which relationships are formal, limited to the individual requirements of each member, and contolled by the corporation itself. Such relationships might be between employer and employee, receptionist and customer, supervisor and staff and of a type that, for example, may also be found in professional bodies, trade unions, the armed forces, goverment etc.

Individuals may therefore be members of a primary group and a secondary group and in fact many individuals are members of more than one primary group and a number of secondary groups.

## Student Activity   No. 20
(i)  Draw up a list of primary groups and secondary groups of which you are a member and compare these with other members of your group.
(ii)  Discuss, within your group, the effects that membership of these groups has upon your behaviour.

## Reference Groups
A classification of groups into primary and secondary categories is helpful in providing us with a broad picture of group behaviour and how this behaviour differs from group to group. There are other group classifications which we need to consider. The reference group is not a group that an individual actually belongs to, it is one which he refers to when he considers his actual position in life. A reference group is the group with which the individual compares his own standing in society. In one sense it may be the group that the individual looks up to in some way or another. Different individuals will possess different reference groups according to their own personality, attitudes, intelligence etc; once again our analysis of individual differences is of relevance here.

Reference groups can be identified in a number of ways: they may be the group an individual refers to in terms of levels of pay or working conditions. An individual in one work situation may refer to individuals in another work situation and use this as a basis for assessing the value of his work and efforts. Kitchen staff may use food service staff as a reference group in this way, arguing perhaps that they should earn more to bring them in line with the gratuities that the waiters and waitresses earn in addition to their wages.

Reference groups may be the groups that individuals refer to in terms of their attitudes and beliefs. Political parties, trade unions and religious groups may all operate as reference groups in this way. So far we have considered the way in which individuals compare themselves to reference groups in an 'upward' direction, but comparison can also take place in a 'downward' direction. The individual may look down on the behaviour patterns of a particular group, perhaps of which he himself was once a member, and in so doing see himself as being in a superior or higher position.

The purpose of a reference group therefore is to enable individuals to define their own position in society in comparison or by reference to other groups.

### Student Activity   No. 21
(i)   Make a list of the reference groups that you personally use.
(ii)  State clearly what it is about these particular groups that you look up or down to eg. financial position, appearance, beliefs, work situations etc.
(iii) Do your reference groups change over time?

### Formal and Informal Groups
The distinction between formal and informal groups is particularly useful in our analysis of group behaviour in the catering workplace. Working relationships, in any industry, are best described using the distinction between formal and informal groups. We will describe each of these in turn.

*Formal Groups*
A formal group exists, normally in a work situation, to carry out certain specified tasks. These tasks will be clearly defined by the organisation within which the formal groups exists and the behaviour patterns of the individuals within the group will be regulated by a set of clearly defined rules. We say therefore that within a formal group, formal control of individual behaviour is exercised. Formal groups are normally related to one another within a workplace by the organisation that embraces them. In this way the tasks, duties, responsibility and area of authority of one group will not overlap with those of another and taken as a whole the functions of formal groups will complement one another and contribute to the overall successful running of the organisation. The following diagram illustrates one of the ways that formal groups are interrelated to form a working organisation. This is sometimes referred to as a hierarchical organisational structure.

So within a hotel, for example, the formal groups that constitute its organisation might be: the kitchen brigade, the restaurant brigade, the reception team, the housekeeping team, porters, cleaning staff etc. All

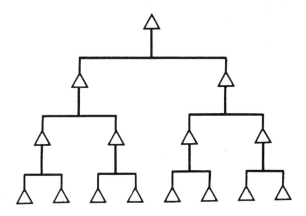

Fig. 4. *An example of Formal Group Structure*

these formal groups will be interrelated and inter-dependant and will all contribute to the efficient operation of the hotel. If the scale of the operation increases then the number of formal groups is also likely to increase. The reception team may be divided into shifts to provide a 24 hour reception service, similarly the kitchen brigade will be divided into specific sections or corners under the authority and supervision of a chef de partie.

Formal group organisation therefore requires close interaction between the various groups and careful separation and co-ordination of duties and responsibilities. Unless this occurs efficiency will not be achieved, because an overlapping of duties and duplication of effort will occur.

### Student Activity    No. 22
With the help of your lecturer draw up an organisation chart showing all the formal groups and the way in which they are connected, in a large-scale, luxury type hotel.

*Informal Groups*
Formal groups come about as a result of the specific design and planning of employers, managers or supervisors; they are therefore part of the personnel policy and are covered by the objectives of management. Informal groups, however, do not have this pre-planned or designed quality; they are the type of group that may be formed to fulfill certain needs that are not met by a formal group. The importance of informal groups can be seen when we consider the fact that no formal system can possibly foresee every future eventuality or be able to predict a sudden change of events. Informal groups develop to satisfy these needs. They may be short-lived, as in the case of the group of stewards, maintenance men and kitchen staff who work

34

efficiently together to replace a soaked carpet when a water-pipe bursts a short time before food service. They may be long lived, as in the case of the hotel manageress and her staff who breakfast together daily, as this is the only time they are all together and able to jointly discuss aspects of the working day.

Both of these examples of informal groups cannot be written into any organisation chart, the first because it is largely unpredictable and the second because it represents a convenient slot in an otherwise busy day in which staff members have to function within their own formal groups.

Informal groups are recognisable in terms of three important characteristics:

(i)   Group norms.
(ii)  Group attitude.
(iii) Group cohesiveness.

We will consider each one of these in turn.

(i)   Within a formal group procedures for carrying out tasks, rules, regulations and so on, will be specified by the group's place within the organisation. In other words formal control is exerted over the behaviour of individuals within the group in terms of the tasks they do, the hours they work, the length of holiday they have and so on. Informal groups operate a system of informal control, where, instead of specified rules or regulations, unwritten laws, better known as norms, control the behaviour of group members. A norm represents the accepted way of doing something within a particular group. So in the staff canteen, everybody will queue for their meal, no matter how long the queue, or in how much of a hurry they might be. The pressure to conform to this norm is quite strong and if it is violated the individual is often viewed with displeasure and scorn. We may take this example a stage further to explain in more detail the operation of norms within informal groups. In a workplace where employees are drawn from a wide range of social and cultural backgrounds this often provides the basis for the formation of informal groups. A problem may arise here in that the norms which help to regulate behaviour in one informal group may not have any influence or relevance to the behaviour of individuals in another informal group. So, in our example, members of one culture, in one informal group may recognise the restraints imposed by queueing, whereas members of another informal group from another culture may have a different set of controls which does not include queueing. In this situation where the staff of an establishment are drawn from a wide range of social and cultural backgrounds care must be taken to ensure that conflict does not occur. This indicates that the existence of informal groups can have positive and negative effects.

35

## Student Activity No. 23

Although all students are members of a formal group defined by the college or department organisation eg. TEC Diploma IX, informal groups usually develop. You are probably a member of an informal group of this kind, draw up a list of group norms which regulate its behaviour. Compare this with other groups you are familiar with.

(ii)  Attitudes are not only represented by individuals but also by groups. The attitudes expressed by an informal group can exert considerable influence upon the behaviour of individuals who are members of that group. The informal group might be a group casually formed to organise a staff children's party for Christmas. The attitude of the group as a whole is based upon benevolence, good-will and a concern to give the children a good time. Once this informal group has become established, in terms of organisation and arrangements, it may be very difficult for any individual to complain about the amount of free time it is taking up, or to try to leave. The group attitude toward this particular cause will have a powerful effect upon the individual, influencing his behaviour.

The force of group attitudes can also influence the individual when an emphasis upon team-work and working together exists, particularly if certain financial incentives are also involved. It is sometimes the case that the combined effect of informal group norms and attitudes is so strong, that non-adherence to them may bring about rejection or social ostracism; what has become known as 'sending someone to Coventry'. This entails ignoring and not communicating with the individual who has violated the accepted mode of behaviour until that person decides to conform. Provided that the informal group norms and attitudes are in line with the formal policy and objectives of the firm then this may have a positive influence.

(iii)  It is often the case that by 'sending someone to Coventry' the group norms and attitudes are strengthened and group members unite together in a show of strength to rid the group of the influence that is challenging these norms and attitudes. This illustrates the way in which group cohesiveness can come about. Although the group is only informal it nevertheless has a strength and unity which often many formal groups do not possess. It is for this reason that management and supervising staff need to carry out regular appraisals of informal group developments so that wherever possible the positive influences of the group may be used for the benefit of the firm as a whole and the negative influences reduced.

## Student Activity   No. 24

Under the headings of 'Positive' and 'Negative' describe the influences of the following informal group practices:
  (i)   Discussing sport and politics during tea-break.
  (ii)  Supervisors and staff meeting regularly for a drink in the local pub after work.
  (iii) Unofficial inter-departmental football matches.
  (iv)  Unofficial inter-firm football matches.


## GROUP INFLUENCES

We have already examined some of the ways in which formal and informal groups can influence human behaviour. It is important to stress that the influence of formal groups on the individual derives from the structure and the function of that group ie. as part of the reception team the junior receptionist will have to work certain hours, receive certain levels of pay and expect certain working conditions. The influence of the informal group is less specific, is not written down and may vary from individual to individual.

### Individual Behaviour

A study by J.L. Moreno attempted to trace the patterns of relationships that existed between individuals in an organisation but that were not necessarily defined by line management or personnel policy. Moreno based his judgements on feelings of individuals toward others in the organisation and compiled what he called a sociogram. This described contacts between individuals based on feelings of attraction, repulsion and indifference. From this analysis Moreno was able to establish the following:
  (i)  . Which individuals were liked and disliked within the organisation.
  (ii)  The group influences on individual behaviour.
  (iii) What groups of individuals might best work together as a team.
The following sociogram will tell us a considerable amount of information about interactions within the group and how the group might affect the individual.

The group is indicated by the letters A to G, each of these representing an individual within it, the line joining two individuals denoting that interaction is taking place between them. Where the lines only have one arrow, as in the case of that joining B and D, this indicates that the balance of the interaction is toward person D. Where the arrows are in both directions, in the case of that joining D and E the balance is equal; they may be friends or have a mutual respect for one another. From observation of the arrows we may therefore tell who is the most popular, or the most informed member of the group and also who is perhaps the least popular and the least well informed member of the

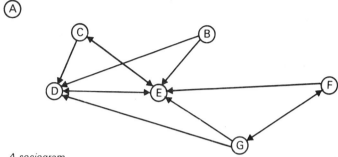

Fig. 5  *A sociogram*

group. In this case person E will represent the most popular or influential member of the group and person A the least popular and most isolated member of the group. It is important that a supervisor is aware of these group interactions, because if the isolation of A has a negative effect then he will have to act in some way to reduce it. Conversely, the popularity of person E should not go unnoticed by the supervisor as it may be possible to give this person responsibilities because of the popularity and respect he has gained from other group members.

### Student Activity   No. 25
Read the example of the use of the sociogram on pages 34-35 of Hotel and Catering Supervision by Gale and Odgers.

Construct your own sociogram; either for a group you know, a group you have worked with or from your own imagination. Use the example above for reference.

### Group Interaction
The analysis carried out so far should clearly demonstrate that groups, whether they are primary, secondary, reference, formal and informal do not act in isolation; there are varying degrees of interaction between these groups. Workplaces, particularly in large-scale organisations, are actually systems of human beings in groups of various types who are interdependant and who link together for the benefit of the organisation as a whole. We have already seen that formally, interaction between groups within an organisation takes place along clearly defined lines which are shown on the organisation chart. However, we

have stressed the importance of informal groups and this can be seen when we consider the way in which they interact with other groups. Informal groups often have a means of communication that is far speedier and more efficient than any specified by the formal organisation. The following diagram illustrates how this may be achieved:

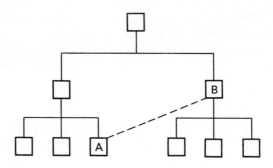

Fig. 6    An illustration of Informal Communication

Each of the blocks in the illustration represent a formal group in the organisation. Each of these formal groups are joined by lines; these represent the lines which formal communication follows and which define what is known as line management.

If formal group A in the organisation has to communicate or liaise with formal group B this would normally follow the lines of the organis- ation chart. However, if the formal channel of communication is pursued time will be used up, waiting for instructions, sending memoranda, making telephone calls etc. The dotted line in the illustration is a channel of informal communication and it may represent a walk down the corridor or a chat between friends, in each case the desired end of communication is achieved much more quickly. The informal group makes a positive contribution to the organisation.

Not all groups necessarily have the goals and ambitions of the organisation at heart. For example, the informal syndicate of brewery landlords who purchase their spirits from the trade supermarket at a reduced rate, rather than from the brewery at the standard rate, or the militant trade union group who are intent upon causing conflict between management and the workforce.

The points that require stressing at this stage and which can be derived from the preceding analysis are as follows:

(i)   Groups of different kinds influence individual behaviour.
(ii)  The influence of the group may be positive or negative.
(iii) Different groups interact with one another.
(iv)  The result of this interaction may be positive or negative.

**Student Activity   No. 26**
Using the illustration in figure 6 as a basis give an actual example in a
work situation of the way in which informal communication between
groups may be more efficient than formal communication defined by
line management.

A study carried out by Elton Mayo, an industrial psychologist, on the
effects of the physical environment on the productivity levels of groups
of workers between 1927 and 1930, produced a set of results which are
highly relevant to this analysis.

**The Hawthorne Experiments**
Mayo and his team carried out their studies at the Hawthorne Plant of
the Western Electric Co. which made telephone switchboards and
related equipment. They carried out a range of experiments which
attempted to measure the relationship between changes in the physical
environment and levels of productivity. The underlying assumption
being that if, for example, lighting conditions were improved, levels of
productivity would also improve. They tested out this assumption by
comparing the productivity of a control group, for which lighting
conditions were not varied and a test group for whom lighting
conditions were varied. Mayo and his team found to their surprise that
the productivity rate of *both* teams increased, and at an equal rate.
   They extended the range of their experiments; not only changing
lighting but also the length of the working week, the length of the
working day, the length and frequency of tea-breaks and so on. Once
again, to their surprise the productivity of the female workers being
observed increased, irrespective of the changes being made. Mayo
was first of all forced to conclude that the changing physical and
working conditions, whether they were improved or worsened could
not be correlated with productivity rate. However, the most important
conclusion drawn from his observations were that over the course of
the experiments, the female workers being studied had become a
social group. They were allowed to participate in the work situation and
take some control, and most important of all because they were being
observed by the experimenters, felt quite flattered and consequently
changed their attitude toward work and actually worked harder.
   Mayo's experiments are significant because they indicate the
importance of the informal group in determining work patterns, rates
of productivity and so on. It was not the individual worker who worked
in isolation for large incentive bonuses or, on the other hand, it was not
the company dictating rates of productivity to which the workers

would inevitably conform. Mayo concluded that work is primarily a group activity, that the groups of workers need not be formal groups set up by management but informal groups, and finally that work rate is not so much governed by the physical abilities of workers but rather by the attitudes, norms and cohesiveness of the group.

## Group Influence within Catering Operations

The Hawthorne Experiments have relevance to the study of human behaviour in all industries and work situations. Hotel and catering operations are no exception to this. Mayo's findings may benefit employers, industrial relations consultants, managers, personnel officers and supervisors alike. Where Mayo considered the way in which group behaviour influenced levels of productivity; within catering operations we have to consider the way in which customer satisfaction may be affected. A variety of different groups exist within most catering operations therefore we should be constantly aware of Mayo's conclusions and be prepared to apply them to human relations within these catering operations.

## ASSESSMENT QUESTIONS

1. Distinguish between formal and informal groups.
2. Distinguish between primary and secondary groups.
3. Describe the nature of reference groups.
4. Explain the following terms in the way that they influence the behaviour of informal groups
   (a) Group norms
   (b) Group attitude
   (c) Group cohesiveness
5. Explain the different ways in which groups can influence individual behaviour.
6. Describe
   (a) The positive influence of a group *and*
   (b) The negative influence of a group.
7. Explain why group influences may be positive or negative.
8. Explain the different ways that groups might interact.
9. Explain the possible effects of interaction between different groups.
10. Explain the way in which different *types* of group might interact.
11. Describe in detail the Hawthorne Experiments.
12. Explain the different ways in which groups can influence catering operations.
13. Assess the usefulness of informal groups to catering operations.

# Social Skills

## THE NATURE OF SOCIAL SKILLS

The analysis of the composition, understanding and application of social skills is of central relevance to the successful operation of any workplace. The Hotel and Catering industry is no exception to this; indeed, as a service industry the need for social skills, in a variety of contexts, cannot be over-valued. We need first of all to define social skills. This will enable us to carry our analysis further.

### Social Skills Defined

Social skills are possessed in varying degrees by different individuals, they may be learned sub-consciously through life or they may come about as a consequence of a specific training programme, carried out by parents, teachers, supervisors etc. In addition social skills represent what is considered to be the appropriate behavioural response to a given person or persons in a range of different situations. Social skills are largely responsible for determining the success or failure of inter-personal relations.

### The Development of Social Skills

All individuals in society possess social skills; if this were not the case then certain individuals would not be members of society. In fact those people who are classified and registered as insane may in one sense be defined as lacking social skills, quite simply the inability to 'get along' with people, to be a 'social animal'.

In a general sense social skills develop throughout life: the process known as socialisation is partly responsible for the development of social skills. A child learns from his parents not to eat peas from the side of his knife and to be respectful and polite when uncles and aunties come to visit. At school, teachers may encourage children to work together as a team, to share laboratory equipment when performing an experiment or to take responsibility in certain roles such as House Captain or Prefect.

Many social skills are also developed independently from the direct encouragement of family or school. Interpersonal behaviour can often be a question of trial and error, with little or no previous guidance having been provided to influence the way in which this behaviour might develop. This may be the case with childhood romances, entering a new set of work relationships, or perhaps visiting another country or region.

The social skills that an individual possesses are therefore influenced by the people he meets in a range of different environments. In addition, however, the factors which contribute to the differences between individuals, dealt with in an earlier section, will also influence the development of social skills. Attitude, personality, intelligence, perception and motivation will all influence the individual's ability to cope with a range of social relationships and situations.

## Social Skills and the Work Situation

A famous industrial psychologist George Argyris has argued that in a range of working situations interpersonal skills are inadequately developed. He argues that people are unable to relate to one another properly and that consequently mutual distrust and feelings of suspicion develop. Relationships tend therefore to develop only on a superficial basis with little honesty or respect for feelings involved; this in turn reduces the commitment that individuals may have to the work situation and ultimately leads to a poor attitude and inefficient working relations.

The development of social skills should enable some of the problems Argyris found to be reduced, possibly even eliminated. We will consider this in relation to the catering workplace and in terms of a number of relevant factors.

## Appearance

Appearance plays an important part in face to face interpersonal contact; it is normally the first point of contact between individuals, before gestures are made, or words are spoken. Although appearance may not give a true picture of the individual, it is often crucial in the effect it has upon individuals who interact with him. Therefore, it may be the case that appearance is a clue to the make-up of the individual which may in turn cause those who meet him to behave in a certain way. It is certainly the case that where casual interpersonnal contact occurs, appearance is of primary importance in creating a certain impression. The catering staff who regularly come into contact with the public must therefore appear in such a way that a favourable impression is made and custom is encouraged.

We will briefly consider the factors that contribute to the composition of appearance. The physique of an individual is often important; an exceptionally tall person for example may appear intimidating and over powerful, in contrast to the small person who may appear weak and insignificant. Hairstyle may provide many indications to the character of an individual. Its cleanliness, length and style may indicate laziness where it appears unkept, a conservative attitude when it is cut short, nearly parted and oiled, or an extrovert personality if it is dyed a bright colour and cut in an unusual style.

Mode of dress can have a similar effect in terms of appearance as hairstyle. Clothes and the way in which they are worn indicate many aspects of character and certain types of clothes are deemed suitable for one occasion or perhaps inappropriate for another. We say therefore that certain expectations, regarding dress and appearance in general, exist. We expect someone to wear a formal suit to a wedding or a funeral but would be surprised to see that person dressed similarly the next day when washing the car or doing the housework.

So, if people do not appear to us in the expected way, our reaction may be one of curiousity, surprise, amusement or annoyance. For this reason staff in catering establishments dress in a particular kind of way, in a 'uniform' fashion so that the expectation and sensibility of customers are in no way offended.

### Student Activity No. 27

Describe in detail what you consider to be the most suitable appearance (ie. in terms of physique, hairstyle, dress etc.) for the following positions in catering establishments:
  (i) Restaurant Manager.
  (ii) Hotel Receptionist.
  (iii) Cocktail Barman.
  (iv) Commis Waitress.
When you have completed your descriptions compare them with others in your group, assessing the advantages and disadvantages of the various suggestions.

## SOCIAL SKILLS AND COMMUNICATION

The aspects of appearance so far considered have been largely visual, we will now examine the manner of an individual and the way in which that individual communicates with others. We often refer to an individual as having a pleasant, or an unpleasant manner, of appearing aggressive or passive. This type of appearance is not so easily discernible in terms of the factors so far discussed (ie. dress, hairstyle, physique etc). It is more meaningful to assess a person's manner in terms of the way he behaves, in terms of the 'tone' of conversation he may use.

### Communication and Tone

In a general sense the way in which we communicate is affected by the 'tone' we use. The tone used will affect the behaviour and the attitude of the individuals with whom we are communicating, although it will be the case that different individuals will react differently to the tone of communication being used. The head chef, dissatisfied with the quality of a certain food preparation may communicate his dissatisfaction in harsh, aggressive verbal tones to the commis chefs who are responsible for it. They in turn may react to this in a submissive or apologetic way, promising to rectify the fault or they may refuse to admit responsibility and challenge the authority of the chef. In each case the tone of the message the head chef is communicating dictates certain behaviour and attitudes; in the first case a submissive form of behaviour and an apologetic or guilty attitude and, in the second case, a rebellious form of behaviour and a challenging, aggressive attitude.

The tone of our communication will therefore convey additional meaning. A complaint about the poor quality of service to the restaurant manager will be all the more forceful, emphatic and meaningful if the tone of the complaint is harsh, aggressive and loud. In contrast, the rather quiet, almost apologetic complaint may do little to influence the restaurant manager to improve the service; it will have had less impact on him.

In considering the tone of the communication we are engaged in, we must attempt to assess the possible response to the use of that tone. A supervisor may decline from using a harsh, abrasive tone to the junior management trainee when he has made the same elementary mistake for the third time, because he knows that the trainee is very conscientious and keen and is also very sensitive to harsh criticism. A lively and enthusiastic description of an idea or new project will often create enthusiasm and interest in someone even though they have not fully grasped the nature of the project. It is the lively and animated tone that generates a response in the listener, almost preparing him to accept the ideas or proposals that are being so enthusiastically outlined to him. This particular use of tone may be invaluable in generating sales of a new product. It conveys an impression to the potential customer that the sales person believes in the product, an impression that would not be conveyed by a rather dull, flat and expressionless description of the product.

## Student Activity   No. 28

Write down a list of expressions you might use to communicate in a certain tone, in the following situations:
  (i)   Making a complaint to a waiter.
 (ii)   Praising the quality of someone's cooking.
(iii)   Expressing gratitude for the offer of a position with a company.
 (iv)   Giving instructions to a trainee who is rather inattentive and lazy.
  (v)   Pointing out the faults in a product that has taken a great deal of time and effort to prepare.
Assess the possible responses to the tone being employed.

## Customer Relations

The need for customer satisfaction is the motivating force behind any successful hotel and catering operation. The elements of customer satisfaction need to be considered and the kind of customer demand needs to be assessed. Questions have to be asked, such as 'What do our customers want?' 'What can our customers afford?' 'What kind of service do they enjoy?' If we can answer this type of question then we are moving towards our goal of achieving customer satisfaction.

Customers of hotel and catering establishments will expect a range of services of a given quality and of a certain price; they will bring with them to these establishments certain expectations. These expectations have to be anticipated, as part of the management task. They will expect in a restaurant, food of a given kind and quality and will expect to pay a certain price for this food. They will also expect a service from the staff of the restaurant, in the form of pleasantness, helpfulness and general efficiency. The service that staff provide to customers can be conveniently broken down into two parts; their physical skills and their mental skills. The first category of skills will include the ability of the chambermaid to clean rooms and change beds or of the waiter to take food orders, relay them to the kitchen and serve the food in the required manner. The second category will include the ability of the waiter to understand customers requests, to decide if cutlery is fit for use or not and to ascertain when food is fit to serve and when it is not.

We may develop this second category further and examine the verbal and non-verbal behaviour of staff to the costumers of catering establishments.

## Verbal Communication

It must be emphasised here that the form of verbal communication that catering staff use to achieve customer satisfaction may not satisfy all customer needs. Individual differences play a part in the response of customers to the most polite and pleasant verbal approach of staff. The difficult customer may be an exception but his needs will also have to be considered and satisfied.

However, there are a number of general remarks that we can·make about verbal communication with customers that will be helpful. We saw in Section B that for communication to be successful there must be a reciprocal relationship ie. the person attempting to communicate will hope to obtain a response from the person he is attempting to communicate with. The waiter who asks questions such as: 'Can I help you Sir?' or 'Would you like to order?' is attempting to communicate in a way that is both efficient and polite. Normally the customer response to such questions would be positive, he is receiving the kind of service he expects.

The verbal behaviour of catering staff should therefore help to promote sales, provide the customer with information about the service provided and present a pleasant, though not over familiar manner. In the majority of cases such an approach would generate a relationship with customers which would be beneficial to all concerned, ie. the firm, the staff and the customer.

## Student Activity No. 29

Give examples of verbal behaviour that would achieve the following:
  (i)   A waitress promoting sales in a restaurant.

(ii)  A hotel receptionist providing information to potential customers.

(iii) A restaurant manager talking to customers in the bar after food service.

**Non-Verbal Communication**

We have already considered the way in which an individual's appearance can influence interpersonal behaviour. The appearance of an individual is a form of non-verbal communication, it is a statement without words of the kind of person we are looking at. Bright and extravagant clothes, for example, may communicate an extrovert personality or a 'devil may care' attitude, without the individual wearing them uttering a word.

The conscious use of non-verbal behaviour by catering staff in relation to customers is a social skill that needs to be cultivated in the interests of providing an efficient service. Therefore, staff who are dealing with customers on a regular basis not only need to develop the physical skills and mental skills specifically related to the job but also those non-verbal communication skills which can contribute so much to the service being provided.

The hotel receptionist will not only be well groomed and of a pleasant disposition but also she will employ a number of non-verbal behaviours in dealing with customers. She will smile or offer a friendly facial expression, she may point to the lifts or the public telephone, she will employ eye to eye contact or perhaps lean toward the customers slightly to indicate attention and awareness.

In the restaurant, the head waiter will offer similarly attentive behaviour, listening carefully to the requests and wishes of customers. He will stand at a discreet distance from the tables, far enough to afford the customers privacy but close enough to be able to offer immediate service. He may also control his staff by using a series of gestures, nodding to offer approval of some action, or discreetly pointing to a table which requires service. In this way his presence will influence the ambience of the restaurant without being in any way obtrusive.

A customer will feel that he is receiving personal service from catering staff if they appear to be listening and paying attention. He will feel that he is achieving a level of communication. The barman in the hotel bar may employ a range of gestures, such as smiles, nods and facial expressions to assure customers that their conversation is witty or interesting. In reality he may be thinking about going home, or last night's match on the television but he does not give this impression to the customer. As closing time approaches, however, he may employ certain non-verbal behaviours to indicate this to the customer. He may wipe glasses or tidy up the drinks servery and begin to glance at the wall clock or his watch a little more frequently.

It is not only important to *appear* attentive when dealing with

47

customers but also to concentrate carefully on what the customer is saying. Without this skill mistakes can be made and the service will suffer. The hotel receptionist who telephones a flight booking for a customer to Dallas instead of the requested Dulles, may not only incur the displeasure of the customer but also her employers who may have to pay the cancellation fee for the ticket. Careful listening skills must therefore be employed at all time to help in the development of relationships with customers.

## Student Activity   No. 30
Give examples of non-verbal behaviour that would achieve the following:
  (i)   The head waiter indicating to a commis waiter that his action was incorrect.
  (ii)  The hotel receptionist indicating to a foreign customer that she understands his request.
  (iii) The hotel manager indicating to a guest that such behaviour is not permitted.

The importance of verbal and non-verbal behaviour therefore lies in the way in which it influences the behaviour of guests. If the speech patterns or gestures of staff are not carefully applied to the customer's needs, then the customers themselves are going to react unfavourably, to the extent that they may eventually take their custom elsewhere. If, on the other hand, the behaviour of staff is polite, friendly and efficient and if their appearance is tidy and well groomed this can contribute to the ambience of the establishment, influencing customers to be friendly and good-natured also.

## Staff Attitudes
The attitude of staff should not be confused with their use of social skills; they represent two distinct though related areas. Staff, for example, may have a very unfavourable attitude toward certain customers but they may disguise this successfully by employing a range of social skills for their benefit. Similarly staff may have an attitude toward work and their employers that is less than favourable but in order to keep their jobs they use certain social skills to give the impression but they are keen, enthusiastic and highly motivated.

This may be contrasted with the highly enthusiastic and conscien tious individual, who has a very positive attitude both to his employers and customers but who has not developed his social skills sufficiently to create a favourable impression with them. His manner and approach may be such that he puts people off, he may not appear pleasant, or he may give the impression of simply trying too hard.

Many factors influence staff attitudes; it is important that supervisors and managers are aware not only of staff attitudes but also the factors that influence them. This awareness improves their ability to control. If a negative attitude appears amongst some staff members, even though they are exercising their social skills in dealing with customers, it is important that supervisors try to find out what is creating this negative attitude. It is important to do this because eventually the strain of masking a negative attitude by the employment of social skills will tell upon the employee, possibly affecting his work in a detrimental manner.

## Staff Position

The position a member of staff holds in an organisation can often influence his attitude to his work. Employees will attempt to negotiate the best wages, holidays, working conditions etc. that they possibly can for themselves. The position that they hold in the organisation may be the key to achieving these things but also it is often the means by which supervisors and management can obtain the best efforts and the right approach from their staff.

Promotion to a higher position in an organisation not only improves an employee's standard of living but also improves his status. Any position will carry with it a certain status, that is the esteem or prestige that being in that position entails. In general terms, the position of head waiter will hold a higher status than that of commis waiter, however, the individual may not value this status if he has held the position for a number of years and feels perhaps that his efforts are not appreciated. Status therefore tends to be attached to certain positions in society and the level of reward given to a position usually reflects that status. Although sometimes a low status position, such as a refuse collector, may accrue high rewards and a high status position, such as a nurse, may accrue low rewards.

From the supervisory point of view the attachment of status to certain positions may act as a motivator for staff. The attitude of staff may be negative but by improving their position within the organisation, perhaps also by giving them extra responsibilities, their self-esteem may increase because they feel their overall status has also increased.

The improvement of an individual's position in the hierarchy of the firm's organisation may not necessarily be linked to an improvement in wages but it will help to satisfy his need for recognition and respect. Abraham Maslow in developing his famous hierarchy of human needs pointed out that once an individual has satisfied his basic, physiological needs for survival, security and safety he begins to 'search out' other, 'higher order' needs. These Maslow classifies as ego or esteem needs and self-realisation and self-actualisation needs (see figure 7).

Maslow argues that individuals not only want to belong to groups but also to be respected within them, in other words to have status. This does not mean that every individual wishes to be a leader but simply to have recognition, praise and approval of the things they do in that position. If the need for status is not fulfilled Maslow points out that inadequacy, feelings of inferiority and helplessness can develop within the individual. Supervisors and managers alike must therefore monitor the status needs of staff to ensure that they are not neglected and to satisfy them wherever possible.

Fig. 7 *Maslow's Hierarchy of Human Needs*

### Student Activity   No. 31

Read the section 'Maslow's Theory of Motivation' in Gale and Odger's Hotel and Catering Supervision pages 56–59. Describe the way in which the satisfaction of status needs can be related to the various categories of catering workers described in this section.
(See Activity 8.)

### The Customer and his Environment

We have considered the different ways that social skills can be successfully applied by catering staff in their behaviour toward customers. The behaviour of staff is of crucial importance in the development of favourable customer attitudes and customer satisfaction in general. Therefore, the implementation of social skills contributes a great deal to the interpersonal communication that takes place between catering staff and customers. We need also to consider the contribution of customers to this interpersonal relationship; their attitude, personality, social background etc will be of significance in understanding this relationship.

The environment that the customer comes from will not only influence his behaviour but it will also affect his expectations of the catering establishment he is entering and the behaviour of the staff he will come into contact with. Catering staff will be anxious to ascertain likely customer behaviour because of their close relationship with customers as a source of income. The successful application of social skills by catering staff may reap immediate financial benefits in the form of gratuities but also long term gain, in the way that satisfied customers will return to the same restaurant or hotel again on a number of occasions. Therefore an awareness of the customer's background will help the restaurant manager, or the hotel receptionist to develop a rapport with the customer. They will be able to anticipate customer demand not only on a general level in relation to wealth, income, education etc but on a more specific level in relation to the particular needs of the individual customer.

The customer's expectations will be shaped by his environment, affecting the way they treat catering staff. A person from a humble social background entering a quality restaurant or hotel for the first time may feel quite overawed by the experience and may look toward staff for guidance, help and advice. In contrast the affluent, seasoned traveller coming from a wealthy background may have a very off-hand and dismissive attitude toward staff, treating them almost as inferior beings or servants. Catering staff will need to be aware of these differences, quickly establish the nature of a customer's background and act accordingly to satisfy the expectations of the customer in question.

**Student Activity   No. 32**
Compile a list of social skills that you might employ for use with the following customers:
  (i)   The working class football pools winner dining in a high class restaurant for the first time.
  (ii)   The elderly couple staying at a seaside guest house .
  (iii)   The group of foreign sportsmen booking into a hotel.
Discuss the contents of your list with others in your group and try to assess the importance of customer environment in determining the social skills used.

**Social Skills in the Different Sectors of the Industry**
We will now consider the application of social skills in the different sectors of the industry. This analysis will bring into focus the special demands of the different sectors and the way in which the social skills required will vary between these different sectors.

*Hotels*
The hospitality provision of hotels is very much dependant upon the way in which those staff who come into contact with the customers employ social skills. In many respects the front office pays a central part in this relationship because perhaps more than any other department it represents the hotel to the guests. All other staff play a part in this relationship and we shall see at a later stage the various skills that each of these groups of staff employ. We may say, in general, that as

part of the commercial sector of the industry hotels encourage the use of social skills to increase sales. In addition, social skills are employed to compensate for the degree of impersonality that computer technology can bring in relation to the treatment of guests. Grand Metropolitan Hotels, for example, award their staff bonuses if they employ good social skills in their relationship with customers, helping them to feel more relaxed in a strange or impersonal environment.

## Restaurants

The commercial value of social skills must also be emphasised in the restaurant sector, where the success or failure of the establishment depends upon the quality of the product and the service provided. Interactive selling skills, which we deal with in detail in Section E, help in the selling of drinks and desserts, an area which often suffers without the careful application of social skills.

The ambience of the establishment not only relates to the decor but also to the way in which staff help to create an appropriate atmosphere. Within the intimacy of a restaurant the way in which staff relate to customers can often be crucial in determining the success or failure of that customer's meal.

## Fast Food Outlets

The requirement of a quick and efficient service can often impose considerable demands upon the social skills of staff in fast food outlets. Where speed is of the essence in providing food for busy city shoppers or office workers in their lunch-break, any mistakes tend to become magnified, appearing much more damaging than in the relatively relaxed atmosphere of a conventional restaurant. Customers have a tendency to be awkward and impatient and any delay, however slight, may cause an increase in tension. Staff therefore have to exercise patience and diplomacy in such situations to ensure that the most disgruntled and irritated customer leaves the establishment with some degree of satisfaction.

Social skills will also be employed in an effective way if staff can create a 'meal experience' for customers in a situation where the major feature may often be rapid turnover of custom and all that is associated with it. A degree of personal contact in the form of a smile or a pleasant comment from the food service staff may well enhance an otherwise cold and impersonal meal experience.

Finally, this kind of social skills approach may also encourage sales. Desserts, sauces and drinks may be ignored in a fast food situation where the customer is primarily concerned with obtaining a rapid service. The friendly approach may encourage the purchase of extras, which will represent an immediate or short term gain and also encourage customers to return to this particular outlet ie. a long term gain.

## Institutional

The institutional sector, which will include hospitals, schools, prisons etc. often has a difficult task in presenting a varied and imaginative style of catering, particularly when budgets may be limited and the customers are captive or regular users. The effect can sometimes be one of blandness, regularity and monotony. Catering staff in this situation, by the employment of social skills, can often create a more friendly and interesting meals experience. In some situations, hospitals for example, meals represent the highlight of the day for many and the exercising of social skills by staff can help to increase the enjoyment of the situation.

Some forms of institutional catering may be limited by smaller reduced budgets, which in turn limits the opportunity of making the meals experience enjoyable, not only in terms of the food but also in terms of the atmosphere in which it might be consumed. This represents another area where motivated staff, through the use of social skills can add enjoyment and quality to the customer's experience of the meal.

## Industrial

Industrial catering in a similar way to most forms of institutional catering, represents an area of essential eating for the customer rather than pleasure or leisure eating, which is more the case for the commercial sector. Nevertheless, customers in the industrial sector will expect a degree of quality in the food service which may be enhanced by food service staff. Canteen staff may help customers by explaining the composition of dishes, and outlining the various choices available. This is a form of social skills which not only improves customer service but also speeds up service in the food servery, helping to improve turnover for the benefit of the establishment as a whole.

In general it should be pointed out that in all forms of catering establishment, whether they be commercial or non-commercial, social skills can be successfully applied, not only to improve customer satisfaction, but also to improve sales and maintain good interpersonal staff relations at all levels of the establishment. In the next section these aspects of social skills will be dealt with in greater detail.

## SELF ASSESSMENT QUESTIONS

1. Define the term 'social skill'.
2. Explain the different ways that social skills can develop.
3. State the factors which influence the social skills of individuals.
4. Describe the way in which individual differences will affect the development of social skills.
5. Demonstrate the importance of appearance in interpersonal behaviour.

6. List the factors that contribute to the composition of appearance.
7. Explain how 'tone' in communication may affect behaviour.
8. Explain how 'tone' in communication may affect attitudes.
9. Describe the importance of verbal behaviours in the development of relationships with customers.
10. Describe the importance of non-verbal behaviour in the development of relationships with customers.
11. Distinguish between the use of 'physical skills' and 'mental skills' in relation to staff ability.
12. Demonstrate the importance of attention and listening in dealing with customers.
13. Explain the way in which attitudes may affect social skills.
14. List a range of staff attitudes that may affect his or her social skills.
15. Explain the relationship between a certain position and the status that that position carries.
16. Describe the way in which position and status can influence the behaviour of individuals.
17. Explain the need for esteem and status as described by Maslow in his hierarchy of needs.
18. Explain the way in which the environment can influence the behaviour of customers.
19. Demonstrate the way in which appropriate behaviour by staff may influence that of guests.
20. Explain with the aid of examples the way in which social skills may be applied in the different sectors of the industry ie. industrial, institutional, fast food, hotel and restaurant.

# Situational Skills

## INTRODUCTION

In Section B we examined the factors that influence interpersonal behaviour, we saw the importance of the roles that individuals play and how these roles differ according to the position an individual holds and the situation in which he is in. We will examine now, in more detail, the way in which different roles interact with one another, in terms of staff interpersonal relations and in terms of staff/customer interpersonal relations.

## STAFF RELATIONS

Staff relations are highly complex, not only in the range of different types but also in the differences that individual's bring to them. In Section B we outlined a range of possible influences that may be exerted upon staff working in catering establishments. For our present purposes we will consider the following:

(i)   The Management influence.
(ii)  The Supervisory influence.
(iii) The Organisational influence.
(iv)  The Group influence.

These influences in no way represent distinct categories and the fact that they overlap demonstrates the importance of individuals in different positions carrying out different roles according to whichever situation they find themselves in. Within the hotel and catering industry different types of social skill will be required by staff in specific positions in the industry.

### Positions within the Industry and Social Skills Required

We are simplifying our analysis of staff relations if we state that different positions within the industry such as head chef, junior receptionist etc. are characterised as having different roles. Our approach to positions in the industry and the roles attached to these positions must therefore be multi-dimensional rather than one-dimensional.

The head receptionist in figure 8 will have a number of formal staff relations (as well as customer relations). So although she will be in the *position* of head receptionist, this range of staff relations will determine that she plays a *number* of roles. We will examine these roles and the different approaches the head receptionist will use as she plays each role.

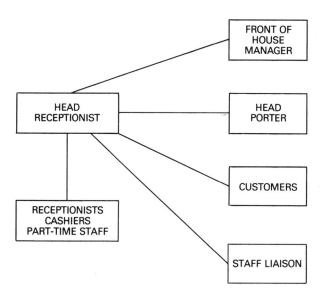

```
                                      ┌──────────────┐
                                      │  FRONT OF    │
                                      │   HOUSE      │
                                      │  MANAGER     │
                                      └──────────────┘

┌──────────────┐                      ┌──────────────┐
│    HEAD      │──────────────────────│    HEAD      │
│ RECEPTIONIST │                      │   PORTER     │
└──────────────┘                      └──────────────┘

                                      ┌──────────────┐
                                      │  CUSTOMERS   │
┌──────────────┐                      └──────────────┘
│ RECEPTIONISTS│
│   CASHIERS   │
│PART-TIME STAFF│                      ┌──────────────┐
└──────────────┘                      │STAFF LIAISON │
                                      └──────────────┘
```

Fig. 8  *The position and formal staff relations of the Head Receptionist*

*Head Receptionist — Front of House Manager (management)*
In this staff relationship the head receptionist will play a largely *subordinate role* which may include, taking orders from the front of house manager or receiving instructions from management. She will also be required to *report back* to the front of house manager providing information, as required, about reservations, shift arrangements, cash-flow details etc.

*Head Receptionist — Head Porter (organisational)*
In terms of the organisation we see that the case staff relations between the head receptionist and the head porter will be horizontal, ie. their positions are approximately equal within the organisation as a whole. The head receptionist in this case will play what is essentially a *liaison role,* ensuring that staff luggage is dealt with efficiently, arranging taxi-services for guests and so on.

*Head Receptionist — Receptionists, Cashiers, Juniors etc. (supervisory and group)*
The head receptionist will play what we may refer to as an *authority role* in relation to the other members the reception team. She will delegate authority, in the form of instructions, from the front of house manager to all other reception staff. She will co-ordinate the different shifts, ensuring that the reception teams work in a balanced arrange-ment; she will oversee the training of the junior receptionist and will monitor bookings, and room availability.

*Head Receptionist — Staff Liaison (general)*

The receptionist desk often acts as the 'nerve centre' of a large hotel, the focal point through which a great deal of communication in a hotel will pass. The head receptionist will monitor this to ensure for example, that telephone contact with the housekeeping staff regarding the availability of freshly vacated rooms is not impeded by telephone calls arranging an inter-departmental darts and pool match in the staff social club. In this case we may describe the head receptionist as carrying out a largely *controlling role.*

The position of head receptionist can therefore be seen as having at least four roles, which it must be pointed out, do overlap but which each carries with it different approaches. The authority which the head receptionist may exercise over the junior reception staff, for example, could not be exercised in the same way over the head porter. Such a position therefore, incorporates the careful and calculated use of different approaches in these different staff situations and the application of a range of social skills.

This example illustrates the way in which one position, that of head receptionist, can be involved in a number of staff situations which will be affected by various management, supervisory, organisational and group influences. In each situation certain social skills will be required. In the subordinate role she plays to the front of house manager, social skills will be exercised in the understanding and receiving of instructions and the ability to act on these instructions given if they cause problems and difficulties. When these instructions are delegated to the rest of the reception team as part of her authority role, she will exercise other social skills such as a friendly but controlling tone of vioice, or the ability to join in and help in times of intense activity.

### Student Activity   No. 33

We have carried out a position/roles/social skills analysis of one position, the head receptionist. Using the organisation chart in Section B, figure 3, for reference, carry out the following tasks:
  (i)   Draw up staff relations diagrams for the position of housekeeper and/or chef de partie.
 (ii)   In each case briefly describe the role relations they enter into with other staff and the different social skills they use in each situation.

### The Demands of a Situation

At any stage during the working day of a catering operation a range of demands will be associated with a particular situation. In the previous example the various situations that the head receptionist will be in (ie. management, organisational group or supervisory) can be affected by a range of events which will create various demands. Such eventualities as staff absences, over booking, computer breakdown, industrial relations problems etc. are all examples where the demands

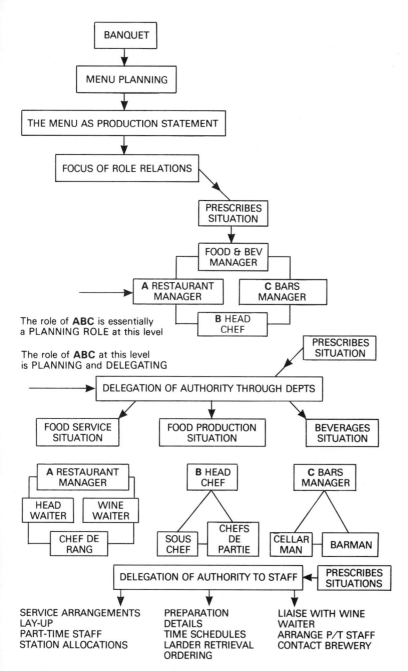

Fig. 9 *Situational Demands resulting from a Banquet*

of a situation are changed, where approaches might differ and where social skills may be tested. Not all eventualities will be of this extreme nature but we need to be aware of them should they arise. Normally, the demands of a situation are anticipated and dealt with as part of the day's routine. We will use a simple example to illustrate the way in which an event which may be part of the everyday routine of a catering establishment can further influence the various situations we have observed, the various interpersonal relationships, the roles that individuals play and the social skills that they will be required to exercise.

### Situational demands resulting from a Banquet

A banquet is being planned by the staff of a large hotel, this banquet will exert specific influences upon the staff and will make demands upon their situational and social skills.

Menu planning will be an important activity and will embrace a larger number of staff, influencing them in different ways. The menu will act as a production statement and will be the focal point which will influence role relations and social skills. Figure 9 will illustrate this point.

We can see that as the menu develops from the original planning stage it creates a range of different situations, all of which place demands upon individuals, requiring them to behave in different ways. The head chef, for example, will play a highly influential role in the planning stage, pointing out the practicalities of food production, making suggestions regarding the composition of dishes and so on. His role will change when he takes details of the planned menu to his sous chef and chefs de partie. At the planning stage he would play an *advisory role,* making recommendations and attempting to influence the balance and composition of the menu. At the food production stage he would play a *delegating* and *controlling* role, giving responsibilities and duties to the various members of the kitchen brigade. As the head chef plays his advisory role, the social skills he exercises may be those of tact and diplomacy as he makes suggestions to the menu planning team. As he plays his controlling role he will exercise a more authoritative social skill, motivating the members of the kitchen brigade, placing demands upon them which are necessary but practical in terms of the skills that they possess and the time that they may have to carry out the various tasks.

This example serves to illustrate the point that routine tasks or occurrences within the day to day running of a catering establishment will place a range of demands upon staff, in terms of the roles they play, their interpersonal behaviour and the social skills that they exercise.

### Student Activity   No. 34

Study the following diagrams and then make notes outlining the demands upon:

(i)   The personnel manager  *and*
(ii)  The food beverage manager.

In terms of the different roles they have to play in different situations and relationships and explain the different social skills they may have to employ.

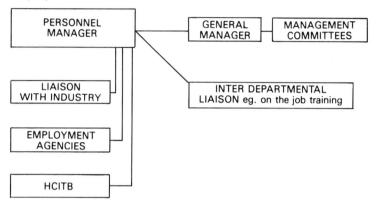

Fig. 10   *The position, roles and formal relations of the Personnel Manager*

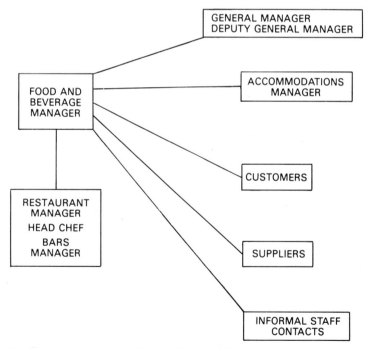

Fig. 11   *The position roles and relations of the Food & Beverage Manager*

## The Demands of an Emergency Situation

Emergency situations of any form will impose demands upon staff at all levels. The staff in many catering establishments work under a great deal of pressure and in circumstances that can often be quite tense. Examples of these high pressure, high tension situations might be during food service or during a busy weekend changeover of customers. Staff will be expected to respond to the needs of these situations and continue to provide an efficient customer service even though they may be under severe pressure.

The ability to respond in this way represents a quality that will be invaluable in times of emergency. In the case of an accident or a fire the staff involved will need to react, quickly and efficiently in an attempt to alleviate the problems caused by such an emergency. Social skills will be employed, not only in dealing with staff who may be injured, comforting and reassuring them, but also in efficiently and politely informing management and the appropriate emergency services about the situation. In addition customers will require careful treatment in an emergency situation, panic would need to be avoided at all costs, so great skill would be exercised in informing them in a clear cool manner of the location of fire escapes and emergency exits, in the event of a fire, for example.

In all such situations staff must be skilled in reducing the bad effects of such an emergency as quickly and efficiently as possible. The application of social skills in such events not only serves to save lives and reduce damage but also to maintain the good 'image' of the firm. Not only will such skilful action maintain or improve the image of the firm in the eyes of the customer but also in terms of employers, the various health and emergency services and the public in general.

## CUSTOMER RELATIONS

It is at this point that we change our perspective on social and situational skills away from the various management, staff and organisational influences themselves, toward the way in which they relate to the customers of catering establishments.

We saw in the last section the importance of staff social skills in providing customer comfort and safety in an emergency situation and also how this might contribute to improving or maintaining the 'image' of the firm. We will consider the 'image' of the firm in more detail.

### The 'Image' of the Firm

It is important that we grasp exactly the meaning of this term. An 'image' in general is a portrayal or reflection of how something is, or appears to be. We therefore talk about individuals or groups of people or organisations or firms promoting or portraying a certain image. In other words, by creating an image an attempt is being made to present a picture or a statement which says 'this is the way I am' or 'this is the way we are'.

A firm therefore will need to present an image to the public which will be attractive and which will draw customers to its various catering outlets. A fast food outlet for example, may wish to promote a clean, sharp efficient image in order to attract the busy customer who does not have time to relax and indulge time in a casual and comfortable environment. Therefore the ambience of the fast food outlet will be one of cleanliness, rapid service and modern efficiency. The staff will reflect this in their manner, their ability to serve food quicky and tidily packaged and their ability to total bills and to give change and receipts. If complaints do arise they will be dealt with quickly and politely, or referred efficiently to management, should they require more official attention. This constant attention to the details of service, thinking about the decor of the establishment, the appearance and manner of the staff and the quality of the product all contribute to the image of the firm.

The manager will be responsible for ensuring that the members of his staff will also be committed to perpetuating the image of the firm and many fast food outlets for example, encourage and motivate their staff by providing incentive schemes, grading systems and efficiency awards. In this context also we may refer back to our discussion of individual differences and emphasise the importance of staff appearance in presenting the image of the firm. Tidy hairstyles and certain types of uniform will help to promote an image for a firm. Restaurants that incorporate a thematic approach to their food service would require their staff to appear in appropriate clothing or uniform to promote the image that represents a certain theme, such as a Wild Western theme or a Mediaeval Britain theme.

Staff members therefore play an important role in perpetuating the image of the firm; many of them are in frequent contact with customers and will therefore be required to exercise social skills which promotes the required image of the firm. The way in which they communicate with, and generally treat, the customers will be a major determinant in perpetuating the firm's image and creating customer satisfaction.

**Interactive Selling Skills**
We may define an area of social skills which directly benefits any commercial catering operation as interactive selling skills. This will be the social skills that a waiter or a barman, a hotel receptionist or a porter will employ to develop a rapport between himself and the customer, which in turn has the effect of generating sales. An interactive relationship is literally one in which action between people occurs. So the member of the catering staff who comes into contact

with the customer will attempt to encourage 'action between' himself and the customer which may in turn promote sales or perpetuate the image of the firm. The staff member who employs interactive selling skills will either be self-motivated, in the case of the waitress working hard to obtain tips for herself or, company motivated, in the case of the ambitious junior receptionist who sees increased bookings as of mutual benefit to himself and the firm. The improvement of the firm's status will be in his interest as it may indirectly lead to promotion for himself at a later stage.

Interactive selling skills may be employed in a number of situations and may operate in a number of ways.

In a hotel restaurant a waiter may develop a friendly but polite relationship with the regular residents who dine at his station. He may use this friendly interaction as means of showing his customers that he is providing them with a 'personal' service, that they perhaps are receiving 'favours', in the form of larger portions or a wider choice. This interaction will tend to generate sales, in the short-term perhaps, by encouraging customers to 'dine out', and in the long-term perhaps by encouraging those customers to use the same hotel in the future.

The publican or barman may generate sales in his public house or bar by developing personal contacts amongst his clientele. By appearing to be 'one of the lads' for example, the landlord of a suburban pub may encourage certain groups of paying customers to return to his pub on a regular basis. He may achieve this by becoming a member of the pub's darts team, or by organising a sponsored run for a local charity. This will help to generate links with the local community, creating interaction between himself and members of the local community which, in turn, will help to generate sales. This sales maintenance will not only be in terms of his regular lunch-time and evening custom but also in terms of providing bar facilities at local functions, providing a functions room for wedding receptions and for meetings of local organisations. The way in which he will be seen to interact in the pub, and in the community will have the net effect of improving or maintaining sales.

A hotel manager by developing social contacts *outside* the hotel may also generate sales *within* the hotel. His membership of the local golf club and his active participation in the local chamber of commerce will have a tendency to attract trade. This may be in the form of the golf club annual dinner and prize presentation taking place in the hotel restaurant or in the form of providing accommodation and catering facilities for the visiting trade delegation to the local area. In each case the way in which the hotel manager has fostered and developed informal social relationships and interaction outside of the hotel has helped to generate sales within it.

## Student Activity   No. 35

Describe clearly the way in which the following may employ interactive selling skills:

(i)     The hotel receptionist.
(ii)    The restaurant manager.
(iii)   The cruise line chambermaid.


## Customer Complaints

The most efficient catering unit will from time to time receive complaints from customers about the service that it is offering. A popular adage that is nearly always employed by those who work in the catering industry is: 'The customer is always right'. It is generally the case that even if all those who work in a catering unit, from the owner down to the part-time kitchen porter, agree that the customer in a given situation, is in the wrong, this point of view will rarely, if ever, be passed on to the customer. Social skills therefore need to be carefully applied in such situations to ensure that customer safisfaction is achieved. A member of staff may feel convinced that he is in the right in a certain situation, but he will be required to accept that the customer is 'always right' and to behave toward him in the appropriate manner. If a customer complains, therefore, the member of staff will respond in every case as if the complaint was valid and justifiable, unless he is told otherwise by his manager or employer.

We will consider a number of situations to demonstrate the importance of staff response to customer complaints.

If a customer complains about the quality of food or service in a restaurant, it is first of all, necessary to ascertain whether the complaint can be justified or not. If it is possible to rectify the cause of a justifiable complaint, then normally the acceptable response on the part of the head waiter or the manager would be to offer apologies and an alternative or improved product. In the case of the unjustifiable customer complaint in the restaurant, staff might respond by treating the complaint as if it was justifiable to ensure customer satisfaction. Such a complaint may however, cause the restaurant manager to point out the customer error but this is unlikely as other customers in the restaurant may become aware of the likely disturbance that might ensue from a disagreement.

Customer complaints in a hotel or guest house, for example, might be directed at other customers. The noisy party-goers arriving back late at the guest-house after a night on the town may provoke complaints from other residents. In this case tact and diplomacy will need to be employed by the guest-house proprietor; he will have to politely but firmly point out the problems caused to other residents when such incidents occur and at the same time be seen by the complaining residents to be acting in some way so that they are to a certain extent appeased by the proprietor's action. The proprietor must judge what is the most expedient course of action so that his operation is affected in the least damaging way. The employment of social skills will be of fundamental importance in such a situation.

### Student Activity   No. 36

Describe clearly the social skills that might be employed to deal with the following situations of customer complaint:

(i) The wealthy hotel resident who continually complains about the quality of the food and service in the hotel restaurant.

(ii) The drunken non-resident guest who complains about being served short-measures in the hotel bar.

(iii) A female member of the reception team who complains about sexual harassment from the night porter during the night shift.

## ASSESSMENT QUESTIONS

1. Explain the different approaches and skills that may be required by different staff positions and roles.

2. Explain how different positions require different social skills in different situations.

3. Explain what is meant when we say that the roles attached to any position are multi-dimensional.

4. Describe the way in which an event or occurrence can influence social skills in a working situation.

5. Explain the way in which social skills will be affected by the demands of different situations.

6. Describe the social skills that may be employed in an emergency situation.

7. Illustrate the employment of necessary social skills in response to a fire and an accident.

8. Explain the meaning of term the 'image' of the firm.

9. Identify the ways in which members of staff can maintain the 'image' of the firm.

10. Explain the meaning of the term 'interactive selling skill'.

11. Demonstrate with the use of examples the way in which interactive selling skills may be employed in the hotel and catering industry.

12. Explain the way in which social skills may best be employed in dealing with customer complaints in a variety of different situations.

# CONCLUSION

Any careful analysis of behavioural studies in the hotel and catering industry must be broken down into a number of component parts. The foregoing analysis can therefore be seen as considering all the elements that contribute to an understanding of human behaviour in a range of specific industrial and commercial situations.

The value of any analysis of behavioural studies in the hotel and catering industry must take into account the context on which the industry exists and the historical dimension of which it is a part. From a contextual point of view behavioural studies in the hotel and catering industry will be influenced by a wide range of social, economic, cultural and political factors. Indeed these external factors which go to make up the context or setting of the industry will be influential in moulding many aspects of the industry as it develops and changes.

These changes and developments will be seen as part of a more general historical perspective. The direction in which the industry is developing and in particular the way in which this affects the individuals who work in it will be of interest to all who are involved in the industry. The historical perspective we take will help us be aware not only of past developments and present conditions but also the way in which change may take place in the future. Factors as diverse and multi-faceted as unemployment, automation, increasing leisure time, computerisation and many others will determine the face of the hotel and catering industry in the future and will influence the behavioural characteristics of its members as these changes take place.

## Biblography and Recommended Further Reading

Manpower Management in the Hotel and Catering Industry: T. Hornsey and D. Dann   *Batsford Ltd*

Hotel and Catering Supervision: K.J. Gale and P. Odgers   *MacDonald & Evans*

Management in the Hotel and Catering Industry: H.V. Gullen and G.E. Rhodes   *Batsford Ltd*

Catering Supervision: A.E. Bevan   *Edward Arnold*

Personnel Management in the Hotel and Catering Industry: M.J. Boella *Stanley Thornes (Publishers) Ltd*

Analysing Catering Operations: G. Cutcliffe   *Edward Arnold*

# Supervisory Studies 1

## STUDY BOOK TWO

# Introduction

The role of the modern supervisor is acknowledged to be of great importance to the successful running of hotel and catering operations. The study of supervisory techniques and approaches is therefore central to the development of our understanding of manpower management in general.

In this study book therefore, we will attempt to come to an understanding of the role of the modern supervisor in the hotel, restaurant and institutional catering trade. We will consider the supervisor's relationship with staff and with other managerial levels within those organisations. This analysis should also provide us with a basis for examining other aspects of management, necessary for a more complete understanding of the manager's role within the hotel and catering industry.

The actual environment that a business operates within will provide us with our first area of study. Such an analysis will give a context or setting within which further investigations may be carried out. We will consider not only the climate within which business operates but also its structure and organisation. From here we can examine the supervisor's role in a little more detail. We will consider the position of the supervisor within the organisation and the way in which his influence may be felt.

An important aspect of the supervisory role is planning and organising the work force to perform in an efficient manner. We will examine what is involved in carrying out these functions, looking at manpower planning, aspects of control, maintenance of standards, performance and so on. This will lead us to an examination of the way in which a supervisor may affect the behaviour of staff for whom he is responsible. His planning, organisational and controlling roles will be greatly influenced by his ability to motivate his subordinates to carry out tasks for the benefit of the operation as a whole. Analysis of communication techniques, working conditions, instructional approaches, industrial relations and employee welfare are all necessary in coming to terms with this part of the supervisor's role.

Finally, in our study of supervisory skills we will need to assess the achievement of success through the efforts of the work force. This is the way in which the effectiveness of the supervisory role can be measured. If results are achieved and seen to improve through the efforts of staff and this in turn can be traced to the skills of the supervisor, then the role of the latter can be said to have been successfully carried out. To this end we will look at manpower planning, in all respects; from drawing up clear and unamibiguous job descriptions, through recruitment and selection procedures, to performance appraisal and analysis.

By using this approach the study guide is intended to break down the supervisory role into its composite parts, to examine each of these in turn and to assess their interrelationships. In this way we can demonstrate clearly the important position the supervisor holds in any hotel and catering establishment.

**Section A**

# Business Organisations

The supervisor will carry out his tasks in a setting. Each setting or context will influence his ability to carry out these tasks successfully. Our examination of the supervisor, his role and the skills he employs, will therefore be preceded by an examination of the setting in which he operates. We will first of all consider the environmental influences on his role, the nature of the business he works in and the organisation of which he is a part.

## THE BUSINESS

In the commercial sector of the industry businesses or firms will be organised in such a way that profits will be achieved for those who own the business. Any restaurant, hotel, fast food outlet or industrial catering establishment will therefore be organised in what is considered the best way for achieving the required margins of profit. Non profit making catering organisations exist in the institutional sector, such as hospital, school and prison catering services. Although these will not necessarily be designed to make profits as such there will be demands placed upon them for efficiency and cost effectiveness. Before we examine the way in which the profit motive influences the organis-ation, we will consider the environment that any business might operate within. This is sometimes referred to as the 'climate' of business operation.

## The Business Climate

The success or failure of any firm or business operation may be crucially affected by the climate in which it operates. For example, a reduction in a nation's educational budget may reduce the quality of educational provision in its schools and colleges and in turn produce less able students. When these students seek employment they may require increased on the job training before they can begin to carry out their job properly. This need for increased on the job training, to be provided by an employer, will affect his ability to maintain profit margins. As a result of a governmental decision the organisation of a firm can therefore be affected.

The nature of the economy of any society will influence the various businesses that operate within it. We will briefly consider the different types of economy and assess the influence they might have upon a business.

### A State Economy

In a state economy, all business activities will be controlled by the state or the government of the country in which it operates. State control usually determines the nature of the business; its profits will normally be channelled back to the state to be further deployed in the running of the economy. Decisions that are made within any business organisation will normally be influenced by the central decision making body.

### A Laissez-Faire Economy

This is sometimes known as a free market economy. It is the kind of economy which is not controlled by the government but by market forces ie. the demands for various goods and services, the prices that may be paid for them and the supply that may exist. An individual business in a laissez-faire economy would not be influenced by state controls and would operate with a degree of independence, competing with other similar businesses and attempting to create profits.

### A Mixed Economy

In reality the existence of state or laissez-faire economics, as described above, is unlikely to occur. Each type is normally influenced in varying degrees by the existence of the other. A state controlled economy will contain within it certain elements of the free market, what may be referred to as elements of free enterprise. Similarly, a laissez-faire economy in which the government claims to play no part will invariably contain some degree of state intervention. In Britain, for example, the mixed economy is represented with a blend of free market trading and nationalised industries ie. those owned and controlled by the government.

Any commercial enterprise will be influenced by this business climate and therefore attention should be paid to the nature of the economy, in the way it influences such things as levels of employment, interest rates, public spending and so on. These in turn will influence the way in which the business functions.

## The Organisation

We must not confuse the term 'organisation' with the term 'the business' or 'the firm'. Each business will possess an organisation but it is confusing to treat the terms as synonymous. Schein defines an organisation as 'the rational co-ordination of the activities of a number of people for the achievement of some explicit purpose or goal through division of labour and function and through a hierarchy of authority and responsibility'.

It should be pointed out at this stage that organisations are usually described as being formal or informal. It is unlikely that a purely formal or purely informal organisation will exist and it is more normal to refer to organisations as being partly formal and partly informal. We will use Schein's definition as the basis for the development of the main characteristics of a formal organisation. These characteristics are as follows:

(i)   An organisational structure which defines the relationships between people in the organisation, in terms of authority, rules, status etc.

(ii)   A divison of labour and function whereby the various tasks to be carried out are broken down into parts and carried out by specialists.

(iii)   Organisational aims or objectives that describe what is hoped to be achieved by the organisation. In other words, its purpose or its goals.

(iv)   Contractual membership which will define the individual's relationship to the organisation, specifying his rights, duties and obligations.

(v)   Formal organisations have a recognisable life-span; a specific starting point and a continuity of purpose and balanced change.

At this stage it will be sufficient to point out that informal organisations possess characteristics which are more or less opposite to those of formal organisations.

We will next consider the business organisation in terms of structure and process, in other words, the way in which it is constructed and the way in which it operates.

### The Business Organisation as a Structure

The following organisation chart represents the structure of relationships, activities and functioning parts that may exist in a large-scale luxury hotel.

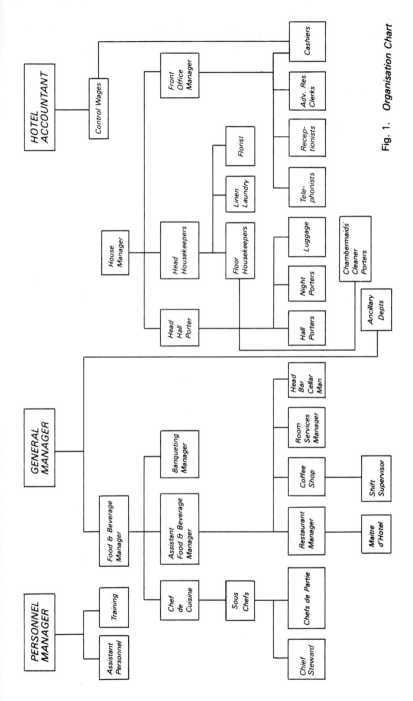

Fig. 1. *Organisation Chart*

74

The organisation chart comes about as a result of planning, development and a range of policy decisions being made at an executive level. In this form the structure of the hotel organisation is defined, each group and each individual in the organisation will know exactly what his duties are and what is expected of him. The business organisation, as a structure, defines what is to be done and who is going to do it.

*The Business Organisation as a Process*
Structures as such are largely static and immovable. That is not to say that they are resistant to change; modifications and alterations can always be made, providing the structure can continue to carry out its functions. Within any structure certain processes will operate and the business organisation must also be seen in this way. The activities of the organisation will take place through the organisational structure, authority will be delegated, tasks will be coordinated, responsibility will be given and communication will occur. In each of these cases a process is taking place. The term 'line management' describes an organisational process and in the organisation chart above certain processes will take place along the 'lines' of the chart. For example, management will use the line for communication, policy transmission, passing orders, giving instructions, delegating authority etc. This will describe organisational processes passing *down* the various lines of the chart. Different levels of the work force may use the 'lines' of the chart for the purposes of communication, feed-back, asking for clarification, reporting back, complaining etc. This will describe organisational processes as they pass *up* the various lines of the chart.

In this way the organisation, as both a structure and a process, is often referred to as a system or a series of sub-systems. The organisation provides a system for communicating instructions, finding decision making procedures and setting up a framework for the successful completion of work.

**Student Activity 1.**
Using the organisation chart in figure 1, explain by the use of examples, the way in which:
(i) Instructions.
(ii) Authority delegation *and*
(iii) Work activities are passed through the lines of the chart.
The same examples can be used to demonstrate how the organisational process operates in the opposite direction.

## THE SUPERVISOR

We next need to consider the position of the supervisor in the organisation. Each organisation will influence the supervisor, and other members of the work force, in a variety of ways but the supervisor, through his position and his functions, can also exert a considerable influence upon the organisation itself. In this analysis therefore we will look at the functions that the supervisor carries out, his position within the organisation and the way in which he influences the behaviour of those working in the organisation.

## The Catering Supervisor

Supervisors are given a wide range of different names, usually depending upon the type of industry or organisation in which they are found. In manufacturing industry, for example, supervisors are normally referred to as foremen, charge-hands or station leaders. In the catering industry supervisors have different names according to the type of organisation they work in and according to the kind of work they are involved in.

So, for example, in the hotel and restaurant sector of the industry we find a number of different supervisory roles being carried out. In the hotel kitchen the different chefs de partie will be given various supervisory duties and in the food service area these duties will be carried out by the maitre d'hotel or the station waiters. In their respective sections and departments housekeepers or floor housekeepers, receptionist shift leaders and coffee shop supervisors will all carry out the duties and responsibilities assigned to the position of supervisor.

In the non-commercial, institutional sector supervisors come in a variety of different forms. In hospitals, prisons and schools the supervisor may be the head cook, the chef supervisor or simply, the catering officer.

An analysis of the functions of the supervisor will help us to recognise him more easily.

## The Functions of the Supervisor

They way in which the supervisor carries out the various functions that are assigned to him must be seen in the context of the environment in which he operates. We have already discussed the importance of the climate of the business, and in addition we will need to be aware of the influence of the organisation and the physical working environment. In this context we may provide a general description of the supervisor's function. He is normally employed to act as a 'middle-man' between management and the work force. He will be responsible for interpreting the orders and instructions of management and passing them on to the work force. At the same time he will also provide feedback from the work force to management, monitoring grievances, communicating information and generally keeping management informed of developments that might be occurring amongst the work force. In the last section we examined the way in which the 'lines' of the organisation carried information, instructions etc. in both directions. Figure two represents the position of the supervisor as the 'middle man' carrying information in both directions in the organisation.

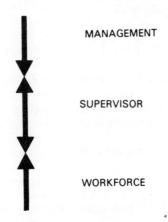

MANAGEMENT

SUPERVISOR

WORKFORCE

Fig. 2   *The Position of the Supervisor in the Organisation*

The 'middle man' position that the supervisor operates from gives him responsibilities, both to management and to the work force, its importance should therefore not be under valued.

We will now consider in more detail some specific aspects of the supervisor's role. We may break down the functions that he carries out into the following areas: planning, organising, operating, directing and controlling. We will consider each of these in turn and examine their interrelationships.

*Planning*
As we have already seen, the catering supervisor may be described in a number of ways according to his position within the organisation. Whatever name he is given within the organisation, his ability to carry out a range of planning activities will accurately reflect his value to the organisation as a whole. If the supervisor carries out his planning role carefully he will ensure that no effort will be wasted, that full production may be achieved, that a good service is provided and that efficiency and profitability are maintained at a high level. Planning results from the intellectual ability of being able to visualise the relationships between elements of the work force, to see the way in which individuals may be placed effectively into the organisation and to change working arrangements, should external factors influence the running of the organisation.

Planning by the supervisor will ensure smooth running of his section of the organisation. It will ensure that over-staffing and duplication of roles does not occur. It will foresee areas of stress or weakness and

77

anticipate future needs. Planning, by ensuring smooth production, will not only bring benefits for proprietors and managers but also for staff, in terms of bonuses, time off and conservation of personal energy. The following diagram demonstrates the value of planning as it allows for the smooth running of the food service operation and in turn enhances customer satisfaction.

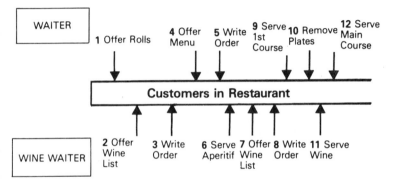

Fig. 3   *Planning smooth customer service in the restaurant*

Careful planning ensures that each of the imputs to the customer is well timed, satisfying customer needs, taking care not to rush customer decisions and unobtrusively offering advice whenever required. This supervisory planning function reflects management decisions, leads to customer satisfaction and is designed to maximise levels of profitability.

**Student Activity   No. 2**
Draw up a planning chart similar to that in figure 3 for the following operations.
(i)   The preparation of the breakfast menu by the kitchen brigade.
(ii)   A room changeover by the housekeeping team.

*Organisation*

If careful planning creates smooth and efficient operation, then organisation creates the framework upon which careful planning might be based. Planning is the supervisory function which looks ahead, assesses situations and describes the most efficient method of dealing with them. Organisation is the supervisory function which creates a structured set of relationships within which members of staff operate.

The task of the supervisor will be to arrange the job titles and activities of the work force into a coherent structure, ensuring that the minimum amount of overlap between them exists, and that the staff he is responsible for can carry out the plans and objectives of the firm in the most efficient manner. It should be pointed out at this stage that the supervisor will have some responsibility for the organisation of equipment and materials, although in the first place, where considerable capital investment might be involved, the decisions regarding equipment might be taken by senior management. This brings us to the actual position of the supervisor in the organisation and should enable us to see more clearly what his exact organising role is within the business organisation. The following diagram demonstrates the position of the supervisor in the organisation, showing what is sometimes referred to as his 'linkman' or 'middleman' role and his position in terms of authority delegation.

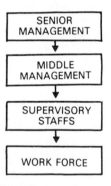

Fig. 4  *Organisation and Delegation*

Senior management and middle management have the ability not only to delegate tasks to lower levels of the organisation but also have the authority to pass on delegating authority, ie. senior management may give authority to middle management to delegate authority to the supervisor. Normally, however, the supervisor will only have authority to delegate tasks to the work force. This represents a distinction between the management's organisational role and the supervisor's organisational role. The ability to delegate tasks to individuals within the work force is therefore a key element of the supervisor's organisational function.

## Student Activity   No. 3

In the organisation of staff and materials for a banquet, show how the organising role of management differs from the organising role of the supervisor. Give specific examples to illustrate your points.

*Operation*

The operation of an establishment is its day to day working, the way in which it operates or works. The operation of any establishment must therefore be smooth, efficient and fulfill the aims of the ownership of the establishment. Supervisors play an important role in this operation. A kitchen in a large industrial catering unit, for example, may be required to be fully operational for 16 hours a day. The catering supervisor will be responsible for operating the kitchen to run efficiently for this 16 hour period. He will be required to draw up suitable split-shift arrangements, design staff duty rotas, arrange for a responsible member of staff to be present at all times, ensure that shift changes are fluent and conveniently managed and generally operate the kitchen so that maximum use of staff and kitchen resources can be achieved.

This example illustrates the role of the supervisor in ensuring that the establishment operates to a maximum capacity, a necessary condition, particularly in the case of the commercial sector when one considers investments made by owners in terms of equipment, staff and general overheads.

*Directing*

We have considered the importance of delegation in the supervisor's organising function, however, delegation will be unsuccessful if it is organised in the wrong direction. In other words an important supervisory function is that of directing individual members of the work force to carry out tasks which they are best suited to do. For example, the delegation of tasks to the kitchen brigade in preparation for a banquet, will be best achieved by due consideration of the skill areas available and directing the different preparation tasks to the best suited areas. The various sections of a large hotel kitchen will be staffed by commis chefs who are most capable of preparing vegetables, making sauces, working with pastries and so on. This deployment of staff will not only demonstrate the supervisor's skills in delegating tasks but also in directing tasks to those most skilled and qualified to carry them out. The parallel between the supervisor and the film director is a close one. The film director will be required to direct actors, film-crew, make-up man, scriptwriters and a wide range of different staff in creating the end product ie. the successful film. The supervisor will be required to employ directing skills in a similar manner.

## Controlling

Any establishment will need to be controlled. If control is not exercised over staff, resources and equipment the establishment will not achieve the levels of efficiency necessary for its success. Supervisors can only successfully control their areas of responsibility if they are given certain standards to which they are expected to adhere.

Standards within a restaurant or a hotel may be set by its owners or management; whereas in an institutional establishment they may be set by nutritional requirements or by government policy. These standards provide the supervisor with guidelines within which to work; he may refer staff to these standards and if they are not complied with they may provide him with a basis for remedial action. Standards are of course arbitrary and some will be easier or harder to achieve than others. The controlling function of the supervisor will be greatly affected by the standards that are set for him.

We should not assume that standards will be imposed upon supervisors entirely from above, governing the limits of his control. A good supervisor will work with management in developing standards that are reasonable and realistic and which impose demands upon the work force that are within their ability to achieve.

The supervisor, in successfully carrying out this controlling function, will therefore be able to accept standards imposed from above, measure the performance of staff in relation to these standards, recommend changes in standards to management and generally work to ensure that control of all aspects of the establishment is carried out. Our analysis of the controlling function is continued in later sections.

### Student Activity   No. 4

Suggest some standards that supervisors might employ for controlling staff in the following areas:

(i)    Food preparation staff and mode of dress.
(ii)   The reception team and the hours/shifts worked.
(iii)  The food service team and the number of restaurant covers worked.
(iv)  The counter staff in a fast food outlet and increased sales.

### Supervisory Responsibilities

The preceding outline of the fundamental functions usually ascribed to supervisors should demonstrate that the supervisor in any organisation will have a number of responsibilities associated with his position in the organisation. The popular image of the supervisor as the link or middle man between management and the work force clearly delineates his responsibilities. In simple terms he will have responsibilities to his superiors and his subordinates. All his actions will therefore be viewed from this dual perspective.

*Responsibilities to Superiors*
The supervisor will be responsible for ensuring that the work force carry out certain tasks correctly. He will be required to act on instructions, receive and carry out orders and generally reflect the management position and the standards that they set. In another sense senior management may see the supervisor as a 'front-line manager' and in this sense his responsibilities may be in terms of defining objectives, motivating staff and exercising his organisational planning and controlling skills. We might say that this represents a more autonomous role in that the supervisor has a higher degree of independence to carry out his assigned tasks. Ultimately, his responsibilities relate to the wishes, objectives and plans of his superiors.

*Responsibilities to Subordinates*
The supervisor by having to fulfill certain obligations and responsibilities to his employers and management superiors, will be constrained to ensure that subordinates carry out certain functions which contribute to the successful running of the firm. The supervisor will nevertheless have certain responsibilities to his subordinates. He acts as their direct and immediate liaison with management, conveying grievances and complaints, asking for clarification, making personal enquiries and generally acting as their representative. He has a responsibility to ensure that the demands that management might wish to impose upon the work force are not too excessive and he will work to protect their working conditions, employment rights and conditions of service.

In his role as the link man the supervisor will have to be aware of his dual responsibilities. He will need to act as a mediator between the often conflicting demands of management and the work force and will therefore need to exercise great skill in dealing with both groups.

## THE ORGANISATION, THE SUPERVISOR AND THE STAFF

Our analysis of business organisations so far has dealt specifically with the business itself, the context in which it operates and the position of the supervisor within it. In this section we will concentrate upon the interaction between the organisation of the business, the supervisors who function within it and the staff who are employed and work for the business. The harmonious interaction of these elements represents the basis of successful and efficient business operations.

### Achievement of Results
The role of the supervisor has been described on occasions as the achievement of results through people. According to this view the supervisors task is to ensure that the objectives of the business, let us say to make profits, are achieved through the efforts of the work force.

This has become a very complex task because the incentives that are available and being demanded by workers requires that the supervisor can skilfully exercise their use. Maslow's hierarchy of needs showed us that once man has fulfilled certain basic or physiological needs he begins to search out certain higher or psychological needs. It may be the case therefore that large sums of money alone will be insufficient to motivate workers; they may require more from their work experience in terms of responsibility, morale boosting, encouragement and attention. The supervisor, as a front-line manager, will be largely responsible for ensuring that these needs are satisfied and that through this needs satisfaction the objectives of the firm are also realised. He will attempt to balance the profit minded approach of the owners of the firm with the human relations approach which considers worker's welfare and well-being. We will examine the achievement of results through people in detail in Section D.

**The Personnel Function**
In many large scale organisations some of the work of the supervisor has been taken over by a personnel manager and, in some cases, a personnel department. The existence of personnel departments in such organisations tends to be a reflection of the size of the organisation rather than that the role of the supervisor has become redundant. By way of contrast, in many smaller firms the tasks of the supervisor would be carried out by the owner of the firm acting in a managerial capacity. The personnel function, therefore, will be carried out by owners, managers, supervisors or personnel staff, depending upon the size of the organisation. Within the hotel and catering industry where a high turnover of labour is common and where a large number of part-time, casual and often unskilled staff are employed the need exists for a specialist personnel staff to take the burden of recruitment, welfare, disciplinary procedure etc. away from supervisors, who can then concentrate upon their front-line management tasks.

Staff relations represents a high priority area in the hotel and catering industry; as a service industry the hotel and catering industry has to employ staff who can not only work to create a product but who, in a sense, are part of the product themselves. Customers pay, not only for a certain quality of product, in terms of catering and accommodation, but also for a quality of service. The personnel function, whoever takes over its responsibility, represents a highly important and significant aspect of successful hotel and catering operations.

*Decision Making*
Decisions will constantly need to be made by supervisors or members of the personnel department. These decisions will vary in importance but will influence the successful operation of the firm in some way or

another. Supervisors may be responsible for staff-training and may be required after a period of induction and on the job training to make a decision regarding the suitability for employment of a trainee or apprentice. The way in which this decision is reached and whether or not it is a correct decision is a measure of a supervisor's skills.

## Job Analysis and Design
The supervisor will have specialised knowledge of the workings of his particular area of responsibility. The chef de partie will have had experience as an apprentice and a commis chef in his particular section prior to taking over supervisory responsibilities. He will therefore be required to exercise skills of job design and job analysis so that the various tasks which his section has to carry out are clearly defined and allocated to members of staff most capable of carrying them out. He will be required to break down the tasks, assigned to his section, into their component parts; in other words carry out a job analysis. This will be followed by the job design, which not only describes the best methods and strategies for carrying out a given job but also specifies and directs the staff most skilled and suitable to carry out the component parts of the job previously analysed.

The personnel manager will carry out analysis on a larger scale but in the same way as the supervisor does in the example above. Where the supervisor deals with one specific area of tasks a personnel manager may deal with the complete range of tasks within the operation. This will be dealt with in greater details in section D which covers performance supervision; at this stage we will outline the areas to which job analysis may be applied.

(i)    Manpower Planning, which deals with the different job categories and the available staff resources.

(ii)    Recruitment and selection of staff based upon the demands of the job and the skills and qualifications of applicants.

(iii)    Job Appraisal will be based upon a previous analysis of the job.

(iv)    Training can only be carried out if job analysis has preceded it, outlining the demands of the job on the trainee.

(v)    Wage levels can be realistically set if the job analysis has been carried out; 'a fair days wage for a fair days work'.

(vi)    Motivation of the staff can be enhanced by job analysis; the analysis may show ways of designing the job so that workers are given more responsibility which in turn boosts their morale.

(vii)    Industrial relations can be maintained at a reasonable level if job analysis has been carried out and as a result the demands and expectations placed upon staff and the rewards they receive are seen by management and staff as being reasonable.

## Quality Control
Job analysis and job design, which is based upon careful observation, interviews, work study and staff appraisal, can only ultimately lead to

control over the quality of product and service given. Any efficient catering operation which is to maintain an image favourable to the public, must consistently provide products and service of high or acceptable quality. Control must be exercised over the factors which contribute to the quality of product and service. The supervisor and the personnel manager will, by means of the procedures outlined above, contribute to the staff aspect of quality control.

In general, high quality service and product will be achieved if attention is paid to all aspects of the personnel function, dealt with in this section. To this end, it is important that consistency and standards are maintained. Quality control cannot be left to chance or allowed to be disrupted by unforeseen occurrences therefore it is common practice for those responsible for personnel practices to consult and draw up what is known as a personnel policy, or a manpower plan. The manpower plan, described in detail in section D, will be a statement (or range of statements) describing practices and procedures to be followed by all staff in the fulfillment of the aims and objectives of the firm. It will also take into consideration the needs of personnel and attempt to incorporate the satisfaction of these needs, within the framework of the firm's objectives.

All the factors described in this section are designed to contribute to the achievement of results through the efforts of people employed in the industry. It is essentially the role of the supervisor and all personnel staff to achieve this end.

## ASSESSMENT QUESTIONS

1. Explain the term 'the business climate'.
2. Distinguish between a state, a laissez-faire and a mixed economy.
3. Explain the importance of the context in which a business operates.
4. Describe the business organisation as a structure.
5. Describe the business organisation as a process.
6. Explain the way in which the business organisation as a structure interacts with the business organisation as a process.
7. List the characteristics of a formal business organisation.
8. Distinguish between the various functions of the supervisor.
9. Explain the way in which the different supervisory functions inter-relate.
10. Explain the relationship of the supervisor to other levels of management.
11. Distinguish between the supervisors' responsibilities to superiors and subordinates.
12. Explain the need for a system of communicating instructions and guiding decisions and work.

13. Explain the phrase 'achievement of results through people'.
14. Define the personnel function.
15. Explain the importance of the personnel function to hotel and catering establishments.
16. Describe what is entailed by job analysis.
17. Explain the importance of quality control.

# Work Supervision

Our analysis so far has demonstrated the importance of the supervisor within the organisational context; we have examined basic supervisory functions and have linked these to the achievement of broad organisational objectives. In this section we will consider the role of the supervisor in specific terms of planning and organising for work performance. We will carry out this examination, first of all, by looking at the way in which the supervisor will plan the work that has to be carried out by his sector of the work force and secondly, by examining the way in which he maintains levels and standards of work performance within his area of responsibility.

## PLANNING THE WORK

A supervisor's approach to the work that his section has to carry out must, above all, be systematic. He must demonstrate to management and workers alike that he is consistent and logical in his treatment of the work to be done. There must be a pattern to his work, his decisions must be consistent and to a certain degree predictable; his activities must therefore conform to a set of pre-determined conditions that have been carefully conceived and laid out. In other words the supervisor must develop, establish and follow plans. By planning the work the supervisor will not only present a work-man like image to management but also he will appear consistent and logical to the work force.

The supervisory functions dealt with in Section A; planning, organising, operating, directing and controlling will all be embraced by the supervisor's planned approach. In planning for a banquet, in organising a duty roster, in operating a split shift system, in directing staff to carry out a range of specialised tasks and in controlling a staff meeting, the successful supervisor will be working to fulfill preconceived ideas of work performance. He will have developed an overall strategy or plan to enable him to carry out all his functions in the required manner. His plans will not be rigid, he will incorporate a degree of flexibility into them to allow for changes in circumstances eg. in the case of a breakdown of a piece of equipment, or in the case of staff absence. Wherever possible his planning will incorporate an anticipation of all possible eventualities that may occur in the work place. In reality this will be difficult to achieve with 100% success, but this should not discourage the supervisor from working toward achieving such a plan. We will next consider the way in which a supervisor may go about planning the work.

## Planning Production and Service

In beginning the planning process the supervisor will have to consider the mutual and harmonious working relationship between three elements: Staff, Equipment, Materials. Figure 5 shows how these elements are connected.

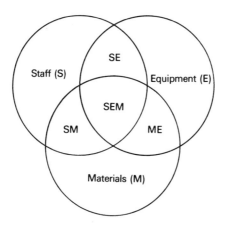

Fig. 5. *Elements of the Planning Process*

Not only will the supervisor need to maximise the capabilities of each element in the planning process, but also he will need to ensure that each area of overlap ie. Staff-Equipment (SE), Staff-Materials (SM), Materials-Equipment (ME), is planned in advance to functional requirements. In addition the area in which all three elements overlap ie. SEM, will require special attention to ensure that production and service can be successfully carried out.

The supervisor, in planning production and service, has to consider many factors in the relationship between these three elements. To illustrate this we will consider some examples.

In the area marked SE supervisors will have to consider the relationship between staff and the equipment. This area of analysis is covered by the study called ergonomics; the way in which man is affected in his working environment by the machinery or equipment he has to operate. The supervisor might consider operating a job rotation where the operation of one machine is repetitive and may become boring. This is a significant consideration where large quantities of food are being produced eg. in a bakery or in a hospital or factory kitchen. Similarly, if an individual experiences difficulty operating a piece of equipment, the supervisor should monitor this and take action to ensure that productivity is not lost, and that the equipment is not damaged or the operator hurt in any way. An important dimension of planning therefore, is being able to carefully match individuals to equipment and the tasks they have to carry out with that equipment.

In the area marked SM supervisors will have to consider the relationship between staff and the materials they use. In kitchens, for example, chefs de partie may have to deal with the problem of de-skilling, where pre-packaged or ready prepared food products are being introduced. The introduction of this type of food will inevitably reduce the level of skills required by kitchen staff, which in turn may have an effect upon job satisfaction and the status of members of the kitchen staff. Clearly, changes of this kind should not be resisted but supervisors are faced with a problem in this area, where de-skilling occurs, because of the use of the convenience food products.

The role of the supervisor, in carrying out successful planning therefore, incorporates the need to ensure that the area SEM in figure 5 is an area of smooth and harmonious interaction between the three major elements he is concerned with.

### Student Activity   No. 5

(i) Write down some of the points a supervisor might need to consider in terms of planning production and service when micro-wave ovens are introduced to the kitchen or a large hotel.

(ii) Write down two illustrations of the technical relationship between equipment and materials (areas E and M in figure 5) that the supervisor might need to consider in the kitchen of an industrial catering unit.

(iii) Discuss the points and examples you have written down with other members of your group.

*The Process of Planning*

In order for the approach of the supervisor to be systematic he must adopt a planning process; action should not take place at random, planned logical steps need to be taken.

We will consider a number of possible stages through which a planning process might develop.

(i) The supervisor will need to be aware of the *objective of the organisation.* In a non profit making, service organisation such an objective might be to provide an efficient service within a given budget. In a commercial establishment, the objective might simply be to maximise the firm's profits. The supervisor will need to work within these objectives; they provide the setting for his work, he will be continually aware of the expectations that the fulfillment of these objectives place upon him. This might entail working toward targets, such as productivity goals or the achievement of a certain standard of service.

(ii) The objectives of the organisation, though clear, may be rather general, as targets for supervisors to aim for. It is therefore important that these general objectives are broken down into *specific goals or targets.* For example, in providing an adequate food service from which profits will accrue, management and supervisors will need to create smaller, separate but co-ordinated work units to achieve the organisational objective. The coffee shop supervisor will set a range of tasks, each having specific targets, for her staff. She will have to ensure that tables are correctly laid up and set, that an adequate supply of crockery is available, that carpets have been cleaned, that sufficient food stuff has been brought from the larder and so on. The coffee shop supervisor will need to set each of these tasks, specify targets and ensure that each are co-ordinated to produce a smooth and efficient service in the coffee shop.

(iii) This can only be achieved by careful *task analysis* on the part of the supervisor. In the previous example, the coffee shop supervisor will need to know exactly, what each of the tasks she sets her staff entails. She will need to know the materials necessary to carry out certain tasks and may need to ask such questions as: 'Do we have enough clean table cloths?' 'Do we have an adequate supply of fresh coffee?' 'Is the supply of cleaning materials sufficient for the week?' She will also need to know at what stage the job should be carried out. She should ensure, for example, that the dining room floors have been cleaned before she instructs staff to begin laying up. She will also need to consider who is the best person to ask to do a particular job. Her understanding of the range of abilities within her staff will enable her to carefully deploy these staff abilities to areas of work for which they are most suited. The supervisor may consider that a job rotation is a practical means of staff deployment but she should also be aware that certain members of staff are better at some jobs than others. She must draw up a balance here between staff being specialists or staff being multi-skilled. Advantages and disadvantages can result from both approaches.

(iv) From this careful task analysis the next logical step in the planning process is the carrying out of *work design.* Work design entails making decisions based upon the preceding target and task analysis. These decisions will specify the answers to questions that might have been set during the task analysis eg. how is the job to be done? At what stage will the job be done? Who is best equipped to do the job? The supervisor will then *specify* the answers to these and other questions and indicate *schedules* for these tasks to be carried out. We will deal with work design, specifications and schedules in greater detail in section C.

(v) The next stage of the planning process is to actually *put the chosen plan into operation* and to invite management and staff to offer comments about the effectiveness of the plan in operation. This in effect is the presentation of the prototype of the plan and after a trial period changes to the plan may be made.

(vi) *Appraisal and modification* will follow directly from (v) above. Any plan will have mistakes; creases will need to be ironed out. It is at this stage that the supervisor will review his plans, consider them in the light of the practical application and the comments that have been made about them. It is unlikely that he will be required to carry out wholesale changes to his original plan. Modifications will need to be made to deal with points that may have been overlooked.

It is important to point out at this stage that the conscientious supervisor will carry out appraisal and modification on a regular basis. This will accommodate the changes that may occur in the working environment which might necessitate alterations to the original plan being made. Appraisal and review of working methods and conditions will enable supervisors to monitor levels of productivity and efficiency and also place themselves in a position whereby staff may approach and consult them on a regular basis.

**The Legal Aspects of Planning**

All work activities within any industry should take place with due consideration of the laws that apply to the work situation. Recruitment procedures within a firm must be drawn up in accordance with the Sex Discrimination Act 1975 and the Race Relations Act 1976. Terms of employment offered must be in line with the Contracts of Employment Acts 1963-72. Legislation exists to cover all aspects of the work situation: health and safety, redundancy payments, labour relations, methods of payment etc.

We will briefly consider some of the legal aspects of planning the work that is to be carried out within hotel and catering establishments.

*The Written Contract*

All employees, if they do not possess a written contract of employment, must possess a written statement of the terms under which they are employed. This represents the initial legal consideration to be made. The Employment Protection (Consolidation) Act 1978 specifies that the written contract or statement of employment must include the names of the parties involved (ie. the employer and the employee), the date of commencement of employment, the rates of pay, method of payment etc. The Act also states the following, which is of specific relevance to the planning of the work:

'... The hours of work; what arrangements exist (if any) for holidays and holiday pay; sickness and sick pay; pensions and pensions scheme; the length of notice required to terminate the contract on either side, the date of termination in the case of a fixed term contract; the title of the job which the employee is employed to perform; whether or not the employer is contracted out of the state pension scheme.'

From this quotation we can see that the supervisor cannot carry out the planning process without first making reference to the contractual obligations of the employee. He cannot, for example, draw up a duty roster if the hours of work specified on it violate those previously agreed upon by the employer and the employee. Similarly, the supervisor should not draw up plans specifying an employee's area of work if this is outside 'the title of the job which the employee is employed to perform'.

*Working Conditions*
In addition to legislation which specifies conditions of employment, the conditions in which employees work are regulated by different forms of legislation. No supervisor can draw up working plans without due consideration of these. In legal terms, employers owe many duties to employees (and third parties such as customers) in respect of health, safety and working conditions.

Within the hotel and catering industry the three major Acts of Parliament which influence the working conditions of employees are: the Shops Act 1950, the Offices, Shops and Railway Premises Act 1963 and the Health and Safety at Work Act 1974. Each of these Acts contain requirements regulating planning procedures that supervisors may draw up. We will briefly consider each of these in turn:

(i)   The Shops Act 1950, despite its name, embraces workers in the hotel and catering industry because it defines a 'shop' as 'any premises where any retail trade or business is carried on'. The term shop includes all catering establishments that sell food and drink to the general public. The term therefore includes, for example, cafes and restaurants but not industrial or welfare catering establishments. In a hotel, for example, because all staff do not deal with the 'general public' they will not be covered by the Act. Those that do, such as receptionists or bar staff will be classed as 'shop assistants' and will be covered by the Act.

The Act makes stipulations about hours that employees may work, length and frequency of meal-breaks, overtime and Sunday working etc.

(ii)  The Offices, Shops and Railway Premises Act, 1963, which covers over 25,000 catering establishments in Great Britain, sets down certain minimum working conditions for employees covered by the Act. Most employees included are:

(a) Shop Assistants as defined by the Shops Act 1950.

(b) Office workers eg. receptionists, cashiers.

(c) Canteen staff working in canteens providing a service to employees in offices and shops.

The Act makes stipulations regarding health and safety. Health provisions include details regarding cleanliness, lighting, temperature etc. Safety provisions include details of working premises, machinery, first aid etc.

(iii) The Health and Safety at Work Act, 1974, is probably the most important Act that supervisors need to be aware of when planning the work. Although the Offices, Shops and Railway Premises Act deals specifically with catering establishments, the Health and Safety at Work Act covers *all* industry laying down general rules covering employee safety at work, and establishing a Health and Safety Executive with powers to inspect premises.

The range and general applicability of the Health and Safety at Work Act 1974 to all industrial premises makes it a compulsory source of reference for the supervisor who is in the process of drawing up plans for implementation in his section of work. The Act covers a wide range of areas; these include protecting employees from defective or dangerous equipment, providing training and instruction for staff, ensuring safe working systems and so on.

## Student Activity   No. 6

Look up the Shop Act, the Offices, Shops and Railway Premises Act and the Health and Safety at Work Act in your college library. Under the headings of 'health' and 'safety' draw up a list of the major provisions of each Act for workers in the catering industry.

## The Implementation of Plans

The supervisor is now in a position to implement and initiate the plans he has drawn up. He has carried through his planning process, which has included a careful appraisal of his plan and he has taken into consideration the legal requirements of the work situation and the employees within it. His plan can now be put into operation. We will consider what this entails.

The initial stages of the planning process show how specific targets evolve from the objectives of the organisation. Menu planning provides us with an illustration of the way in which this works. The general objective of a hotel restaurant may be, for example, to maximise the quality of food and service and to ensure acceptable levels of profit for proprietors. In order to achieve this objective numerous targets or goals may be set by management and supervisors. The menu as a production statement will   generate these targets and the recognition of these targets will generate the need to achieve these targets. This is demonstrated by figure 6.

Fig. 6. *Target Achievement*

The targets that any menu will allow us to identify may be listed as follows:

(i)   The courses of the meal.
(ii)  The dishes that form these courses.
(iii) The associated alcoholic beverages.
(iv)  The service of (i), (ii) and (iii) above.

The preparation and service of these, represent targets that have to be achieved. We need to examine the process whereby the targets that have been identified become the targets that have been achieved; in other words the implementation of plans to fill the gap between the two boxes in figure 6.

Figure 7 is a more complex version of figure 6 and represents the way in which plans may be implemented.

We will go through the various stages of the diagram in turn. The various chefs de partie in the hotel kitchen will have identified targets which are component parts of the menu. The sauce chef, for example, will have to prepare a variety of stocks, sauces and gravies which will complement the dishes on the menu. The fish chef will prepare various fish dishes, fish sauces and garnishes in line with the requirements of the menu. In each case the chef de partie will carry out a task analysis and make decisions on how to delegate tasks to the various commis chefs, stewards or apprentices in his section. The larder chef, for example, will have studied the menu and will realise that certain raw materials are required for the menu. He will delegate tasks according to these requirements ie. different members of staff will dress and prepare different raw materials as required, such as poultry, meat, fish, salads, hors d'oeuvre etc. Each of these will be specialist task areas requiring individual skills. Finally, the larder chef will be expected to co-ordinate the tasks under his authority ensuring that the various raw materials are dressed and prepared in line with the production schedule of the menu. When this is done the larder chef will have achieved his target.

Each chef de partie in his supervisory capacity will need to carry through his plans in this way. The production of the menu represents

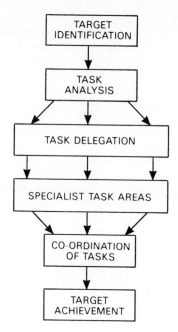

```
        ┌─────────────────┐
        │     TARGET      │
        │ IDENTIFICATION  │
        └─────────────────┘
                 │
                 ▼
        ┌─────────────────┐
        │      TASK       │
        │    ANALYSIS     │
        └─────────────────┘
         ╱       │       ╲
        ▼        ▼        ▼
    ┌─────────────────────────┐
    │     TASK DELEGATION     │
    └─────────────────────────┘
      ╱      │      │      ╲
     ▼       ▼      ▼       ▼
    ┌─────────────────────────┐
    │   SPECIALIST TASK AREAS │
    └─────────────────────────┘
       ╲      │       ╱
        ▼     ▼      ▼
        ┌─────────────────┐
        │  CO-ORDINATION  │
        │    OF TASKS     │
        └─────────────────┘
                 │
                 ▼
        ┌─────────────────┐
        │     TARGET      │
        │   ACHIEVEMENT   │
        └─────────────────┘
```

Fig. 7.  *Plan Implementation*

the focus of attention and the various parts of the menu represent different targets for different chefs de partie. It will be the role of the chef de cuisine to ensure that the activities of the various chefs de partie are co-ordinated into a continuous and fluent process of food production.

The example we have considered here demonstrates the way in which any supervisor may implement and initiate the plans that he has drawn up for the staff in his section.

**Student Activity   No. 7**
Using figure 7 as the basis for your answer show how:
  (i)   A head waiter would implement plans for ensuring that his waiters/waitresses had prepared their mis en place.
  (ii)  A head shift receptionist would implement plans to deal with a Saturday changeover in a busy seaside hotel.

## MAINTENANCE OF STANDARDS

We have now examined the planning process from its earliest stages through to its implementation and the achievement of targets and objectives. The supervisor, in carrying out his planning role, is therefore

95

in a critical position in terms of the achievement of the firm's objectives. Figure 8 shows how these objectives are achieved.

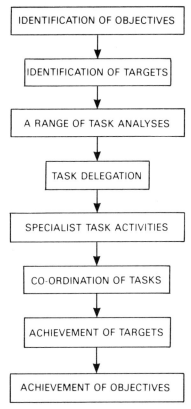

Fig. 8  *Achievement of Objectives*

Through successful planning the supervisor places himself in an important position in the achievement of the firm's objectives; he achieves this through his systematic approach to task analysis and delegation and co-ordination with other sections. The standard, having been achieved, has to be maintained.

**Direction and Control**
The supervisor will be in a position where he will often have to direct the activities of his staff. An important aspect of his role in terms of the achievement of objectives, as shown in figure 8, is his detailed knowledge of his staff which allows him to delegate tasks to them. In dealing with this delegation the supervisor is *directing* the most suitable staff to their respective specialist areas. In order to achieve this the supervisor must have a close working knowledge of his subordinate's mental and

physical skills. He will have worked with his staff; he may have carried out a work study which indicates to him the strengths and weaknesses of his staff in different areas of work. His ability to direct staff will therefore be based upon experience of both his staff and the jobs which they can do.

If the supervisor has successfully implemented plans and they are seen to be operating effectively, then he has to ensure that they continue to do so. Control, therefore, represents the means by which successful planning and operation is sustained. The supervisor has realised the firm's objectives, he has created plans to reach the targets demanded by these objectives. He has, however, to constantly check to ensure that the plans are being carried out in the form that they were originally conceived. Checking becomes a system of control. In the same way that planning was justified because it provided a systematic approach to the work, so control is justified because it provides a systematic means of ensuring that plans are correctly implemented and standards are being maintained.

*A Feedback System*

The success of any communication process is dependant upon ensuring that the message being sent is received and acted upon in the intended manner and form. One means of establishing if this is the case is by obtaining feedback. We may ask the person with whom we are communicating certain questions to establish if understanding has taken place, eg. 'Is that clear?', 'Do you understand?' Similarly, the implementation of plans requires the same kind of feedback system. The supervisor needs to be constantly aware that the plans that he has put into action to achieve certain objectives and targets are being acted upon correctly. This enables him to exercise control.

The flow chart in figure 9 demonstrates a feedback system that a supervisor might employ to exercise control of subordinate's work in his section.

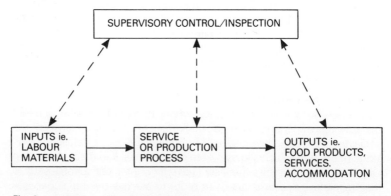

Fig. 9. *Supervisor's Feedback System*

The diagram shows that the supervisor is in direct contact with each stage of the production or service process within his section and is therefore able to exercise control over it. This form of control can be described as a continual work-study exercise. Plans have been implemented and the supervisor has to carry out inspection procedures to ensure that the plans are effective. This represents a means of control: the supervisor, by being in direct contact with all aspects of the work of his section, is able to implement corrective procedures if necessary and to encourage and maintain those procedures that are affective and which contribute to the overall efficiency of the organisation. We will continue our analysis of feedback systems in section C.

The supervisor's ability to control the work of his section is of critical importance to the effective running of the organisation as a whole. For example, if the speed at which his section produces is faster or slower than other sections in the organisation, the productive flow will in some way be disrupted, either creating a pile-up or a shortage of goods. In addition supervisory control must relate to quality and quantity, and must also have some influence over managerial decisions. If, for example, the quality of fried foods being produced in the kitchen is in some way inferior because of the malfunctions of the deep-frier, then the kitchen supervisor will need to exert pressure on management to ensure that the defective frier is either repaired or replaced. Control therefore relates to materials, equipment and staff.

### Student Activity No. 8
Explain the most effective form of control a supervisor might employ in the following situations:
  (i)   The coffee shop supervisor becomes aware that the quantity of food and drink passing between the kitchen and the restaurant does not tally with the waiter's cash receipts.
 (ii)   The turnover of waiting staff in a hotel is unacceptably high; the head waiter has to remedy this situation.
(iii)   The quality of food produced in the school canteen kitchen begins to deteriorate, despite no staff changes or apparent equipment malfunctions. What should the kitchen supervisor do?

### Induction
In the same way that the quality of food a chef is able to prepare is dependant upon the quality of raw material he obtains from his supplier, so the standard of work a supervisor is able to maintain in his section is dependant upon the staff he is able to employ. We have seen that the supervisory role embraces the smooth and efficient functioning of the three overlapping areas of materials, equipment and staff. The success of his function in relation to staff will be eased if the quality of staff he employs is high and if he also concentrates upon carefully inducting staff into his section and the organisation as a whole.

It is not sufficient, however, to simply employ high quality staff. New staff will be required to fit into the organisation; more specifically, they will be required to fit into a particular work group. The importance of group influence is highlighted in section C of Behavioural Studies for Hotel and Catering Operations. The work group which an individual enters lays down informal procedures based upon the attitudes and norms of the group. The newcomer will be expected to conform to these and this will be encouraged by the supervisor, particularly when the motivation of the group is in line with objectives of the organisation as a whole. Therefore, the supervisor will not only be required to provide the newcomer with information related to the job, ie. formal considerations, but also information related to the social context of the work situation ie. informal considerations. Induction therefore can be seen as having two general functions:

(i) The provison of information about the jobs.

(ii) An alignment of the newcomer to the objectives of the firm.

We will consider some of the specific elements of these two general functions.

*The Provision of Information*

As previously indicated we may subdivide the information a supervisor may provide a newcomer into formal and informal categories. We will deal with each in turn.

(i) Information related to the formal procedures within the work place will vary from one place of employment to another but we may refer to legal requirements which provide us with guidelines for formal induction procedures. In the first place information must be supplied regarding the Contract of Employment and also the terms and conditions of employment, as specified by the Employment Protection (Consolidation) Act 1978 (for details see previous section). A code of practice as specified by the 1971 Industrial Relations Act provides any supervisor with a sensible basis for the content and approach of an induction process. This code of practice lists the following information, which needs to be provided:

(a) The requirements of the job and to whom the employee is responsible.

(b) Disciplinary rules and procedures eg. dismissal or grievance procedure.

(c) Trade Union membership policy.

(d) Promotion and training policy.

(e) Social and welfare facilities.

(f) Fire, health and safety regulations (under the 1974 Health and Safety at Work Act, the provision of training, instruction etc. in this area is a specified duty of employers to employees).

(g) Communication and consultation procedures.

In addition to the above, supervisors might also be required to provide new employees with information about the firm, its history, organisation and products as well as giving them a thorough and complete tour of the workplace.

(ii)  Information related to informal procedures will be seen as being complementary to the information provided in (i) above. The introduction and acceptance of the newcomer must be achieved as quickly and completely as possible, not only for the success of the organisation but also for the benefit of the individual. One important reason for high labour turnover in some establishments is the inadequate provision given to the needs of the new employee during this introductory period. The supervisor can carry out a range of tasks to achieve this aim:

(a) Introduce himself, giving his name and where he may be easily found.

(b) Introduce the new employee to the rest of the group, giving their names and their relative positions in the group.

(c) Explain clearly the newcomer's role within the group, and what his duties will be.

(d) Explain clearly where he will work and provide him with information regarding the location of important places eg. locker room, equipment stores, toilets etc.

(e) Explain clearly working regulations eg. time and duration of tea-breaks, overtime requirements etc.

## Student Activity No. 9

(i)  Draw up a list of details that you would provide the new employee with during the induction period.

(ii)  Using your understanding of informal group influences, draw up a list of possible problems that may be associated with in this area.

(iii)  Discuss your ideas with the other members of your group.

The reasons for induction should now be clear; it should be carried through until the newcomer is fully integrated and accepted into the work group, whilst ensuring that disruption or changes to the successful working organisation are kept to a minimum. In other words induction is of fundamental importance to the maintenance of work standards. Without careful, thorough and complete induction, standards within the work place will inevitably suffer.

## Levels of Attainment

The logical extension of the induction process for the supervisor is to carry out performance analysis. He is responsible for productivity and service in his section, ensuring that standards are maintained, therefore he must constantly be able to analyse and appraise the performance of his subordinates. We will consider in detail in section D the way in which performance analysis and appraisal is carried out. At this stage we will examine the required attainment levels set by supervisors or management.

We have already seen the importance of supervisors setting realistic attainment targets for their subordinates and also the role of the work group in setting what it considers to be realistic levels of achievement (Mayos' famous Hawthorne Experiments demonstrate this latter point). In carrying out this task, supervisors must consider the suitable method of improving poor performance in a group and reducing the amount of errors that are made. The approach of the supervisor in these situations has to be carefully worked out. A stern, direct, authoritarian approach to poor performance or errors might be effective with some subordinates and ineffective with others. In deciding what approach to take the supervisor must consider the personality and attitude of the staff that he is dealing with and also the leadership style he should adopt. We will consider this latter aspect in section C.

*Maintenance Factors*
We will now refer to Herzberg's Motivation – Hygiene Theory which demonstrates the importance of establishing and maintaining the ''hygiene'' factors in any working establishment before the ''motivational'' factors can be fully developed. These relate to performance; the former have to be established before motivation can take place.

The Health and Safety at Work Act 1974 is designed to provide a framework for the health and safety of all workers. Employers, through managers and supervisors have a duty to providing information, instruction, training and supervision in all matters relating to health and safety and, in addition, to ensure that working conditions permit this.

*Routines*
An effective means by which supervisors can achieve satisfactory hygiene levels for the work force is through the establishment of practices or routines. If, during the planning process, the supervisor develops routines for such important areas as: cleaning, equipment maintenance, hygiene levels, safety requirements etc. he is more likely to be able to control the maintenance of standards within his section. Through the induction procedure staff can become familiarised with such routines, recognising them as a necessary part of their daily work schedule.

**Student Activity   No. 10**
   (i)   Draw up a cleaning routine that a school meals kitchen supervisor might implement for staff:
       (a)  On a daily basis.
       (b)  On a weekly basis.
       (c)  On a monthly basis.
       (d)  On an annual basis.

(ii) Draw up a set of fire regulations and instructions for use in your college to be placed in strategic positions. You should indicate such things as: emergency exits, muster-points, procedures to be followed etc.

Our examination of maintenance factors and the establishment of a range of work routines is continued in section C, where a more detailed examination of the work environment is carried out.

## ASSESSMENT QUESTIONS

1. Explain the need for a systematic approach to work in terms of the main supervisory functions.
2. Explain the interrelationship between staff, equipment and materials in the work situation.
3. Outline the ways in which the planning of production and service may take place.
4. Explain the main elements of the planning process.
5. List the main pieces of legislation associated with work planning.
6. Explain the relevance of the legislation above in the maintenance of work standards.
7. Explain the problems associated with the implementation of plans.
8. Describe the way in which work may be initiated: from having first of all identified a target to having achieved that target.
9. Outline the way in which plans may be implemented and work initiated.
10. Distinguish between direction and control and describe their different roles in the work situation.
11. Explain the need for direction and control in relation to the performance of subordinates.
12. State what you consider to be the main reason for the induction of workers.
13. Explain some of the more important considerations a supervisor might need to make in drawing up a programme of induction.
14. Explain the importance of a 'follow-up' to the induction programme.
15. Describe the role of the supervisor in the maintenance of work standards and required levels of performance.
16. Describe some of the problems that might be associated with the correction of errors and the improvement of performance amongst the work force.
17. Explain the usefulness of establishing routines for maintenance, cleaning, hygiene and safety standards.
18. Explain the importance of health, safety and hygiene factors at work.

## Section C

# People Supervision

The successful application of supervisory skills and practices can only be carried out after a careful consideration has been made of those people to whom these skills and practices are to be applied. In this section therefore we will concentrate upon the skills of the supervisor, directly in relation to the people he is supervising. We will consider the way in which individuals and groups within the work place are influenced by the supervisor and how the demands of different situations are relevant to this influence.

## BEHAVIOURAL ANALYSIS

In a previous study 'Behavioural Studies for Hotel and Catering Operations' we saw the importance of analysing and understanding human behaviour and its relevance to hotel and catering operations. In this section we will carry out a behavioural analysis which concentrates upon the relationship between the supervisor and his subordinates in the hotel and catering work place. We need to be aware of the way in which a supervisor may affect the behaviour of subordinates for whom he may be responsible.

### The Achievement of Organisational Objectives

Any organisation is designed to achieve certain objectives in the most effective and efficient manner. As we saw in section A the business organisation will be designed with specific objectives in mind and the supervisor has an important role in helping to achieve these objectives. He will be required to organise and motivate the section of the work force for whom he is responsible, ensuring that they achieve their allocated tasks in a specified time, according to certain standards and in conjunction with other sections and departments of the business organisation. The objectives of a business organisation may be primarily concerned with profit whereas the objectives of a welfare or institutional organisation may be primarily concerned with the provision of a service. Levels of staffing will be affected by the objectives of the organisation. Where profit is the primary objective staff levels may be kept to a minimum to reduce costs. In contrast, overstaffing may possibly occur in a hospital canteen or an oil-rig kitchen to avoid a break down of service in the case of staff shortages, caused, for example, by sickness or injury. In each case the supervisor will be required to organise and motivate his staff to achieve any given organisational objective.

The staff of a large hotel kitchen will be required to achieve specific objectives relating to the production of food required by guests at certain times during the day. The production of food for a 5 course evening meal will require careful timing and co-ordination, as well the achievement of correct quantities and the desired quality. The various chefs de partie responsible for each area of food production will organise and motivate the various stewards, porters and commis chefs within their section to achieve this objective. In addition, the chefs de partie will work in close conjunction with one another. For example, the soup chef will ensure that the soup prepared does not clash with subsequent courses and will act as an 'overture' to the main courses. The roast chef should ensure the timing of his roast dish is correct; in the case of poultry, for example, he should allow time for the bird to stand prior to carving. In general, dishes should not be allowed to go cold or over cook during the course of food service. If this is achieved then the supervisory skill of the individual chefs de partie has been successfully employed.

Supervisors will not only be required to exercise organisational skills, as in the previous example, to achieve certain objectives, but also certain motivational skills. We will consider the role of the supervisor as a motivator of staff and briefly consider the different ways in which he may exercise leadership skills.

## Leadership Styles

All individuals respond to certain stimuli in a variety of ways. All individuals are different and therefore they will be motivated in different ways and by different things. Maslow's hierarchy of needs shows us that individuals, according to their position in life, are motivated to fulfill certain needs. On the basis of this hierarchy of needs it would probably be useless for the supervisor to attempt to motivate the low paid kitchen porter with the prospect of promotion if his immediate needs were purely basic and in terms of wages to pay for food, heating and rent for himself and his large family.

Not only do individuals respond to certain motivational factors in the fulfillment of personal needs but also they respond differently to the approaches of managers and supervisors within the organisation. The leadership style that supervisors adopt is extremely important, therefore, in terms of motivating subordinates to work. We will consider some of the basic leadership styles and examine the advantages and disadvantages of each.

### Authoritarian

This style of leadership is the most common form and represents a management or supervisory approach which takes sole responsibility for decision making and requires powerful individuals to exercise authority. A supervisor using the authoritarian or, as it is sometimes known, autocratic style of leadership would hold the view that any form of consultation with subordinates is a sign of weakness and that he should possess sole authority over the decisions that are made concerning his area of responsibility.

The advantage of the authoritarian style of leadership is that decisions can be made quickly, without laborious consultations. This may be seen as particularly important within hotel and catering operations where often the need for a quick decision is necessary to deal with an emergency or unforeseen circumstances. If the approach of the authoritarian leader is direct, positive and fair then he may well be able to motivate his staff to achieve goals for him. This is because the work force sees his approach as being fair, consistent and predictable and who therefore have respect for the authority of the supervisor in question.

The disadvantageous effect of the authoritarian style of leadership is that it can make the work force feel inferior and uninformed. They may feel that their contribution is taken for granted and this may have the effect of lowering morale and the motivation to work. It is important that if this is the effect of the supervisor using the authoritarian leadership style then he should change his approach because its net effect may be to decrease productivity and the efficiency of the work force as a whole.

**Student Activity   No. 11**
Draw up a range of specific examples that might occur within a hotel and catering operation to show:
 (i)   The advantages.
 (ii)  The disadvantages of supervisors using the authoritarian leadership style.

*Democratic*
This leadership style is designed to allow the workforce to participate in the decision making process and to delegate authority to other individuals within the organisation. Consultation and discussion between the different members of the work group would be encouraged by the supervisor in an attempt to use the knowledge, skills and experience that individuals within the work group might possess.

The advantage of the democratic style of leadership for supervisors is that it has a tendency to raise the interest of the work force in the day to day tasks in which they are engaged within the organisation. It is likely that this kind of approach may raise motivational levels amongst the work force, making them feel a part of the organisation and that their contribution is being valued by supervisors and managers alike.

The main disadvantage of this style of leadership is that it tends to be slow and is therefore inappropriate for certain tasks. It may be highly suitable where the compilation of duty rosters, overtime schemes and work study programmes are considered but quite inappropriate in terms of emergency or extreme pressure eg. during food service.

## Laissez-Faire
The main approach embodied in the laissez-faire leadership style is of allowing the operation to function in a free and apparently uncontrolled manner. The laissez-faire approach, which literally means 'leave well alone', depends for its success upon a group of workers who are highly motivated and who can be trusted to take decisions, work hard and achieve objectives with limited supervision.

The laissez-faire style can have its advantages, providing that it is not the excuse for lazy or inefficient supervisors to abdicate their duties and responsibilities. Staff may feel highly motivated because their supervisor has left them free to carry out certain tasks and make certain decisions. The negative effect of this style of leadership is that it does not give the inspiration and charisma that can be provided by an individual leader, consequently the work force tend to drift and behave aimlessly, not fulfilling their allocated tasks. Inexperienced members of the work group may suffer from a lack of direction, guidance and, most of all, supervision. Great care must therefore be exercised by supervisors if the laissez-faire approach is to be effectively employed.

## Supervision and Leadership
In practical situations it is unlikely that the leadership style employed by a supervisor will adhere rigidly to carry one particular type. The skilful supervisor must bear in mind the following when using a given leadership style:
  (i)   The differences that exist between individuals in the workforce.
  (ii)  The interpersonal relations between group members.
  (iii) The influence of the group on individuals within it.
  (iv)  The employment of appropriate social skills.
  (v)   The situation in which his leadership style will be exercised.
According to the influence of the above factors the successful supervisor will blend, modify and adapt different leadership styles in an attempt to fulfill the objectives of the organisation.

**Student Activity   No. 12**
State which leadership style, or blend of leadership styles would be most appropriate in the following circumstances:
  (i)   A junior manager taking over an experienced group of workers.
  (ii)  A staff meeting called to consider the setting up of a time, motion and work study exercise in the kitchen of an industrial catering unit.
  (iii) The supervisor dealing with the situation where a member of the work group has been 'sent to Coventry' by the rest of the group.
Discuss your conclusions with the rest of your class.

**Formal Communication**

We saw in section A the way in which a system of formal communication operates through the organisation of any work place. The organisation chart shown in figure 1 represents a structure which is designed to allow formal communication to take place. The organisation chart is made up of lines which describe the passage of formal communication both 'up' and 'down' the organisation. Along these lines a wide range of messages, decisions, instructions, orders and a complete cross-section of communication will pass. The system is described as being a 'formal' system of communication, because it represents the official structure of communication designated by management.

The supervisor holds a particularly important position in this chain of formal communication; he represents the link between management and the work force (see figure 2). He therefore has the formal position of acting as the middle man, transmitting formal messages in both directions.

Much of the communication that the supervisor involves himself in will be carried out on a face to face, oral basis, giving workers instructions or relating grievances to management. So, although the method of communication may appear to be relaxed or informal, the message itself represents a formal part of the communication process. The value of formal communication lies in the fact that it is the official network of communication, within the organisation. Although it is often carried out verbally, in the form of face to face contact, formal communication is often transmitted in the written form. For this purpose a variety of methods can be used eg. business letters, memoranda, instruction leaflets, reports, posters etc. Each must be considered in terms of its effectiveness in putting the intended message across.

As a general rule written communication is used for the following type of information:

(i) Complex or complicated information that may be incorrectly intepreted in an oral form eg. recipes, duty rosters.

(ii) A message intended for large numbers of emloyees eg. notice of a meeting, details of holiday arrangements. (Duplicate copies can be circulated to all departments and sections).

(iii) Where other forms of contact are difficult to achieve, eg. the communication between two reception shifts may be based in an exchange of memoranda.

(iv) Legal relations normally require written communication, eg. a contract of employment is normally formalised in writing.

(v) Business relations between companies for purposes of stock control, invoicing and accounts procedure, eg. bin cards, carbon copies, packing notes, invoices etc.

(vi) Standard forms are often used to routinise required information, eg. in the case of industrial accident firms use an accident report form for recording details of an accident in the work place.

(vii) If it is important that no misunderstanding of information occurs then written communication will be preferred, eg. fire, first aid or emergency procedure notices, placed in strategic positions for a considerable period of time.

The examples of formal written communication above will depend for their success upon the choice of an appropriate method of communication. Careful consideration must be given to the choice. The most commonly used method of written communication in large organisations is the memorandum, or 'memo' as it is normally abbreviated. The 'memo' is a simple and straightforward means of recording and transmitting a wide range of information. It normally takes the form of the example shown in figure 10 but different organisations modify the basic type according to their needs.

| **ELMBOURNE HOTELS** — *Memorandum* | |
|---|---|
| FROM: | TO: |
| MY REF: | YOUR REF: |
| PHONE EXT: | DATE: |
| **SUBJECT** | |

Fig. 10   *An internal memorandum*

A supervisor may use memoranda for a variety of purposes. He may send memos to staff in his section outlining the new overtime or shift work schedules or perhaps to notify them for a pay-rise or a change in holiday arrangements. Alternatively he may send a memo to management requesting a day off to attend a one day conference on personnel management, or perhaps to recommend one of his subordinates for a promotion within his section. Memo's should be short, direct and deal with one matter only; if a number of topics are to be dealt with a similar number of memos should be written.

**Student Activity   No. 13**
(i) Write memo's to convey the following information:
   (a) A request to your supervisor for the afternoon off to attend a family funeral.
   (b) Informing staff of working arrangements over the Christmas holidays.

     (c) Informing management of staff disciplinary procedure carried
         out.
(ii)  Either individually or in small groups design and draw up standard
     forms for the following functions.
     (a) Internal promotions.
     (b) Accident report.

## The Motivating Role of the Supervisor

The importance of the supervisor in his motivating role was stressed in 'Behavioural Studies for Hotel and Catering Operations'. In that study book we saw also the importance of distinguishing between the motivation of individuals and the motivation of groups. Motivation is not something we can universally apply; different individuals and groups will be motivated by a wide range of different things. We will briefly examine some of the more significant factors that a supervisor needs to be aware of when considering the motivation of individuals and groups.

### The Motivation of Individuals

A supervisor, by creating a favourable environment, can encourage individuals to motivate themselves. McGregor's Theory Y points out that individuals will be motivated to work hard and take on extra responsibility provided that they are committed to the goals of the organisation in which they are working. In contrast, McGregor's Theory X points out that individuals are disinclined to work if they do not recognise and accept the goals of the organisation. They therefore have to be pressurised and persuaded by means of incentives and bonuses to work hard. The major motivating task of the supervisor, in relation to individuals therefore, is to attempt to achieve some degree of alignment with the goals of the organisation. This will motivate the individual to work to satisfy his own individual needs and in so doing the needs of the organisation also.

In figure 11 we see a classification of some of the needs that an individual may be motivated to fulfill.

| INDIVIDUAL NEEDS (PERSONAL) | INDIVIDUAL NEEDS (WORK RELATED) |
| --- | --- |
| 1. Self Expression and Individuality | 1. Sense of Achievement within the Work Environment |
| 2. Provision for Dependants | 2. Job Responsibility and Control |
| 3. Achieve Self Satisfaction | 3. Adequate Payment and Recognition for Job Done |
| 4. Achieve Group Identity and Respect | 4. Promotion and Personal Development |

Fig. 11   *Classification of Individual Needs*

Any supervisor must therefore pay attention to the individual needs of his subordinates. He must be prepared to listen to them, discuss grievances and act upon them where possible, allow participation in work schemes, give praise for achievements and generally be aware of his subordinate's position and needs within the organisation.

## The Motivation of Individuals in Groups

Mayo's famous Hawthorne Experiments showed us the powerful influence that group norms can place upon the individual. It is often the case that the objectives of the group may be contrary to the personal objectives of individuals and those of the organisation in which the group functions. If this occurs group practices may have a counter-productive effect upon the achievement of organisational goals. A supervisory function of crucial importance therefore, is that of influencing the formation of group attitudes and norms so that the organisation as a whole will benefit from the practices that these attitudes and norms engender.

The supervisor's function in this case is essentially one of manpower management, he must be aware of informal practices that are set within the group and attempt to adapt these to the objectives of the organisation. His relationship with the group should be sufficiently personalised to enable him to be involved in setting group standards and objectives, to ensure that the whole group is involved and works as a team, and to help maintain levels of motivation and morale at a high standard. Moreno's work on informal group relationships and influences (see section C, Behavioural Studies for Hotel and Catering Operations) shows us clearly the way in which, for example, individuals within a group or work team may become socially ostracised, or 'sent to Coventry'. A supervisor must therefore be aware of the dynamics within the group and ensure that all individuals within the group are able to fit in. A key role that a supervisor has to play in achieving this objective is, as we shall see in section D, the careful recruitment of staff. This should be carried out not only in relation to an individual's potential job skills, but also in terms of his potential to fit in and accept the norms and practices of the group he will be working with.

The supervisor may therefore have to carry out the following tasks/appraisals:

(i)   Ensure that the right people are working together.
(ii)  Ensure that the allocation of tasks is fairly distrubuted.
(iii) Ensure that a fair and unprejudiced reward system exists.
(iv)  Set clear work standards in terms of quality, quantity, time taken, safety standards etc.
(v)   Instigate consultation procedures, allowing staff involvement in decision-making eg. overtime or split shift arrangements.
(vi)  Set up a grievance procedure, allowing staff a direct channel of communication should problems arise.

## Student Activity    No. 14

Discuss the following situation in your group; suggest methods of dealing with it. An enthusiastic trainee receptionist frequently takes on extra responsibility and works over her allocated time. This has the effect of violating the group practices of the reception team as a whole who also see her enthusiasm as a means of currying favour with management. Should her supervisor, encourage her in these practices and possibly damage group unity or should he recognise the group's standards and discourage her from taking on this extra work?

## Work Design, Specifications and Schedules

The objectives of the organisation, which we have already considered, will be achieved through the co-ordination of work throughout the workplace. A supervisor and the group for which he is responsible will be allocated tasks and areas of responsibility within this organisational framework by management. The supervisor will therefore be required to carry out work design, to specify standards and requirements and to ensure that schedules are met.

The work design that the supervisor will engage in must first of all be linked and co-ordinated with other sections eg. in a hotel, the reception team will work in liaison with the housekeeping team as guests book in and out of rooms. The supervisory functions of planning, organising, operating, directing and controlling will all be integrated as part of work design, in terms of drawing up required specifications and schedules and ensuring that they operate in the practical work situation.

Our examination of the planning process, in section B, showed us the place of work design in the context of the supervisor's overall planning function. the supervisor having carried out objective, target and task analyses is ready to design the work to be done; the preceding analyses provide him with an awareness of the setting or context for the work and a detailed knowledge of the work requirements themselves. He can design tasks for his subordinates which will be fitted to their practical skills, which will take into consideration the materials and equipment available and which will be co-ordinated with the work of other sections or departments.

The important elements of successful work design are setting specifications and schedules for the work to be done. We may talk about the supervisor specifying standards in terms of the following:

(i)     Quality of work done.

(ii)    Quantity of work done.

(iii)   Time taken to achieve (i) and (ii) to required specifications.

The specification of quality and quantity within a given time schedule depends upon the number of staff, the equipment and materials they have to use, the motivation of the staff, the incentives that may be provided, the working relationship with the supervisor and many other factors. A supervisor must not only ensure that external specifications are adhered to, eg. in terms of the requirements of the Health and Safety at Work Act 1974, but also that those which he sets his staff himself are realistic and practical. In other words, the targets and performance requirements of management must be within the achievement capacity of the work force. If this is not the case negative results will occur. Staff may work an unofficial go-slow as a form of objection to unrealistic productivity targets, or because they are concerned that improved efficiency may lead to redundancy or even greater demands upon their work output. An extreme negative effect of management and supervisors setting unrealistic targets and goals is that of industrial sabotage. Huw Beynon in his study 'Working for Ford' gave examples of workers stopping the assembly lines and damaging cars so that they could slow the production process to what they considered was a realistic pace and also as an attempt to assert some control over their working environment.

Supervisors must therefore pay considerable attention to work design, they must ensure that the specifications that they set down and the schedules that they stipulate are realistic and within the potential of the work force.

## The Work Environment

Favourable conditions must exist within the work environment if the work design, specification and schedules dealt with above are to be successfully implemented. Herzberg's work on motivation shows us that before the work force can be motivated to achieve certain goals or targets set by management, certain minimum requirements regarding the work environment have to be met. He referred to 'maintenance' or 'hygiene' factors as being non-motivational but setting the standard and expectations of the work force in terms of job conditions and the work environment. These maintenance factors might include the following:

(i)    Adherence to basic legal health and safety requirements.
(ii)   The position of the individual within the organisation.
(iii)  The physical environment, in terms of heating, lighting etc.
(iv)   The provision of adequate leisure or recreational facilities.

The work environment and the conditions in which individuals are expected to work and achieve the objectives of the organisation must reach certain standards. If the context in which individuals are expected to work is favourable, then supervisors and management may advise means of motivating staff to work beyond the minimum level of requirement.

## Student Activity   No. 15

List the necessary maintenance factors that staff may require in the following work environments (an example is given in each case to help you compile your list).

(i)   The hotel kitchen (eg. regular and consistent supply of clean hot water for pot wash purposes).

(ii)  The coffee shop (eg. conveniently placed fresh water supply for filling up pitchers).

(iii) The reception team (eg. changing room facilities close to the reception area for staff use).

## A SITUATIONAL ANALYSIS

The supervision of people takes place within a range of situations; individuals behave differently in different situations, and react differently according to stimuli in these situations. For supervision to be effective it has to be able to predict with a degree of certainty the way in which people will behave in certain situations. An important means by which supervisors may be able to predict the way in which their subordinates are likely to behave in certain situations is through the setting up of training procedures.

Effective staff training enables supervisors to predict the way in which subordinates will behave. In other words training encourages a conformity to certain accepted standards and should create consistent, and therefore predictable, behaviour patterns. For example, a drill instructor in the army can predict with a high degree of certainty that when he gives an instruction to his drill-squad they will all behave in exactly the same way, following his instruction precisely and accurately.

Staff training is therefore an important aspect of a supervisor's duties, if successful it will bring benefits to both employers and employees in the work situation.

### The Benefits of Training

The benefits of training may be classified under the headings of 'employer centred' and 'employee centred'.

*Employer Centred Benefits*

Despite the heavy investment required employers invest in training because it does bring rewards. Production and service will invariably prosper under a carefully conceived training programme. Material wastage will be minimised and the likelihood of damage to equipment because of operator inexperience will be reduced. The commercial benefits of this are self-evident. We have already seen that under the Health and Safety at Work Act 1974 certain minimum standards of training and instruction in terms of health, safety and hygiene are mandatory. Although this provision clearly benefits employees it also benefits employers in that lost production, damage to plant, industrial accidents etc. will be minimised, thus maintaining production and service at acceptable levels.

## Employee Centred Benefits

As the last point demonstrated, training can be mutually beneficial to employers and employees. For example, the achievement of good performance not only increases productivity but also may improve staff morale and create incentives to achieve improved results. Training clarifies an individual staff member's position within the organisation, in terms of the actual work he is required to do and his relationship to other workers. Training will therefore engender good performance in individual workers which in turn may be rewarded in the form of bonuses, perks or promotion opportunities. In other words, employees may benefit in financial and status terms from a training programme.

## Identification of Training Needs

The high level of 'investment' involved in training requires, first of all, a careful analysis of training needs. Such an analysis would show, for example, the need for personnel training in a situation where new technology was to be installed in a catering operation. The implementation of computer technology instances the need for staff training programmes in computer operation. In fact, unless new and fully trained staff are to be employed, existing staff will need to be trained in the principles of computer operation before the computer terminals and keyboards are installed.

New methods and approaches also create training needs. The induction of cuisine nouveau in many restaurants requires that kitchen and dining room staff are fully trained in its methods or production and service. A college of further education catering department offering a vegetarian and whole food catering course will need to train its staff in all aspects of this type of catering in advance of running the course.

In section D we shall see that an essential feature of any successful staff selection and recruitment procedure is the drawing up of detailed job descriptions, enabling the individual members of staff to know exactly what they are expected to do in their jobs. The applicant for a job must be matched against the job description; if the applicant does not match the job description, in the sense that his qualifications and experience would not enable him to carry out the job, then the employer has one of two choices. The first of these is simply to not offer the applicant the job; the second of these is to offer the applicant the job with the provision that the applicant undertakes a training programme which will fully equip him for the job.

Training needs can therefore be identified by comparing the experience, skills and abilities of an individual employee with the requirements of the job in which he is engaged, or is likely to be engaged in the future.

## Training Methods

The choice of training method is an important factor in the success of training. Students and trainees will know the merits and de-merits of different types of training method; they will find it easy to respond and learn by the use of one method and difficult when another is used. Employers must pay careful attention to the type of training method they decide to invest in for their staff. Without this careful attention training may be inappropriate or misdirected and very costly.

*The Location of Training*
The place where training occurs can have a significant effect upon its success or failure. There are three main types of location:
  (i)    On-the-job training.
  (ii)   Off-the-job training.
  (iii)  A mixture of (i) and (ii) above.
We will consider each of these in turn in an attempt to assess their relative merits or de-merits.

  (i)    On the job training occurs at the employee's place of work. In the hotel and catering industry, where much of an employee's work is carried out in direct contact with customers, on the job training represents the most realistic means of enabling staff to work with customers. By this means they may develop practical skills under pressure and also learn to develop social skills beneficial to their overall capability. The instructing role of the supervisor in this situation has to be played very carefully. The supervisor should not allow the trainee to be over-exposed to difficult situations and should therefore allow him to slowly develop skills and confidence. Indeed, supervisors themselves may need to undergo a training programme before employers allow them to help with the training and instruction of staff in their section.

  (ii)   'Off the job' training takes place away from where the employee actually works although it may take place on the premises of his employer. Therefore we say that 'off the job' training may be either internal or external. If it is internal it will be carried out away from the actual job location but on the premises, and under the authority of the employers eg. the firm's own training school. If 'off the job' training is external it will be carried out by an outside body. It may take place in a college of further education or a local skills centre, or it may take place on the firm's premises in their training centre but be organised and run by an outside organisation such as the Hotel and Catering Industrial Training Board (HCITB).

  (iii)  Some trainees will undergo a mixture of on and off the job training. An example of this may be a trainee manageress working for a large hotel chain, who not only is trained in the running of a number of firm's hotel operations but who is also attending a college on a day release basis to complete her HCIMA finals. The identification of training needs will also help establish which training location will be most suitable to satisfy these needs.

115

*Methods of Skill Training*
There are a variety of different methods of skill training, each of which are designed to create changes in the performance of behaviour of the employee being trained. Once again, the identification of the need is important because the most appropriate training method must be matched to it. We will outline the various methods of skills training that might be employed.

(i) *Demonstrations* are a means by which a person who possesses certain skills shows them to those who do not. This is a particularly useful method in the teaching of manual skills eg. following a recipe or using a piece of equipment.

(ii) *Skills Practice* is a method of training which is often linked to the demonstration. In other words, once the demonstration has been completed by the instructor trainees have the opportunity to practice their skills to see if they can match them with that of the instructor.

(iii) *Talks and Lectures* depend for their success upon the ability of the trainees to take and complete well structured and relevant notes. Talks and lectures are normally given by experts in a particular field and are usually designed for the attendance of a large number of people. They are often supported by the use of visual aids and hand-outs.

(iv) *Simulation and Role Play* is used in an attempt to re-create an actual situation for the trainee to exercise skills, so that he will be prepared for the 'real life' situation when it occurs in the work place. It is useful in the teaching of social skills in such areas as customer relations, interview techniques and developing interactive selling skills.

(v) *Seminars, Tutorials and Discussions* are used to enable the trainee to participate in the learning process. In the tutorial for example, the trainee may be expected to present a prepared paper on a topic that he has researched and the other trainees may then be invited to discuss aspects of the paper. Seminars normally involve a larger number of trainees than the tutorial but in each case learning is achieved through participative activity ie. discussion.

(vi) *Case Studies* are used by instructors to familiarise trainees with a particular case, which has features from which the trainee may learn. A supervisor on a training course may be expected to consider a number of case studies on manpower problems in the industry.

(vii) *Programmed and Distance Learning* enables trainees to obtain information from sources such as a computer data bank, libraries, television etc. at their own convenience. A high degree of motivation is required here on the part of the trainee because he is normally expected to carry out his research in his own time. Trainee managers, for example, may be encouraged to watch and make notes from an Open University programme on industrial relations.

Many other methods may be used in the training process, such as in-tray exercises, research projects and business games, the effectiveness of each will depend upon the versatility and general teaching abilities of the instructor or trainer and the motivation of the trainee to learn.

## Student Activity   No. 16

Select what you consider to be the most suitable training method for the following:

(i)   The introduction of computer technology at the reception deck.
(ii)   The supervisor learning industrial relations law.
(iii)   The pastry chef learning new techniques.
(iv)   The station waiter learning how to deal with difficult customers.
(v)   The experienced and mature chef who is expected to learn vegetarian cookery techniques.

After you have selected what you consider to be the most suitable method(s), compare your answers with the rest of your group and discuss the relative merits of your answers.

## The Value of Feedback

In section B, we stated that: 'The success of any communication process is dependant upon ensuring that the message being sent is received and acted upon in the required manner and form'. Training methods employ a range of different communication techniques which are intended to improve trainees performance or influence their behaviour. The demand for feedback is based upon the need to ascertain whether or not the method of training has been successful. For example, the demonstration method of training can only be assessed in terms of skills practice; allowing trainees to practice the skills that have been demonstrated to them. The demonstrator/trainer can then determine whether or not the trainee has acquired the skills that were demonstrated. This is a form of feedback.

All the training methods described above which incorporate a participative approach employ a feedback system. A discussion, for example, may follow a lecture, in which the trainees are asked to comment upon the points that the lecturer dealt with. The comments that the trainees give about the lecture are an indication of how much the trainees understood and they therefore represent a form of feedback. The value of feedback therefore is based upon what it tells us about the learning process; it indicates to us whether or not the method of training has been effective.

## Student Activity   No. 17

(i)   Draw up a detailed feedback system which will review the effectiveness of the training methods employed in Activity No. 16. Discuss your results with others in your group.

(ii)  Draw up a list of feedback methods that are employed by your college lecturers.

## Trade Unions, Job Security & Welfare

In this final section we will consider the position of the supervisor in relation to trade union activity, the job security of employees and their welfare at work. In order to place this examination into a perspective, we should reflect upon the supervisor in his intermediary position, as the link-man between senior management and the work force. His knowledge and experience of both the management and the work force puts him in a unique position of mutual representation.

It is common knowledge that trade union activity in the hotel and catering industry is at a low level and therefore, in general terms, the supervisor is not greatly affected by the presence of trade unions. Where subordinates are in a trade union it will be the responsibility of the supervisor to establish a working relationship with the union shop steward or branch representative. This working relationship should help to defuse any point of production resistance which may develop amongst the work force, in that any problem that might arise will be noticed immediately and promptly acted upon. In addition, supervisors and managers are made responsible by the Industrial Relations Code of Practice for ensuring that management is kept informed of employees' points of view and 'of the problems which they may face in meeting management's objectives'.

A supervisor therefore has an important role to play in industrial relations. In addition he can operate to ensure that employees can discuss such things as their welfare at work, their job security and other matters with their employers and their representatives. The successful enactment of this role places considerable demands upon the skills of the supervisor in relation to both management and his subordinates.

## ASSESSMENT QUESTIONS

1.  Explain the way in which staff may best be motivated and organised to achieve organisational objectives.
2.  Identify the various leadership styles.
3.  Explain the various methods of formal communication.
4.  Explain the value of the different methods of formal communication.
5.  Describe the way in which a supervisor can motivate workers:
    (a) As individuals.
    (b) In groups.

6. Distinguish between work design, work specification and schedules.
7. Explain the importance of:
   (a) Work design.
   (b) Work specification.
   (c) Schedules.
8. Explain the way in which worker's performance can be affected by working conditions and the work environment.
9. List the various needs for training of hotel and catering workers.
10. Explain the benefits of training:
    (a) For employers.
    (b) For employees.
11. Explain the way in which training needs may be identified.
12. List the various methods of training.
13. Distinguish between 'on the job' and 'off the job' training.
14. Assess the value of different methods of training.
15. Explain the importance of feedback in relation to the success of different methods of training.
16. Explain the way in which a supervisor's work may be affected by trade unions and/or employees' associations activities.
17. Describe the factors that influence job security at work.
18. Describe the role of the supervisor in relation to the welfare of employees.

# Performance Supervision

Performance supervision brings together the elements of supervision so far discussed. We have considered the supervisor's role in planning and organising for work performance and we have examined the way in which a supervisor may attempt to influence the behaviour of his subordinates in a variety of organisational situations. In this section we will deal with the way in which a supervisor contributes to the achievement of results through people. We will consider his role in terms of performance supervision; first of all dealing with the way in which the work force is selected and deployed, secondly by considering the way in which he sets levels of performance and ensures that they are maintained.

## MANPOWER PLANNING

Manpower planning is the means by which managers and supervisors draw up a plan for the future labour force of the organisation. The essential features and the importance of planning have already been explained in the context of the supervisor's role. Here we shall see how it is applied to obtaining the most suitable staff for the job and ensuring that the performance of staff in these jobs is maintained at the desired level.

In large scale organisations manpower planning will be carried out by managers and supervisors, in smaller organisations, employers will be involved in the drawing up of the manpower plan. No organisation, large or small, complex or simple, can afford to operate without a carefully conceived manpower plan. We will consider the necessary phases in developing a manpower plan.

### Prediction
The manager or supervisor has to be able to forecast the likely manpower needs of the organisation in the future. This will demand an acute knowledge of the operation of the organisation and an awareness of the way in which it is intended to develop in the future. The role of proprietors and senior managers in manpower planning is therefore an important one.

The prediction of future manpower needs can be classified into two categories: demand and supply forecasting, we will consider each of these in turn.

*Demand Forecasting*

This category of prediction entails asking two relatively simple questions: 'What is the future size of the manpower force likely to be?' and 'What is the quality of the future manpower force likely to be?' However, the answers to these questions are not quite as simple and before they can be given, some knowledge of the direction in which the organisation is going has to be obtained. A simple example will illustrate this point. The proprietors of a large hotel chain intend to install computerised communications and finance systems into all their hotels over a five year period. The effect of this will be seen in terms of the quantity and quality of the future manpower force, ie. the demand for ledger clerks, reception and check-out staff will diminish but the skills of those that remain, or who may be employed in the future, will have to be in line with the new technology.

**Student Activity   No. 18**

Explain the effect that the following will have upon (a) quantity and (b) quality in the demand forecasting of manpower in each establishment.

(i)    The introduction of microwave ovens into a restaurant kitchen.
(ii)   The extension of a catering companies work into banqueting, special functions and other forms of outside catering.
(iii)  The seaside guest house operating a six-month summer season instead of the usual five month season.

*Supply Forecasting*

In the previous case we considered the way in which prediction was affected by the possible future demands of the organisation; in this case we consider the way in which prediction is affected by the supply of labour to the organisation. In the previous case, for example, the introduction of computer technology into the operation of hotels would only be feasible if an adequate supply of suitably qualified labour was available. This supply of labour may come from two sources. In the first case the supply will come from external sources ie. the national (or international) labour market and will be affected by such things as government policies, educational provision, economic conditions, population migration and a wide range of other factors, largely beyond the control of individual establishments. In the second place, supply will come from internal sources, ie. from within the organisation or the company itself. This supply will be regulated by the firm and will affect such things as training policy, both on and off the job, selection and promotion procedures and more generally the attitude of staff to the firm. If, for example, there is a shortage of adequately trained staff on the external labour market, it may be the case that management in a firm may attempt to improve their internal training facilities. The size of the organisation is a crucial factor here. A small firm may not be able to afford the high capital cost involved in setting up internal training facilities and programmes and would therefore be dependant upon the quantity and quality of supply from the external market.

**Student Activity   No. 19**
Discuss in your group the specific effects that the following might have upon supply forecasting in terms of the future manpower force of a particular establishment.
(i)   A change of government.
(ii)  The opening of a new hotel and catering department at the local college of further education.
(iii) High levels of seasonal unemployment.

**Evaluation**
The manager or supervisor, having carried out a range of careful predictions, has now to evaluate the most suitable course of action to take. Decisions have to be made on the basis of these predictions, targets have to be recognised, objectives considered and possible future costs appraised. Evaluation can be a difficult and complex process embracing a number of related factors. This following example will help to demonstrate this point.

An industrial catering firm may decide to introduce a wide range of convenience food products into their operation. They will then have to consider the effects this might have upon their kitchen staff who are skilled to do more complex preparation tasks not required by the implementation of convenience food products. Not only will they be faced with the problem of de-skilling of staff but also the cost of paying for a work force that is over-skilled for the lower level tasks involved. Careful evaluation of these and other related aspects needs therefore to be carried out before any new manpower plan is implemented. The manpower plan should integrate with the work of the other departments and should fall within the financial constraints of the firm as a whole. No manpower plan can be implemented without a consideration of costs. These can be substantial, covering the areas of recruitment, selection, induction training (or re-training), wages and salaries, staff accommodation and welfare, the administration of manpower and so on.

**Control and Review**
Once the complex task of evaluation is complete and plans have been implemented, managers and supervisors have to exercise control and reviewing techniques to ensure that their implementation is effective.

We have considered the controlling function of the supervisor in some detail, manpower planning entails a considerable element of control. Control is exercised over the activities of the work force, providing guidelines for behaviour and also ensuring that the manpower plan is being carried out.

Supervisor's, in supervising the work, are carrying out a continual informal process of review, watching to ensure that the manpower plan is being effectively implemented. In addition, the manpower plan will incorporate a formal, periodic process of review, whereby updating, modification and structured alteration to plans may be carried out. The review may be short or long term, depending upon the scale and scope of the manpower plan and the size of the organisation for which it is used. The review should take note of such things as recruitment needs, over-manning, under-staffing, inefficient work procedures, redundancy possibilities, training requirements and so on.

**Staff Recruitment**
The successful implementation of a manpower plan is very dependant upon a work-force that is capable of fitting into its requirements. recruitment and selection procedures can help to achieve this and over a period of time the staff selected will be matched with the planning requirements. Problems exist in this area when a new manpower plan is adopted, perhaps when new management takes over, because staff may not be adaptable in terms of the requirements of the new manpower plan.

*Job Descriptions*
Staff recruitment will be carried out in terms of the needs of the organisation. The organisation chart in figure 12 will clearly define certain areas of work; each area of work will be defined by specific and accurate job descriptions. This will ensure that each member of staff knows the exact requirements of their job and that no overlap of duties occurs. It also provides management with a clear description of a particular job when vacancies occur and new staff have to be appointed. The value of the job description cannot be under-estimated

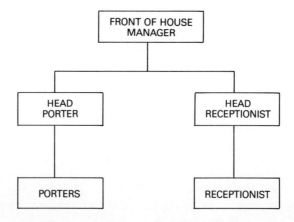

Fig. 12 *Front of House Organisation*

because around it revolves recruitment procedures, training require-
ments, performance appraisal, induction approaches and many other
organisational functions covered by the manpower plan. The following
classifies the main elements that a good job description should include:
*Job Title*
*Department*
*General Area of Work*
*Responsibilities to*
*Responsibilities for* i) *Staff;* ii) *Equipment;* iii) *Materials*
*Communication Links* i) *Vertical;* ii) *Horizontal.*
*Main Duties*
*Authority*
Using these categories we may write a job description for a Head
Receptionist.

*Job Title:* Head Receptionist
*Department:* Front of House
*General Area of Work:* Reception
*Responsibilities to:* House Manager
*Responsibilities for:* i) All Reception Staff; ii) All front-office equipment
*Communication Links:* i) House Manager, All Reception Staff; ii) Head
Porter; iii) Housekeepers
*Main Duties:* Day to day running of reception office to include
checking in guests, allocating rooms, maintaining guest accounts,
checking out guests, dealing with guests' enquiries and complaints,
communication with guests, handling guests mail and messages.
*Authority:* Control of the reception function.
Fig. 13   *Job Description for a Head Receptionist*

The thoroughness of a job analysis, as described in section A ensures
that the job description is an accurate breakdown of all aspects of the
job and that the minimum of overlap between jobs is maintained.


**Student Activity   No. 20**
Using figure 13 as a model, draw up detailed and accurate job
descriptions for the following:
   (i)    Kitchen Porter.
   (ii)   Fast Food Counter Assistant.
   (iii)  Head Barman.
   (iv)   Chambermaid.
Job descriptions should be given to all employees when they are
recruited, along with the various contractual details specified by the
Contracts of Employment Act 1972. This ensures that any confusion
about the requirements and limits of any job are kept to a minimum.

*Job Specification*

Having drawn up an accurate description of the job to be carried out, the manager or supervisor must next give careful consideration to the kind of person he wants to do that particular job. In other words he must, as part of his manpower plan, *specify* the kind of person required for the job described. This is known as drawing up job (or employee) specifications.

The job or employee specification gives details of the attributes that an individual must possess to fulfill the demands of the job description. The only limits that may be imposed upon the drawing up of detailed and comprehensive job specifications are those contained in legislation such as the Sex Discrimination Act 1975 and the Race Relations Act 1976. Bearing in mind, therefore that job specification cannot exclude potential employees because of their gender or ethnic background we can draw up a list of criteria that may be used.

(i)   Physical characteristics eg. height, weight, health.
(ii)  Mental characteristics eg. attitude, personality, intelligence, health.
(iii) Qualifications, reflecting education and training.
(iv)  Experience, that which is relevant to the job in hand.
(v)   Skills, including experience of the physical, mental and social skills required to carry out the job.
(vi)  General interests which may be relevant to the post eg. sporting activities, community interests.

The range and detail of the job specification will depend upon the job itself and the requirements of the manpower plan.

**Student Activity   No. 21**

Draw up what you consider to be a comprehensive set of job specifications for employees' suitable for the jobs described in Activity No. 20. Consider carefully:

(i)   The various headings you use.
(ii)  The details included under each.

*Recruitment Considerations*

Recruitment will be carried out to fulfill the requirements of the organisation and its manpower plan; the drawing up of accurate job descriptions and job specifications should facilitate this. The need is simple; the right people have to be recruited for the right job. Without this, inefficiency and extra costs will be created. The role of the supervisor at this stage is crucial; more than anyone else he will have knowledge of what kind of person fits a given kind of job. His work will involve a constant job analysis, looking at the various tasks and procedures involved, the various responsibilities that the job entails and the attributes of the individual who carries out that job.

This knowledge and familiarity with what a job entails and the attributes of individuals required to do these jobs, places the supervisor in an important position in the development of the manpower plan. From this position the recruitment and selection policy of the firm can develop; drawing on the knowledge and experience, through consultation, of supervisors in all departments of the organisation.

**Staff Selection**
It is at this stage that we may distinguish between recruitment and selection. The process of carrying out job analysis, job descriptions and job specifications are all embraced by the recruitment procedure. From these three elements the advertisement for a particular post may then be drawn up and this can be said to conclude the early stages of staff engagement according to the manpower plan.

Systematic selection follows initial recruitment; the advertisement will attract a range of candidates both internal and external from which the suitable applicant will be selected.

**Student Activity   No. 22**
Draw up lists of the advantages and disadvantages of recruiting and selecting staff:
(i)   Internally.
(ii)   Externally.
Discuss the contents of your lists with other members of your group.

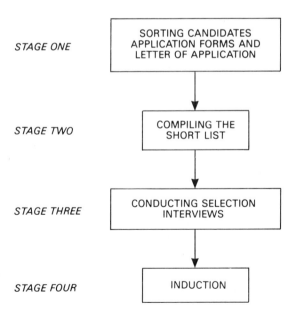

*STAGE ONE* — SORTING CANDIDATES APPLICATION FORMS AND LETTER OF APPLICATION

*STAGE TWO* — COMPILING THE SHORT LIST

*STAGE THREE* — CONDUCTING SELECTION INTERVIEWS

*STAGE FOUR* — INDUCTION

Fig. 14   *The Selection Procedure*

The staff selection procedure can be summarised in a diagrammatic form. Figure 14, shows the stages through which the selection procedure may be carried out.

The importance of a systematic approach to staff selection cannot be over-emphasised. The hotel and catering industry traditionally suffers from a high rate of labour turnover, this may partly be attributable to poor selection procedures at the outset. Systematic staff selection, in accordance with a carefully conceived manpower plan, can help to reduce the often damaging effects of high labour turnover, ie. high re-training costs, low staff morale, lack of continuity etc.

In addition to helping reduce a high incidence of labour turnover, systematic staff selection procedures are particularly useful in establishments where multi-skilling is employed. If, for example, it is intended that the person to be employed is to carry out the duties of a waitress and a chambermaid, the various stages of the selection procedure will reveal whether or not she is capable of carrying out the tasks required by both skill areas.

The supervisor himself may gain indirectly from the systematic selection procedure. His involvement in terms of carrying out a job analysis and contributing to the compilation of job descriptions and job specifications has already been dealt with. This involvement with management and the manpower plan is good for his morale. In addition, if the selection procedures reduce the amount of labour turnover within an establishment, supervisors have a greater opportunity to build up the work of their section and to improve its prestige within the organisation. When labour turnover is high, the morale of the supervisor may be affected because not only are his ambitions and personal development threatened but also the quality of his own job may be undermined by having to engage in the training of new staff on a fairly regular basis.

It can be seen from the preceding analysis that there are a number of systematic approaches to the recruitment and selection of staff. These arguments apply to the selection, upgrading and promotion of staff on an internal basis, within the organisation and on an external basis, in the recruitment, selection and appointment of new staff to the organisation.

## LEVELS OF PERFORMANCE

The careful development and application of a manpower plan is designed to help with the achievement of results through the performance of the work force. We have so far examined the way in which carefully conceived recruitment and selection procedures enable management and supervisors to obtain staff who are suitable and who will fit in with the manpower plan. The next stage in the successful implementation of the manpower plan is to ensure that the work force can meet the demands of the organisation and achieve levels of performance that are in line with the objectives of the organisation. In order to achieve this end not only must the objectives of the organisation be realised but also small scale targets and goals must be set and achieved by different sectors of the work force. These goals and targets may be in terms of levels of productivity or in terms of quality of service. In both cases supervisors will be expected to set goals for which the subordinates in their section will be expected to aim. In other words the supervisor will be setting standards to which his work group will be expected to adhere. He will engage in a continual process of measurement, examining and appraising the work of his group to ensure that it reaches the standards he has set. In setting these standards for his subordinates to aim for the supervisor is in turn helping to achieve the objectives of the organisation of a whole.

Organisational objectives might be rather generalised to act as a means of motivating the work force. For instance, the achievement of satisfactory profit margins as an objective may be difficult for a worker to interpret, so the supervisor will be expected to translate this into operational terms, setting clearly defined standards of achievement in quantity and quality terms.

**Performance Assessment**
In section C we saw that instruction and training could only be effectively carried out if a system of feedback and assessment was available, enabling the supervisor to measure whether behaviour patterns had been changed. The achievement of results through people requires the same type of analysis. By carrying out an assessment or appraisal of worker performance the supervisor is exercising control. Standards have been specified and defined in the form of targets for the workforce, and by assessing whether these targets and standards are being achieved and maintained the supervisor is exercising control over the activity of the work force. Through using the various feedback systems outlined in section C, the supervisor is able to appraise the performance of his subordinates and in this way exercise control.

*Methods of Assessment*
Assessment or appraisal, as a means of control, is designed to measure whether or not standards are being maintained. It provides the basis for action or performance modification if standards are not being maintained. Therefore the method of assessment that is used is critical in the system of control. We will briefly consider some methods of performance appraisal and assessment.
(i)   The Open Ended Report is used by supervisors who wish to write a free-ranging and relatively unstructured appraisal of staff in the

## MAYFLOWER CATERING CO.
*PERFORMANCE APPRAISAL FORM*

EMPLOYEE'S NAME.............................................

EMPLOYEE'S POSITION.........................................

DEPARTMENT/SECTION.........................................

SUPERVISOR/MANAGER'S NAME..............................

| TICK APPROPRIATE BOX | EXCELLENT | GOOD | SATISFACTORY | POOR | COMMENTS |
|---|---|---|---|---|---|
| TECHNICAL SKILLS | | | | | |
| INTERACTIVE SELLING SKILLS | | | | | |
| SOCIAL SKILLS | | | | | |
| EFFORT | | | | | |
| ENTHUSIASM | | | | | |
| INITIATIVE | | | | | |
| ABILITY TO GET ON WITH | | | | | |
| (a) CUSTOMERS | | | | | |
| (b) OTHER STAFF | | | | | |
| (c) MANAGEMENT/SUPERVISORS | | | | | |

Fig. 15   *A Performance Appraisal Form*

129

work situation. Such a report has the advantage of not restraining what the supervisor includes but it has the disadvantage of often being vague, rambling and unspecific. The supervisor who uses the open-ended report is relatively free to include and exclude details at his own discretion and this may mean that the value of the appraisal is limited.

(ii) The Closed Grading or Ranking system of assessment is used by supervisors to classify the work force into a range of performance grades or ranks. Grade One, for example, may classify the top 10% of the work force, Grade Two the next 10% and so on down to Grade 10, which classifies the bottom 10% of the work force. Although this method provides a specific assessment grading system it is rather subjective in that the supervisor may use whatever criteria he chooses for ranking the work force. Person 'X' may be better in one respect than person 'Y', but in another respect may be worse.

(iii) Rating systems of assessment are favoured by some supervisors because they provide a more detailed and more objective system of appraisal than the previous two methods. In this system the supervisor rates the employee's work in a specific area. Figure 15 is an example of a ranking system that a supervisor may use in a range of work situations.

This type of assessment does allow for more specific details to be given about worker performance and its format lends itself to being modified and used for a variety of different purposes. For example, a large company is likely to use a similar form for the assessment of supervisors and might include such categories as: organisation skills, planning abilities, staff liaison skills etc.

We have dealt with three methods of performance assessment or appraisal here, each has its advantages and disadvantages, which should be considered when they are used in a practical situation.

## Student Activity   No. 23

(i) Using your notes for reference, draw up a method of assessment that may be used by a coffee shop supervisor for appraising staff performance.

(ii) Discuss the relative merits and de-merits of your finished work with other members of your group.

Whatever method of assessment is chosen it should be used in conjunction with the appraisal interview. Not only will this provide the supervisor with a more detailed profile of the employee in question but also will enable the employee to discuss the various comments and criticisms that may have been made about him. The method of assessment should not only serve as a means of observing worker performance but also should be used to help to modify that performance in the future. the supervisor's report should indicate both the good and bad points about an employee's performance, so that the good points can be sustained and the bad points improved upon. Performance modification can be brought about by a variety of approaches; it is up to the supervisor to recognise which will be most suitable in a given situation. If an improvement in performance is required a supervisor might use a strict, authoritarian approach to achieve this but in other situations he may use more delicacy and tact in pointing out a worker's deficiency in a particular area. The supervisor has to exercise considerable skill therefore in the area of performance modification.

**Student Activity No. 24**
With reference to the different attitude and personality types dealt with in section A of Behavioural Studies for Hotel and Catering Operations draw up a range of different approaches that a supervisor might use to modify worker performance. Use the following headings to classify your results.

| ATTITUDE/PERSONALITY TYPE | SUPERVISOR'S APPROACH |
|---|---|
| 1.   LAZY/EXTROVERT | STERN, OFFICIAL, PROVIDE SPECIFIC GUIDELINES |
| 2. | |
| 3. | |
| 4. | |
| 5. | |
| 6. | |

**Internal Influences on Performance**
Within the firm itself many factors will influence worker performance; we have already seen, for example, that the approach of the supervisor is critical in modifying worker performance. The motivation to work, or to perform to given standards in a work situation relates to the needs that an individual can identify with. We will consider the effects of the following factors on the motivation of individuals to perform according to the standards of the work situation.

*Working Conditions*
In section C we saw that the nature of working conditions is critical in relation to worker performance. A work environment which lacks adequate health, safety, welfare and social conditions will not have a motivating or positive effect upon worker performance. In contrast if attention is paid to the improvement and maintenance of good working conditions then this provides a basis for satisfactory worker performance.

131

## Wages

Employees are paid for their labour and efforts in the form of wages. Wages can be referred to as the basic pay of an employee; these are often determined by the Wages Council and should be agreed upon when the contract of employment is made and paid to the employee on a regular basis. Basic pay is rarely the only form of payment that an employee receives and in this sense 'basic pay' can be seen as a 'right' rather than a motivating factor as such. The hotel and catering industry is characterised by a complex system of payment. We have considered the wages that a worker receives; other forms of payment also exist.

## Subsidised Lodging and Food

This represents a common form of payment in many catering establishments and is often given as a major reason for relatively low basic rates of pay that many catering workers receive.

## Gratuities and Services Charges

These can act as a form of incentive for catering workers, particularly those who are in direct contact with the customer, to work hard and improve their performance. 'Tipping' places a very special relationship between catering staff and customers and again is often used as a reason for paying catering workers relatively low basic rates of pay.

## Fringe Benefits

Unofficial recognition exists within many hotel and catering establishments that 'knock offs' and 'fiddles' operate as a supplement to staff income. The arguments regarding the value or desirability of such practices will not be pursued at this stage, although it has been argued that 'fiddles' are not only beneficial to the staff who are engaged in them but also to supervisors and managers who can use the practice as an excuse for dismissing a member of staff should one be required.

## Formal Incentives

The basic rate of pay for any job is usually supplemented with incentives, which are, quite simply, inducements to encourage staff to improve levels of performance. Incentives can take the form of commission rates for restaurant managers, promotion possibilities for supervisors, productivity bonuses for food preparation staff, annual increments, piece rates etc.

Careful planning is required on the part of managers and supervisors alike to ensure that any payment or reward scheme is implemented fairly and that it brings about the desired results in terms of worker performance. In addition, the supervisor should be aware of the 'individual contracts' that staff make with customers and ensure that these are not damaging to the quality of production or service in his section.

## Student Activity No. 25

Go to the Hotel and Catering Section of your college library and carry out research on the payment system in catering establishments. With particular reference to 'individual contracts', 'fiddles', 'backhanders' and 'knock-offs'. Write a short essay discussing the advantages and disadvantages of such a system for performance and quality of work.

## External Influences on Performance

In section A we considered the business climate in which any catering establishment has to operate and we stated there that external factors will influence levels of performance within any organisation. The performance of any individual employee, and the work force as a whole, cannot therefore be seen in isolation from external factors. These can be many and varied. We will instance a few to indicate the diverse range of external influences on worker performance.

### Personal Life

The personal life of an individual employee is particularly important here. A supervisor should not pry into an employee's personal life but he should make himself available to his subordinates should counselling or advice be required. If an employee has an unstable or problematical personal life his ability to perform to his full capacity will be limited. An emotional crisis in the home, such as a death in the family or a divorce, financial problems and so on can all contribute to this.

### Cultural Background

Increasingly hotel and catering establishments employ workers from a wide range of ethnic and cultural backgrounds. Consideration of this will have to be taken by employers and supervisors as certain cultural characteristics could affect worker performance eg. the need for Mohammedans to fast during Ramadan. Religious practices, eating habits and modes of dress are all cultural characteristics which although external to the work situation could influence performance within it.

### Political, Legal and Economic Factors

These three may be taken separately but they are inter-linked so we will consider them collectively. The political system and the governing body in a society will exercise a controlling influence over the members of that society. They will determine economic policy and they will enact certain laws to regulate the behaviour of members of society. Therefore any business organisation or work environment will be influenced by these external or outside influences.

## Grievance and Discipline

We have emphasised in this section the way in which results may be achieved through the performance of workers and the way in which performance may be modified to adhere to the objectives of the organisation. From time to time situations occur in the work place where workers feel they may be wrongfully treated; they may, for example, have been dismissed for allegedly not fulfilling the targets set by management. In this situation it is important that a clearly defined grievance procedure is available for workers to follow should they feel they have been unfairly treated.

Similarly, if workers are found to be at fault in the work situation, violating the terms of their contract, then disciplinary procedures should be made absolutely clear, so there is no doubt as to the path that should be followed.

ACAS, the Advisory, Conciliation and Arbitration Service lays down a code of practice designed to deal with grievance and disciplinary procedures. It is intended that disciplinary practices and grievance procedures will be adhered to and respected by both employer representatives and trade unions alike. If the guidelines set down by ACAS are adhered to then a clear framework for grievance and disciplinary matters is provided. The value of this for both employers and employees is that there is no doubt about the practices and procedures to be followed. Grievance and disciplinary practices and procedures work best when they are recognised and agreed upon by both management and the work force. We shall be examining, in some detail, in study book 3 the way in which grievance and disciplinary procedures are set up.

## ASSESSMENT QUESTIONS

1. Describe basic manpower planning theory.
2. Explain the way in which manpower planning theory is applied to specific working situations.
3. Distinguish between demand and supply forecasting.
4. Distinguish between a job description and a job specification.
5. Demonstrate the use of job descriptions.
6. Demonstrate the use of job specifications.
7. Explain the importance of recruiting the right people for the right job.
8. Distinguish between recruitment and selection.
9. Explain in detail the need for systematic selection of staff from within the organisation and from outside it.
10. List the different stages of the selection system.
11. Explain the importance of clearly defined standards and objectives.
12. Explain the importance of measurement in relation to standards and objectives.
13. State the need for clearly defined standards, objectives and measurement.
14. Explain the importance of performance appraisal.

15. Explain the various ways of assessing performance in workers and supervisors.
16. Expain the relative merits of different methods of performance assessment.
17. Define performance modification.
18. Explain the different ways in which performance modification may be achieved.
19. Explain the relevance of control in relation to performance appraisal.
20. Explain the need for performance feedback.
21. Describe the way in which pay, working conditions and systems of reward may affect worker performance.
22. Indicate a range of outside influences that may affect the performance of the workforce.
23. Explain the value of clearly defined grievance and disciplinary procedures.

# Conclusion

In this study we have attempted to place the supervisor firmly in the context of the hotel and catering work situation in all its diverse forms. We have attempted to address the difficulties associated with the position of supervisor in terms of the achievement of organisational objectives through the performance of the work force. In doing so the importance of the supervisor in all his roles should be clearly demonstrated; if he is successful the contribution of the supervisor will be of value to employers and employees alike.

The maintenance of this important and influential role will depend upon the supervisor's ability to keep abreast of the constant and sometimes radical, changes that affect the industry and the establishments within it. He will need to find solutions for the current problems of the industry, such as high levels of pilferage and labour turnover, the need for multi-skilling, improvement of staff shortages and wage levels. Above all he will need to be adaptable to change. His methods will need to embrace the increasing levels of computerisation and automation that are being introduced into the industry and his social skills technique will need to be developed within the context of the increasing heterogeneity of societies.

It is hoped that this study book has clearly demonstrated the position and importance of the modern supervisor in the hotel and catering industry, so that a future examination of the techniques he employs and his role in general can be carried out more thoroughly.

# BIBLIOGRAPHY AND RECOMMENDED FURTHER READING

Manpower Management in the Hotel and Catering Industry: Timothy Hornsey and David Dann  *Batsford Ltd*

Manpower Problems in the Hotel and Catering Industry: G. Mars, D. Bryant and P. Mitchel  *Saxon House*

The Social Stigma of Occupations: C. Saunders  *Gower Publishing Group Ltd*

Catering Supervision: A.E. Beven  *Edward Arnold*

Staff Management in the Hotel and Catering Industry: J.P. Magurn  *Heinemann*

The Supervisor's Handbook: J. Reay  *Northwood Books*

Management in the Hotel and Catering Industry: H.V. Gullen, A.G.E. Rhodes  *Batsford Ltd*

Hotel and Catering Supervision: K.J. Gale and P.F. Odgers  *MacDonald & Evans*

Personnel Management in the Hotel and Catering Industry: M.J. Boella  *Stanley Thornes (Publishers) Ltd*

# Supervisory Studies 2

## STUDY BOOK THREE

# Staffing and Staff Development

Staffing is an area of fundamental concern for employers, managers and supervisors alike. The existence of high levels of labour turnover in the hotel and catering industry provides a clear indication of the need to pay particular attention to staff in all hotel and catering operations, irrespective of their size, structure or complexity. Our early analysis of supervisory studies for hotel and catering operations, demonstrated the need for developing a manpower plan or a personnel policy to deal with all aspects of staffing in a given operation. In this section we will consider some of the practical difficulties experienced in the implementation of personnel policies and by the same procedure further demonstrate their value.

Our analysis will therefore come to terms, first of all, with the criteria used for evaluating staffing needs and how a process may be developed to meet these needs. We will follow this by demonstrating the way in which we may achieve a continuing process of individual and organisational evaluation and development.

## STAFFING NEEDS

An awareness of staffing needs is not something that should come about as a consequence of a member of staff performing inefficiently or resigning at short notice; it is something employers and their management and supervisory representatives should permanently possess. This awareness represents an essential element in the skills and abilities of managerial and supervisory staff; an absence of which, it is often suggested, contributes to the high levels of labour turnover in the industry. Staff may be appointed without careful consideration of organisational requirements and may find themselves mis-placed and unable to fit in. In 1969 the Hotel and Catering Economic Development Committee published a report called 'Staff Turnover' which showed that in the first few weeks of employment over 70% of hotel and catering workers left that employment. In the same way that the director of a stage play may mis-cast an actor in a particular role, so may a manager, through insufficient awareness of staffing needs, incorrectly recruit a member of staff into a section of the organisation.

It is important therefore, from the point of view of reducing labour turnover and the costs associated with it in terms of advertising, interviewing, training etc, that we identify the criteria for evaluating staffing.

**Evaluating Staffing**
Staffing needs will exist in terms of quality and quantity; a certain number of staff possessing certain skills and experience will be required to carry out a number of tasks. The range of tasks will largely be determined by the organisation. An organisation chart showing staff deployment and 'lines' of communication will clearly indicate the number of staff and their relationship to one another in the organisation. Job descriptions can be drawn up when the organisation chart is completed, ensuring the minimum of overlap between the different jobs described. This in turn allows for the appropriate job specifications to be compiled. If careful and thorough recruitment and selection procedures are carried out and the man power plan is fully implemented, then staffing needs should not only be specifically described but also fully met.

We may identify the following as being important criteria in the evaluation of staffing.

*The Labour Market*
The labour market can be further classified into the internal and external markets. It is from these sources that labour can be recruited. In practice, managers within the hotel and catering industry prefer the external market as a source of labour. Only 1% of managers use promotion within the organisation as a method of recruitment; reliance on the external market being much preferred. A wide diversity of staff is employed within the hotel and catering industry and therefore a range of different labour markets are used. The quality of the labour market must therefore be considered when staffing is being evaluated.

*Organisational Needs*
The organisation represents the framework upon which the establishment operates, therefore its needs are a primary consideration in staffing evaluation. If a vacancy for a position occurs then this represents an organisational need that has to be fulfilled, according to the requirements of the job description. Organisational needs will fluctuate in line with other changes, such as, the installation of new equipment, or the use of different materials and will normally be translatable in terms of numbers and skills of staff.

*Costs*
The objectives of the firm will normally reflect the needs for suitable margins of profit or levels of cost effectiveness and therefore any form of staffing evaluation must be carried out with this in mind. Cost restraints impose strict demands upon staffing evaluation because if it is not effective, as pointed out earlier, unacceptable levels of labour turnover may occur, resulting in extra costs of recruitment, selection, induction and training. This criterion is particularly important because

140

ineffective staffing evaluation may also result in poor staff morale, insecure industrial relations and an overall loss of working efficiency.

*Future Developments*

Evaluation of staffing cannot be carried out without some reference to possible future developments. Manpower planning should therefore not only incorporate carefully conceived recruitment and selection procedures but also various means by which employment termination, redundancy, retirement and so on may be systematically and fairly carried out. In this way new staffing requirements may be more easily met, if the need for new skill areas, a reduced labour force or staff redeployment should occur.

This represents the main criteria to which we need refer when carrying out staffing evaluation. We will continue our analysis by examining the practical implications of staffing evaluation and the way in which we develop a process to meet staffing needs.

**Sources of Labour**

We may classify labour sources, broadly speaking, into three categories ie. local, national and international. The decision to recruit staff from a given source will depend upon the position that is vacant and what the source of labour has to offer. The choice may be influenced by such things as level of unemployment in a particular region or levels of skills training available. The local market is usually relied upon for the provision of part-time or unskilled staff. In contrast, managerial staff may be appointed, using a national source of supply. In some cases, where the acquisition of visas and work permits allows, staff appointments are made on an international basis.

The following is a list of possible sources of labour supply, it is not intended to be exhaustive, merely to demonstrate the wide range of sources that are available. Careful consideration of the staff potentially available from each source should be taken before that source is used to recruit.

(i)     National press.
(ii)    Local press.
(iii)   Trade press.
(iv)    Employment agencies.
(v)     Job Centres.
(vi)    Skill Centres.
(vii)   Colleges of Further Education.
(viii)  Universities, Polytechnics, Colleges of Higher Education.
(ix)    TV and radio (national and local).

**Student Activity   No. 3.1**

(i)   Add any sources of labour that you can think of to the list above.
(ii)  Specify from which labour source you would be most likely to recruit the following staff.

141

(a) Hotel manager.
(b) Public house manager.
(c) Head chef.
(d) Cleaning staff.
(e) Part-time banqueting staff.
(f) Kitchen porter.
(g) Chambermaid.
(h) Junior receptionist.
(i) Commis waiter.

(iii) Discuss your recommendations with the rest of your group.

We next have to consider the way in which we implement a given source of labour; we have to employ the most effective means of obtaining suitable labour from our chosen source. The most common means by which this is achieved is by the use of the advertisement. Whatever source of labour is implemented an advertisement will need to be drafted, the design of which will attract the right type of staff. The drafting of the advertisement will be based upon detailed knowledge of the job description and the job specification. We will briefly consider these before examining the way in which the advertisement is drafted.

## The Use of Job Descriptions

In Section D of the previous study book we provided an outline of the details of a job description which will have general applicability to a range of positions within the hotel and catering industry. We will use this model as the basis for drawing up actual job descriptions for an unskilled and a sub or semi-skilled job. (See figure 1 and figure 2).

**JOB TITLE:** Catering Assistant

**DEPARTMENT:** Works Canteen

**GENERAL AREA OF WORK:** Assistance in the main food production kitchen

**RESPONSIBILITIES TO:** Canteen Supervisor

**RESPONSIBILITIES FOR:**    (a) OTHER STAFF: None
    (b) EQUIPMENT: Cleaning and storage of kitchen utensils
    (c) MATERIALS: Maintenance of the contents of the food store.

**COMMUNICATION LINKS:**    (a) VERTICAL: Canteen Supervisor
    (b) HORIZONTAL: i) Other catering assistants; ii) Delivery staff; iii) Food service staff

**MAIN DUTIES:** (a) Assist with food preparation, as specified by the Canteen Supervisor.
    (b) Care and attention of kitchen utensils.
    (c) Clean and tidy food store, carry out regular checks (form of stock control).
    (d) Assist with unloading of goods for the food store.
    (e) Ensure food delivered is of the required quantity and quality.
    (f) Complete stock records when delivery is complete.

**AUTHORITY:** Limited to stock records unless otherwise specified by Canteen Supervisor.

Fig. 1. *A job description for a Catering Assistant (unskilled)*

**JOB TITLE:** Breakfast Cook

**DEPARTMENT:** Food Production

**GENERAL AREA OF WORK:** Preparation of Breakfast Menu

**RESPONSIBILITIES TO:** Roast Cook

**RESPONSIBILITIES FOR:**    (a) OTHER STAFF: Kitchen Assistant
                                      (b) EQUIPMENT: All equipment used during breakfast preparation
                                        (c) MATERIALS: Maintaining stock in his area of work

**COMMUNICATION LINKS:**    (a) VERTICAL: Roast Cook
                                        (b) HORIZONTAL: i) Vegetable Cook; ii) Night Cook

**MAIN DUTIES:** (a) Preparation of specified breakfast menu
                 (b) Participation in the breakfast menu planning
                 (c) Supervising work of Kitchen Assistant
                 (d) Stock Control and ordering
                 (e) Helping with the preparation of the lunch/dinner menus during morning
                 (f) Preparation of staff breakfasts

**AUTHORITY:** Limited to his area of food production, authority may be delegated by other Cooks.

Fig. 2.   *A job description for a Breakfast Cook (semi-skilled)*

Each of these job descriptions not only defines clearly the work entailed by each position but also firmly establishes that position in the organisational hierarchy. This latter point will be particularly important in large establishments where clarity of line management is a necessity.

### Student Activity No. 3.2
Draw up clear and detailed job descriptions for the following posts:
- (i) Kitchen Porter.
- (ii) Chambermaid.
- (iii) Junior Receptionist.
- (iv) Commis Waiter.

Use figures 1 and 2 as your models, ensure that the details you include are accurate and do not overlap with other areas.

### The Use of Job Specifications
We need to be able to specify the kind of person we require to carry out the job we have described. We should specify characteristics relating to physical make-up, education and training, work experience, personality etc. and ensure that we do not specify characteristics beyond the requirements of the job. Such an approach may lead to over-skilling, job dissatisfaction and ultimately to an increase in labour turnover.

    Figure 3 shows a job specification for the position of catering assistant as described in figure 1.

**JOB TITLE:** Catering Assistant
**INDIVIDUAL CHARACTERISTICS**
1. PHYSICAL
    (a)    Sex: N/A
    (b)    Age: 18+
    (c)    Appearance: Clean/Tidy
    (d)    Health: Good general condition, no hereditary or recurring diseases
2. QUALIFICATIONS/EDUCATIONAL EXPERIENCE
    (a)    Basic literacy and numeracy skills
    (b)    Basic cooking training eg. to CSE/GCE Standard
3. WORK EXPERIENCE
    (a)    Any relevant kitchen/food preparation experience
4. PERSONALITY
    (a)    Ability to get along with others*
    (b)    Honesty*
    (c)    Attitude to work*

    *All to be endorsed by relevant Testimonials and References from previous employers or educational establishments.

Fig. 3    *A job specification for a catering assistant*

## Student Activity   No. 3.3
Draw up job specifications for one unskilled and one semi-skilled job that you produced job descriptions for in Activity 2.

## The Advertisement
The job descriptions and specifications that we have produced, provide us with the basis for drawing up the advertisement for the vacant post. It may not be necessary to include all the details of the job and the prospective employee for reasons of expense, but it will be important to include information which will attract the right kind of candidate.

There are three basic types of press advertisement that are normally used and TV or radio advertisements will be modified versions of these. The type of advertisement used will depend upon the type of jobs being advertised, the type of press medium being used and the funds available. The most eye-catching, but also the most space-consuming and therefore the most expensive type of advertisement, is the *Display advertisement*. This will be designed to be visually attractive and to appeal to a particular type of applicant; these are often used for advertising management posts.

The *Part Display advertisement* is simply a less extravagant version of the Display advertisement and may contain more factual information than the previous type. This is often used when applicants need to be provided with more detail about the job.

The type of advertisement most commonly used in obtaining staff for hotel and catering establishments is the *Classified advertisement*. This is an essentially informative advertisement, with the only display normally being bold type-face or underlining on the first line of the advertisement. Classified advertisements are relatively cheap, easy to assemble and normally achieve quick results. Figure 4 is an example of a classified advertisement that may be used to advertise the vacancy for a Canteen Assistant, that we considered in the previous examples.

CATERING ASSISTANT, WORKS CANTEEN, BYRNE BEARINGS, ROEHAMPTON, SW15. General kitchen and stores work duties. Applicants over 18, experience an advantage. Apply in writing to the Catering Supervisor.

Fig. 4   *A Classified advertisement for a Catering Assistant*

It will be noted that in figure 4 the information we have included gives the essential details required to advertise the post and nothing else. The information in the advertisement can be classified in the following way:
  (i)   Job Title.
  (ii)  Name and Address of Firm.
  (iii) Elements of Job Description.
  (iv)  Elements of Job Specification.
  (v)   Contact Authority.
The advertisement may be more detailed, as in the case of the classi-fied advertisement for a breakfast cook in figure 5, but the way in which it is classified remains the same.

EXPERIENCED BREAKFAST AND VEGETABLE COOK. Applicants will be responsible for organising and supervising break-fast preparation also to carry out other kitchen duties. Telephone Cambrian Hotel, Port Isaac 4079 for an application form.

Fig. 5   *A Classified advertisement for a Breakfast Cook*

**Student Activity   No. 3.4**
Using the job descriptions and job specifications you produced in activities 2 and 3 as a basis, produce classified advertisements for:
  (i)   An unskilled *and*
  (ii)  A semi-skilled post.

## Selection of Candidates

As we saw in the earlier study book, the advertisement for a job is the culmination of the recruitment procedure, bringing together the elements of job analysis, job description and job specification. From the point that the advertisement begins to attract candidates for the job the selection procedure begins. The early stages of this procedure are concerned with sorting out the applications of the candidates and compiling a short list for interview. This can be a difficult task and the most straight forward approach is to simply sift candidates into 'probable', 'possible' and 'rejected' categories, aiming to draw up a short-list of between 5 and 8 candidates. If we have more than 8 'probables' then our sifting out will need to be more strict; if we have less than 5 'probables' then we may need to select from our list of 'possibles'.

It may be felt that such a selection procedure is too simple and leaves too much room for error; if this is the case, more complex methods of sifting candidates can be carried. Figure 6 is an example of a form we might use in conjunction with the application to grade candidates more methodically than in the previous example.

| Candidates Name | Qualifications | Experience | Personal Qualities | Combined Grading | General Comments |
|---|---|---|---|---|---|
| 1. | | | | | |
| 2. | | | | | |
| 3. | | | | | |
| 4 | | | | | |

Fig. 6  *Candidate Selection Form*

*GRADES*

A  80% Excellent
B  65% Above Average
C  50% Average/Satisfactory
D  35% Below Average
E  20% Poor

This form can be adapted to satisfy the selection criteria of a variety of different jobs and its format might also include space for grading candidates on the basis of such things as: recent courses attended, posts of responsibility held, reference details etc. In addition, the percentages attached to each grade may be adapted to satisfy other functions, should the need arise. The additional value of such a system of grading is that once the most suitable candidates have been selected the form can be taken to the interview, along with the candidates' application form, so that further notes and adjustments can be made through the course of the interview.

## Conducting the Interview

Carefully conceived and carried out recruitment and selection procedures can founder on ill prepared, badly conducted interviews. Inexperienced and poorly prepared interviewers can, through the poor conduct of an interview, lose suitable candidates for jobs. The first stage to examine when we are able to conduct interviews therefore, is the planning stage.

### Planning the Interview

Staff carrying out interviews may ask themselves a range of general questions before they enter the interview room. The following are some of the more important of these:

Am I familiar with the Job Description and the Job Specification of each candidate?

Have I examined the candidates' selection form?

Have I compiled a list of *specific* questions based upon the candidates' application?

Do I have access to information that the candidates might require?

Is the room in which the interview is to take place fully equipped for this function? ie. is it comfortable? are there likely to be no interruptions?

If we can provide the answers to these general questions then we have progressed through the first stage of planning the interview. Our earlier question: 'Have I compiled a list of *specific* questions based upon the candidates' application?', takes us into the next planning stage of the interview. We need to compile a comprehensive and detailed list of questions along the lines suggested by this question. Our questions have to be structured in a way that the candidate's answers will inform us whether or not he is suitable for the job in question. In other words; does his application fit the company's requirements? In order to ascertain this, questions will also have to be structured to find out if the candidate possesses what the company requires.

Questioning along these lines might embrace such areas as: the suitability of the candidates' qualifications and experience for the job, the candidates' personality and attitude and how it might fit in with the rest of the staff, the appearance of the candidate and its appropriateness for the job, the candidates' interest in the job and a consideration of whether or not he is a genuine applicant, the references and testimonials of the candidates need to be considered to assess whether they contain any implicit meanings. All of these considerations provide the basis for the specific questioning the interviewer might undertake.

**Student Activity   No. 3.5**
Use the information in the last paragraph to help you draw up a list of questions to ask candidates at interview:
- (i) For an unskilled post *and*
- (ii) For a semi or sub skilled post.

You may compile your questions under the following headings:
- (i) Suitability of Candidate's Qualifications.
- (ii) Suitability of Candidate's Experience.
- (iii) Suitability of Candidate's Personality/Attitude.
- (iv) Candidate's interest in the job.
- (v) Your own headings(?).

*The Interview as a Two-way Experience*
No interview will be successful unless communication takes place within it: the interviewer and the interviewee must therefore interact. We have seen that the interviewer, for his part, has a large number of questions that he wishes to ask. These questions must be structured in such a way that the interviewee does not simply provide 'yes' or 'no' answers, they must be relatively open ended and demand a response. The interviewee's response will enable the interviewer to obtain a picture of the suitability of the interviewee to the post in question. This activity may be helped by the use of an Interview Grading Form, as illustrated in figure 7. When the interviewer is satisfied that he has investigated an area in sufficient depth, by the use of his questions, he can grade the interviewee accordingly by ticking the appropriate box on the form.

## INTERVIEW GRADING FORM

CANDIDATES NAME:

| CRITERIA | A | B | C | D | E |
|---|---|---|---|---|---|
| APPEARANCE<br>QUALIFICATIONS<br>EXPERIENCE<br>PERSONALITY<br>ATTITUDE TO WORK<br>ATTITUDE TO JOB<br>PERSONAL INTERESTS<br>OTHER QUALITIES | | | | | |
| COMMENTS: | | | | | |

Fig. 7  *Interview Grading Form*

The preparation of the interviewer in this two way experience must embrace the ability to be able to answer interviewee's questions. Genuine candidates will want to know details about the job for which they are applying; the interviewer must be fully prepared to answer these questions. He must therefore anticipate what these are likely to be and have the relevant information within easy reach should the questions arise.

Interviewees are likely to ask questions about the hours and the number of shifts they will be expected to work, holiday entitlements, social facilities and so on. The ability of the interviewer will be taxed by the kind of questions he may be asked in the interview situation.

**Student Activity   No. 3.6**
Prepare a bank of information that would enable you to answer questions about the unskilled and semi-skilled jobs that we have been dealing with throughout this chapter. The areas of questioning that your information might be suited for are as follows:
  (i)   The job duties, responsibilities.
 (ii)   Working conditions: wages, hours, shifts, fringe benefits.
(iii)   Social/welfare facilities.
(iv)   Promotional prospects.
 (v)   Use your job descriptions for reference.

*The Structure of the Interview*
The initial planning considerations that we made involved concentrating upon the kinds of questions the interviewer should ask and being prepared to answer questions that the interviewee might ask. This approach will help to eradicate two weaknesses of the interview situation:
  (i)   It will ensure that the limited time available is well and beneficially used   *and*
 (ii)   The element of bias or prejudice inherent in all communications may be reduced by an early objective analysis.
A further weakness of the interview situation is that it is a largely unnatural experience for all concerned; it is therefore to the advantage of both interviewer and interviewee if this unnatural element can be reduced. A major contribution the interviewer can make here is to structure the interview. He may employ an approach, in the early stages, of making the interviewee feel relaxed, talking in general terms about his journey, the weather etc. to help establish a rapport between them. This approach is not simply for the benefit of the interviewee's comfort and well-being; a nervous candidate, lacking in confidence may, when relaxed, offer explanations about himself which may not hitherto have been forthcoming.

This awareness, that it is important to create a relaxed atmosphere, should also make us realise the need for structure or to give some shape to the interview. Obviously, the phase we have just described will come in the early stages of the interview. Figure 8 is an example of the way in which the interview may be structured to ensure the most effective means of achieving its intended objectives.

By working through a structure of this kind the interviewer will provide a logical sequence for the interview; the interviewee will be able to discern the 'shape' of the interview and will not be caught off guard by questions asked abruptly and at random.

**Interview Structure**

1. *Introductory Phase*
   (a) Welcome candidate.
   (b) Ensure he is not kept waiting.
   (c) Interviewer introduces himself.
   (d) Adopts a relaxed, friendly manner.
   (e) Ask general, easy to answer questions.

2. *Analysis of the Application Form*
   (a) Ask questions that provide clarification.
   (b) Ask questions that follow from the form.
   (c) Encourage interviewee to expand upon material in the application form.
   (d) Attempt to elicit information about the interviewee's attitude to work, to past employers, reasons for leaving jobs and general personality characteristics.

3. *Analysis of Aspects of the Job*
   (a) Ask questions which indicate a candidate's skills in a particular area or situation. eg. 'How would you deal with a case of continued staff absence and lack of punctuality?'
   (b) Ensure that the candidate is fully aware of what the job entails.
   (c) Questions should be searching and demanding at this phase.
   (d) A degree of pressure may be exerted to test the candidate's suitability.

4. *Closing the Interview*
   (a) Summarise main areas of the interview and confirm these with candidate.
   (b) Offer the opportunity to ask further questions.
   (c) Ensure that all the candidate's questions have been fully answered.
   (d) Slowly bring the interview to a conclusion asking questions like 'When would you be able to take up employment?' 'Have your travelling expenses been dealt with?'.
   (e) Inform him of date by which he will hear the result of the interview.
   (f) Thank the candidate for coming to the interview.

Fig. 8   *An example of an Interview Structure*

The interviewer should, through this structure, establish a rapport with the interviewee, he will show a willingness to listen to the interviewee's answers and comments and will, from to time, refer back to earlier points in the interview or to answers given by the interviewee. All these approaches re-affirm the structure of the interview, providing a sense of order and efficiency.

## Student Activity   No. 3.7

Use the material developed in activities 3.2, 3.3, 3.4 and 3.5 as the basis for an interview simulation in your group. With the help of your lecturer and the participation of other students carry out interviews for:

(i)  An unskilled post  *and*
(ii)  A sub-skilled post.

This activity is designed to demonstrate your understanding of what is entailed by the selection process as a whole and your interviewing ability for the posts in question. The use of video recording equipment may help you to assess your abilities and recognise your good and bad points.

The interview or interviews, having been completed, leave the interviewer or the interviewing panel with the need to make a choice from all the persons that they have interviewed. This may be a simple and straightforward activity in the case where one candidate is far superior to the others. In other cases more protracted deliberation may be necessary. Whatever the case, the decision should not be rushed, the selected candidate should be the best. When selection has been made the successful candidate should be informed in writing, he should be notified of his starting date and to whom he should report. The unsuccessful candidates should be informed in writing of the decision and thanked for their application and for their interest in the post.

**The Induction Process**

The importance of the supervisory role cannot be over-emphasised when the induction process is examined. Great care, attention and effort has been injected into the recruitment and selection procedure and therefore the induction process should be conducted with similar diligence. Induction, as we saw in section B of the previous study book, represents an important element of the manpower plan and therefore as a thorough and complete process, needs to be carefully conceived.

It is important at this stage that we clearly distinguish between *induction* training and *job* training. Induction training refers to the process by which the new employee is introduced and made familiar with the total work environment. Job training refers to the learning and adoption of skills relevant to the job and the carrying out of tasks embraced by the job. It is likely that the new employee will undergo induction training and job training at the same time and will probably not be aware that the two training programmes are operating in tandem.

On the job induction will take a similar form for all employees within a given section or department of the workforce, irrespective of the job that they have been employed to do. In contrast, on the job training will be specific to the requirements of each job and this will be reflected in the training programmes that are conceived and developed for this purpose.

*Developing an On-Job Induction Programme*
In the previous study book we considered the main elements of an induction programme. We may summarise these elements in the following way:

(i) The legal framework of induction as specified by the Terms and Conditions of Employment in The Employment Protection (Consolidation) Act 1978 and the code of practice contained in the 1971 Industrial Relations Act. Also the working conditions as defined by The Health and Safety at Work Act 1974.

(ii) The provision of information about the company: its history, its organisation and its objectives.

(iii) The 'geography' of the work environment, including the location of important people, places and things.

(iv) The supervisor responsible for induction, will be in charge of the section of the work force in question and will need to introduce himself and establish a relationship with the new comer.

(v) Introduction of the new comer to all members of the work group that he is to join.

The size of the organisation will be a major determinant in deciding who carries out the induction process. In small organisations a manager or supervisor may well carry out the whole induction procedure. In larger organisations induction will be divided into two interrelated parts, *primary* induction and *secondary* induction. *Primary* induction, covering 'i', 'ii' and 'iii' above, will be carried out in a large organisation by the company's personnel department. *Secondary* induction, covering 'iii', 'iv' and 'v' above, will be carried out in a large organisation by the supervisor of each section. It will be noted that 'iii' is included in both primary and secondary induction, this is because, in the first instance, the 'geography' of the firm as a whole would be dealt with and, in the second instance, the 'geography' of the new comer's specific work area would be dealt with.

With drawing up on-job induction programmes attention should be given to areas of special needs eg. disabled people, school-leavers and immigrants. Each of these groups may have special needs and care should be applied when dealing with them.

**Student Activity No. 3.8**
Design an on-job induction programme that a catering supervisor of a school's canteen kitchen might use for the induction of new staff. You may assume that the catering supervisor has responsibility for primary and secondary induction.

Your programme should be carefully timed, giving a longer time period to difficult or more important areas, allowing flexibility, should problems arise, and indicating when and how frequently supervisory checks are likely to occur.

You should refer to the information in this section in the development of your programme. You should also refer to the information contained in section B of study book 2 and for detailed information on the legal requirements relating to induction you should refer to the Law section of your local or college library.

*Developing an On-Job Training Programme*
On-job training will be carried out as a part of, or in conjunction with, the on-job induction programme. The nature, level and content of on-job training is very dependent upon the level of skills, knowledge and experience the potential trainee possesses. It must be assumed that the trainee will be equipped with at least a minimum amount of basic skills to enable him to benefit from the training programme.

Any training programme that a supervisor might devise for staff in his section must be conceived within the control of the training plan for the whole organisation. Progressive employers and managers alike will encourage the implementation of training programmes, whether they be for new staff entering the organisation, or for existing staff who are being trained in new methods, or to use new equipment. However, training does take time and does cost money, so training programmes must be carefully conceived and thoroughly employed. In an industry which is characterised by high labour turnover, staff training can be a substantial cost to a hotel and catering establishment.

We found that with the induction programme the size of the organisation was an important factor in determining the content and operation of the programme. The same is true with training programmes; in a large organisation training may be carried out by specialist training officers and instructors, in a small organisation training may be carried out by supervisors or the operatives themselves. The ability to train someone to learn a skill is something that is not always easily acquired; that is why the designing of an on-job training programme is an invaluable aid to all those involved in the training of staff.

The level and complexity of skills being taught are also factors involved in the effective running of an on-job training programme. We may generalise here and say that as the level and complexity of skills increases so the task of training becomes more difficult.

The success or failure of the training programme will also be largely dependant upon the motivation and the attitude of the person being trained. An enthusiastic trainee, eager to learn new skills, will make the task of the training officer so much easier. In contrast, the simplest of skills will be difficult to teach if the trainee lacks motivation, has a poor attitude to work and is relatively reluctant to learn.

We may summarise at this point and say that the initial design stage of a training programme must take into consideration the following factors:

(i) The company training plan (if one exists).
(ii) The skills the trainee possesses.
(iii) The costs of training.
(iv) The role of the trainer/supervisor.
(v) The kind of skills being taught.
(vi) The motivation of the trainee.

We will now consider the specific details of the on-job training programme; we have made initial considerations and identified training needs, now we have to clearly indicate what trainers and trainees will actually do. The following represents the main features of a systematic training programme, details of which might vary slightly from job to job but which are, in principle, basic to any training programme.

(i) What is the training programme designed to achieve? *Objectives* must be written and trainees must be aware of these objectives.

(ii) A *training timetable* must be drawn up, including details of dates, times and the location of training. In addition trainees should be given an indication of how long a particular element of training should take (see figure 10).

(iii) The *parts* of the training programme must be identified for the trainee, ie. the tasks that are to be dealt with (see figure 9).

(iv) The *method of training* must be considered and chosen. (See section C of study book 2).

(v) The *method of assessment*, which will be linked to number iv above.

(vi) The *trainees should be identified,* and their names should be written into the training programme.

If figure 9 we see an example of the kind of form that might be used to record the training of staff in carrying out particular tasks.

## TASK TRAINING RECORD

Trainee's Name:...............    Task:..........................

Job Title:....................    Trainer:......................

Section/Department:...........    Date of Training:...............

Training Location:..............    Duration of Training:.............

| Task | Training Objective | Method of Training | Method of Assessment | Objective Achieved | Trainers Comments |
|------|-----|-----|-----|-----|-----|
|  |  |  |  |  |  |
|  |  |  |  |  |  |

Fig. 9 *An example of a Task Training Record*

The task training record shown in figure 9 can be used for each individual task the trainee has to learn to carry out. If there are a number of tasks that a trainee has to learn then these will be incorporated into a systematic programme which may be recorded on the kind of timetable demonstrated in figure 10.

## STAFF TRAINING TIMETABLE

| Trainee's Name | Task 1. | Date | Task 2. | Date | Task 3. | Date | Task 4. | Date | Task 5. | Date |
|---|---|---|---|---|---|---|---|---|---|---|
| | | | | | | | | | | |
| | | | | | | | | | | |
| | | | | | | | | | | |
| | | | | | | | | | | |
| | | | | | | | | | | |
| | | | | | | | | | | |
| | | | | | | | | | | |

Trainers Signature:                    Programme Completion Date:

Fig. 10  *An example of a Staff Training Timetable*

By implementing task training records and staff training timetables, similar to those illustrated in figures 9 and 10, the training programme can be presented and operated in a systematic manner.

**Student Activity  3.9**
(i)   Design an on-job training programme that might be used for the purpose of training junior reception staff in a large hotel.
(ii)  Design an on-job training programme that might be used for the purpose of training counter assistants in a fast food outlet.
Training needs in any organisation will vary, as the organisation changes and as external factors influence its development. For this and other reasons, the final stage in any training plan or programme is the review procedure. The training staff should examine from time to time if the programme continues to be effective, if it is achieving the desired results and if staff can be seen to have benefitted from taking part in it. Recommendations arising from review procedure should be implemented as quickly as is expedient and any new training needs that may be identified, as a consequence of the review, should be catered for.

**Student Activity   No. 3.10**
With the help of your tutor design and carry out a piece of on-job training for a task or tasks you are familiar with, in one of the college training areas ie. restaurant, coffee shop, kitchens, reception area or

housekeeping area. You will need to plan your training carefully, taking into consideration the objectives you wish to achieve, the methods you are going to use, assessment procedures and so on. Record your findings on a task training record and discuss your results with:

(i) The trainee (ie. a student from another course).
(ii) Other students in your group *and*
(iii) Your tutor.

## ORGANISATIONAL AND INDIVIDUAL EVALUATION

We have so far represented training as a means by which organisational needs can be met. We have recognised that training needs exist and that systematic procedures are necessary to fulfill these needs. These training needs will not be constant and as the organisation and the business environment in which it exists changes so also will its training needs. If efficiency is to be maintained therefore a process of organisational and individual evaluation must take place to ensure that the organisation develops to keep abreast of changes that may be occuring.

The role of the supervisor, in co-ordination with other supervisors and management, is particularly important here. The supervisor will be in direct contact with the jobs that are being carried out within the organisation and will be able to see whether they are being carried out effectively or not. He may well be involved in staff training programmes and will be able to see how individual staff members are coping with the demands of a particular job. It will be the supervisor who will be required to appraise the work situation, should changes be recommended and he will be required to implement these changes, should managerial decisions be made. In the second part of this section then, we will consider job content and its relationship to organisational needs, and the importance of different forms of job appraisal, job rotation and the maintenance of staff development.

*Job Content*
The function of job descriptions has already been dealt with in this and other sections, they provide clear and explicit guidelines for carrying out the job, or in other words, they describe the content of the job. So the job description of a catering assistant in figure 1 gives details of the content of the job, indicating that, for example, the catering assistant will 'assist with food preparation as specified by the canteen supervisor'. We need to consider what this actually entails, what will the catering assistant actually be expected to do when he or she is assisting with the food preparation, as specified by the catering assistant?

Any job is clearly made up of a number of related tasks which the individual has to carry out, these tasks, in turn, will be related to the tasks that other individuals in the organisation carry out and also to the

156

equipment and material that the individual has to work with. Without going into detail, we can see how complex the job can be, even though it may superficially appear to be simple and straightforward. In order to understand any complex job it can often help to break it down into its component tasks, to examine what these comprise of and to see how each is related to the other. Not only does this activity help us to understand the job and its component tasks but also it helps us to evaluate if it is being carried out effectively and if it is contributing to the overall efficiency of the organisation. There is therefore, both an organisational and an individual need to review job content, to ensure that the optimum use is being made of the individual's labour, materials and the equipment being used. This process is often referred to as work study. We will briefly consider what is entailed by the process of work study and how it is relevant to hotel and catering operators.

*Work Study*
F.W. Taylor in his principles of 'scientific management' also developed the concept of work study and, since Taylor's original idea, work study has become an important and integral part of supervisory and management work.

Work study can be broken down into two component parts:
(i)   Method study or method improvement   *and*
(ii)   Work measurement.
Method study is quite simply an analysis of the methods employed to carry out a given task and an attempt, as a consequence of this study, to make improvements in the method of carrying out the given task. Work measurement is simply a process of time study, of establishing, through observation, how long a particular task takes the individual worker to carry out. Work measurement enables the observer to establish what percentage of time an individual worker allocates to certain tasks and from this allows him to build up a picture of job content.

We will return to the example of the catering assistant who is carrying out one of his tasks ie. that of assisting with food preparation, as specified by the canteen supervisor. We will consider one aspect of this task and examine what is involved in vegetable preparation. Figure 11 is an example of a job chart that the canteen supervisor might draw up for the purpose of carrying out this task.

The application of the principles of work study to the job of vegetable preparation shown in figure 11 is relatively straightforward. Method study would involve observation and detailed analysis of each step of the operation in an attempt to establish if any improvements could be made. For example, it may be observed that cleaning down, as part of activity vii, is a superfluous activity and can be left until final cleaning down in activity x. This may not only represent an improve-

# JOB CHART

**DEPARTMENT:** Works Canteen
**JOB TITLE:** Catering Assistant
**TASK:** Vegetable Preparation
**TASK BEGINNING:** Instructions from Canteen Supervisor
**TASK ENDING:** Clean up work area; approval from supervisor.
ACTIVITIES:
    (i) Write out stores requisition for materials.
    (ii) Go to Supervisor's office to obtain signature of approval.
    (iii) Go to food stores, fill out order for vegetables.
    (iv) Carry vegetables to work preparation area.
    (v) Wash all vegetables thoroughly in sink.
    (vi) Pick over, clean and peel all vegetables.
    (vii) Throw away all vegetable peelings and parings, clean work area.
    (viii) Cut up all vegetables to required dimensions for cooking (ie. slice, dice etc.).
    (iv) Reserve vegetables until required for cooking.
    (x) Clean work area, utensils etc.

Fig. 11 *Example of a Job Chart*

ment in the method of working but also, when work measurement is carried out, may also represent a saving in time. This may only account for a few minutes each time the job is carried out, but over an extended period, say a financial year, and costed against the catering assistants' wages, this may represent a considerable cost saving.

## Student Activity No. 3.11

(i) Using the details from the job descriptions you devised in activity 3.2 draw up a job chart similar to that shown in figure 11 for a set of activities that make up that particular job.

(ii) When your job chart is complete, circulate it amongst your group, for them to carry out a work study on it. Use this as a basis for a group discussion on job content.

Work study represents an approach that may be employed by managers and supervisors to satisfy an organisational need, ie. to review job content to ensure optimum levels of productivity and efficiency. However, there are certain constraints attached to the achievement of this end: standards of performance have to be maintained to ensure that the service the customer expects is always given and that the job satisfaction for the employee must not be damaged. The second of these two constraints indicates the individual's need to review job content. A waitress in a coffee shop may, for example, find her job satisfying; she may work a certain number of covers in a given meal period and provide a good customer service. The coffee shop supervisor might, as a consequence of employing work study methods, recommend that the content of her job is altered. He may suggest, for example, different methods of serving rolls or retrieving utensils from the sideboard, in an attempt to increase productivity by increasing the number of covers she serves in the meal period. This may have the effect of increasing productivity but lowering the job satisfaction of the waitress, perhaps because she finds the new method difficult. The result of this may be to lower the quality of food service because the waitress herself feels less job satisfaction. In this case the coffee shop supervisor should recognise the problem and attempt to rectify it. The individual worker also has to be able to recognise the aspect of her job that is causing problems and perhaps suggest to her supervisor that changes could be made.

## Staff Development

In the last example, we saw how changes that were made to the job that an individual worker had to do affected the level of satisfaction she obtained from doing the job and, also, the damaging effect that this might ultimately have upon the customer service being provided. This represents one simple example of the way in which a supervisor's actions might damage the worker's approach to the job.

Staff development represents the way in which members of staff see their role within the organisation progressing in the future. A worker who experienced changes in working conditions which appeared to diminish the status of his role might feel that his career was not progressing ie. staff development for him was not taking place. Supervisors then must pay careful attention to the means by which they might maintain staff development in their particular section of the work force. We will consider some of the ways in which staff development can be achieved and maintained.

### Performance Appraisal

We saw in section D of study book 2, the need for performance appraisal in relation to the objective of achieving results through people. No organisation can effectively operate unless regular and systematic performance appraisal takes place. There are a variety of methods which can be employed to achieve this end. In this sense performance appraisal fulfills an organisational need but it also has an important staff development function. Appraisal can indicate to the sensitive and perceptive supervisor areas of staff discontent. He may recognise, for example, that a qualified and skilled trainee is becoming increasingly frustrated carrying out the same repetitive, mundane tasks. He may decide, as a consequence of careful appraisal, that some form of staff development should take place for the trainee in question.

An appraisal of staffing records may reveal to a supervisor that labour turnover is particularly high in one section, or for one trade. Further appraisal of this section of the work force or specific trade area may provide him with an indication why. Staff may feel they are isolated from the rest of the work force and that their chances of promotion are limited, they may feel that the equipment they have to use is old and outmoded, they may feel they are not receiving justifiable reward for their labours and so on.

Careful performance appraisal therefore reveals areas in which staff development may be generated and improvements in working conditions and customer service ultimately improved. Appraisal and follow-up discussions with staff involved can, therefore, bring benefits all round.

*Job Rotation*
A number of factors related to the content of jobs can lead to job dis-satisfaction: workers may feel their job is unchallenging, that there is no potential for growth or creativity associated with the job, that they have little responsibility and that what they are doing is receiving little recognition. Clearly, performance appraisal will help the supervisor to recognise certain symptoms in his staff but he still has to come up with cures to help alleviate the problems. One approach which has been suggested is that of employing job rotation, whereby amongst a group of workers, various jobs are 'rotated' or changed from time to time, giving staff variety in what they do and preventing them from losing interest or getting bored.

Job rotation is not possible where high levels of specialist skills are involved; it would be hard to imagine successfully operating a job rotation between a hotel accountant, its head chef and the house-keeper! However, where skills are of a relatively low level, job rotation may be possible. Job rotation therefore must be linked to multi-skilling; it will not function unless the work force involved have the skills, no matter how low level, to carry out the tasks involved. Many small catering operations employ staff with multiple skills eg. chamber-maid/waitress, kitchen assistant/bar staff, therefore by the same logic larger oganisations can employ similarly skilled staff and rotate them through the range of their skill areas to help maintain interest and job satisfaction. In addition, the ability to carry out a number of skills, rather than be specialised in one skill creates more promotion possi-bilities for staff involved, another factor contributing to improvements in staff development. This form of job rotation can create benefits for the staff and also the organisation, because if staff see that they can achieve *within* a given company, they will have less of an incentive to leave to better their career, thus reducing labour turnover with all its associated costs.

**Student Activity   No. 3.12**
Draw up a job rotation system that may be practically employed in a working establishment that you are familiar with. Indicate the periods for which staff may carry out jobs, showing also split-shift and weekend working arrangements.

## Job Enlargement

Job rotation represents a possible means by which the disaffected worker, with a relatively low level of motivation, may be given increased job interest which in turn will encourage him to work more efficiently. With careful attention to the question of multi-skilling and a recruitment and selection procedure which reflects this, it should be posible, with low-level task areas, to achieve a working job rotation system. Such a scheme may be part of a wider job enlargement programme instigated by managers or supervisors. Such a scheme would have the twin objectives of providing an area of staff development and of enhancing overall organisational efficiency.

We have defined job enlargement as the means by which an individual's job is broadened, providing increased satisfaction of his social or egoistic needs. It should not be confused with job enrichment, which implies growth and a movement away from the present job area, by means of promotion. Job enlargement is a process by which, at a given level of the organisation, an individual's job is widened by introducing into it an element of responsibility. The idea of job enlargement is based upon McGregor's Theory 'Y' which in turn is based upon the principle that if you remove restraints from the work force and create areas of responsibility for them they will be motivated to work harder. We may illustrate this by reference to an example.

Breakfast preparation for 40 covers in a small sea-side hotel may normally be carried out by the chef and a kitchen assistant. The chef may decide to offer the opportunity of carrying out the preparation of the breakfast menu to the kitchen assistant in an attempt to provide job enlargement for him. The skill area of the kitchen assistant will not be changed, he will be carrying out the same tasks as he normally would under the chef, but he will have a personal responsibility to ensure that the breakfast menu is correctly prepared. Such an approach could provide an increased level of motivation on the part of the kitchen assistant without endangering the success of the operation, as, in such establishments, the chef would normally be resident in the staff quarters of the hotel so that he would be able to deal with any emergencies, should they arise.

Job rotation and enlargement schemes, by enabling a greater level of participation and involvement in the work on the part of the individual, provide the opportunity for the workers to become more self-reliant and to express themselves more fully in the work situation. The famous Volvo and Saab experiments both demonstrate that in work areas where a high degree of repetition and low demands upon worker responsibility exist, the introduction of 'flexible team systems' or group working schemes has improved worker motivation and morale as well as increasing overall productivity.

**Student Activity   No. 3.13**

Go to your college library and look up the Volvo and/or the Saab experiments, then complete the following tasks:

(i)   Write a brief summary of what the experiments involved, how they were structured and what they achieved *and*

(ii)   With the use of a practical example demonstrate the way in which similar methods might be applied in the catering work place.

*Staff Records*

Any systematic supervisory approach to appraisal which recommends changes in the work situation, such as a job rotation scheme, must be based upon a careful and thorough recording system. A supervisor who, as a consequence of careful appraisal, records increasing labour turnover in his section, will be able to provide management with an accurate breakdown of the trends in question. Such an approach is to be preferred to a purely verbal account which is more likely to be open to misinterpretation.

Supervisors, particularly in large-scale organisations, are increasingly being required to keep records. These are used to inform managers and proprietors alike of the day to day operation of the various sections within the organisation. The supervisor may be required to keep the following records:

(i)   Personal record file.

(ii)   Employment records.

(iii)   Training records.

(iv)   Performance records.

(v)   Staff turnover records.

(vi)   Stock inventories.

(vii)   Equipment maintenance records.

(viii)   Fire, health and safety records (inc, accident report forms).

Any supervisor who has to keep all the above records will clearly be involved in a detailed administrative set of tasks which will consume larger amounts of his time. We will briefly consider what is involved in the supervisor keeping a personal record file; this should give us an indication of how involved comprehensive record keeping can become.

The personal record file is an up to date record of all relevant details of each individual worker in the supervisor's section. In smaller organisations this personal record file may incorporate the employment, training and performance records (ii, iii and iv above). Figure 12 is an example of a personal record file that a supervisor might use.

```
┌─────────────────────────────────────────────────────────────┐
│                  CAMBRIAN HOTEL GROUP                         │
│                  ──────────────────────                       │
│                  Personal Record File                         │
│                  ────────────────────                         │
│  NAME:.......................................................  │
│  ADDRESS......................................................  │
│          ...................................................  │
│          ...................................................  │
│          ...................................................  │
│  TELEPHONE No:................................................  │
│  Age:........ Yrs........ Mths │ Date of birth:...../.../......│
│  Sex:.......................... │ Marital Status:..............│
│  Nationality:.................. │ NHI No:......................│
│  Dept:......................... │ Date Started...../.../......│
│  Job Title:.................... │ Wage/Salary:.................│
│  Date Leaving:...../.../...... │ Reasons for Leaving..........│
└─────────────────────────────────────────────────────────────┘
```

Fig. 12  *An example of a Personal Record File*

It should be noted that the personal record file in figure 12 can be easily appended to include additional information ralating to performance, punctuality, absence, holiday arrangements, disciplinary action and so on. It is important that staff records are kept; how they are constructed and what their specific details are will be dependant upon the needs of the organisation and the intentions of the supervisor or manager who is compiling the record.

**Student Activity   No. 3.14**
Using the personal record file in figure 12 as a reference or starting point draw up a detailed personal data file which includes space to record details of staff performance, punctuality, absence, holiday arrangements and disciplinary action. Ensure that the lay-out of your file is clear and provides sufficient space for the inclusion of all relevant information.

Finally, it should be pointed out that the employment record that a supervisor normally keeps is a duplicate copy of the contract of employment that all staff in his section are given when they are employed by the firm. The legal basis of such a contract can be found in the Employment Protection (Consolidation) Act 1978 and the contract should clearly indicate all aspects of the terms and conditions of employment.

The quantity and nature of the staff records kept by the supervisor will vary according to the size and complexity of the organisation in which he is working, but in order to achieve any consistency in his methods and to maintain a clear perspective on his subordinates, staff records of some kind will always be kept.

**Student Activity   No. 3.15**
Research the following sources to obtain examples of the following types of staff records:
  (i)   A personal record card — Personnel Management in the Hotel and Catering Industry — M.J. Boella.
  (ii)  A merit rating form (performance record) — Hotel and Catering Supervision — K. Gale and P. Odgers.
  (iii) An induction check list — A Manual of Staff Management in the Hotel and Catering Industry — J.P. Magurn.

**Systems of Wage Payment**
We have seen that the financial incentive is not the only means of motivating staff but it is essential in providing the basic remaneration necessary for employees and their families to live. If we follow Maslow's line of reasoning, wages provide for the basic first order needs in the needs hierarchy, after which other factors such as job satisfaction, responsibility and the satisfaction of social needs become predominant.

Wages in the hotel and catering industry are not as straightforward as they are in other industries; they are complicated by a number of factors. These factors include: tipping, service charges, accommodation and meals on duty that are provided for staff as an extra benefit to their wages. Wages represent a slight conflict area in some sectors of the industry, not only because of the systems of 'individual contracts' that employees often enter into with employers but also because of the generally low wages paid in the industry. The Wages Council and The Payment of Wages Act 1960 set basic minimum wages but these are often considered to be unacceptably low by some sectors of the industry. Wage costs are particularly high in the hotel and catering industry because of its high labour intensity. The relatively low level of trade union involvement in the industry has meant that wage improvement negotiations have been relatively piecemeal and where improvements to income have been made it has not been in terms of improvements of basic wages. Increasingly, throughout the industry, incentive and bonus schemes are being implemented by management as incentives for the work force. Examples of these may be sales bonuses to receptionists, end of season bonuses to staff to encourage them to work out the season, profit based bonuses to kitchen staff and a variety of other forms.

Supervisors must pay careful attention to the system of payment employed; any dissatisfaction with the system of payment will be made known to them at an early stage and they will be expected to remedy any faults that the system may have. To this end, supervisors should attempt to anticipate the effectiveness of a particular system of wage payment and recommend to management or employees that it be implemented. This highlights an important aspect of the supervisor's role; it is one which, if not carefully dealt with may damage all the care and effort that has gone into recruiting, selecting, inducting and training staff. Supervisors should therefore be sensitive to employees' feelings about the system of wages and ensure that they liaise with management to ensure that the system does not become a damaging bone of contention between employers and employees.

## ASSESSMENT QUESTIONS

1. Define staffing needs.
2. Identify the main criteria for evaluating staffing.
3. List the sources of labour available in the employment of hotel and catering staff.
4. Distinguish clearly between a job description and a job specification.
5. Draw up a job description for an unskilled position.
6. Draw up a job description for a semi-skilled position.
7. List the main component parts of a job specification.
8. Design a classified advertisement for an unskilled position.
9. Design a classified advertisement for a semi-skilled position.
10. Distinguish clearly between a classified, semi-display and display advertisement.
11. Compile a list of questions that you might use in the course of a selection interview for an unskilled position.
12. Compile a list of questions that you might use in the course of a selection interview for a semi-skilled position.
13. Explain the main problems associated with selection interviewing.
14. Explain in detail the way in which you would structure a selection interview.
15. Distinguish clearly between induction training and job training.
16. Describe the main elements of an on-job induction programme.
17. Describe the main elements of an on-job training programme.
18. Explain the difficulties involved in designing an on-job induction programme.
19. Explain the difficulties involved in designing an on-job training programme.
20. Give an explanation of the way in which you would go about recording the details of an on-job training programme that you have carried out.
21. Define job content.

22. Explain the organisational need to review job content.
23. Explain the individual need to review job content.
24. Define work study.
25. Explain the way in which work study can contribute to the satisfaction of organisational skills.
26. Define staff development.
27. Show the way in which appraisal, job rotation and job enlargement may contribute to staff development.
28. Explain the importance of staff records as part of the supervisor's role.
29. Explain the systems of wage payment normally associated with hotel and catering establishments.

# The Techniques of Supervision

In the previous section we emphasised the importance of the supervisory role in relation to both organisational and staff needs. These must be made, as far is possible, compatible with one another so that efficiency is maintained at an acceptable level. This compatibility is not always achieved and problems inevitably arise in the most well organised establishments. The techniques that the supervisor employs are crucial in ensuring that the effects of day to day problems that may arise are kept to a minimum. In this section we will consider some of the practical techniques that a supervisor might employ in coming to terms with daily problems. We will carry out this analysis by examining the practical aspects of his controlling function, his application of relevant legal knowledge and his ability to communicate with staff in interview situations.

## THE CONTROLLING FUNCTION

The supervisor who can exercise control within the context of the organisation is a long way toward achieving the functional requirements of his role. In the previous study book we defined supervisory control as: 'the means by which successful planning and operation is sustained'. We noted also the importance of implementing 'feed back systems' at all points of the production or service process to ensure that the targets and therefore the objectives of the operation, were being achieved. In this section we will examine in more detail the practical aspects of the controlling function of the supervisor by looking at the compilation of work rosters, work schedules and other controlling techniques. We will also assess the different supervisory styles that might be employed in carrying out the controlling function.

### Work Rosters

A work roster may be defined as a visual display of the various periods of work or duty that are to be carried out by staff, in a given section, over a given length of time, normally a working week. Work rosters will display, as graphically as possible, the working arrangements of a section or a work team over this period of time. They will therefore have to take into consideration the following factors, in relation to the organisation of the work:

(i)   The number of hours an employee can work.
(ii)  Full-time staff and/or part time staff.

(iii)   Shift demands eg. split-shifts.
(iv)   Days off.
(v)   Relief work and cover for absent staff.
(vi)   Statutory breaks eg. lunch, tea.
(vii)   Overtime arrangements.

In a work unit that operates on a standard 9 o'clock to 5 o'clock working day for 5 days a week with very little variety of demand or production a work roster would be fairly straightforward to compile. Figure 13 is an example of such a work roster; showing work periods and staggered lunch-breaks. It should be noted that a roster of this type would be drawn up for each day of the week and should be drawn large enough to accommodate overtime working if required.

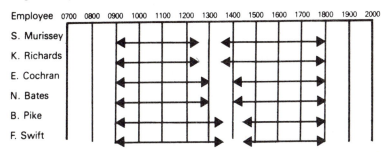

Fig. 13   *An example of a Work Roster*

Catering establishments rarely work in such a simple, uncomplicated manner, the working day is made up of busy and quiet periods, as is the working week in many establishments. Split shift arrangements are often employed, for example in establishments that offer bed, breakfast and an evening meal and, in establishments where multi-skilling is used, the work roster will reflect the different tasks the employee carries out. In addition, the work roster will show the working arrangements of temporary or relief staff, training or staff development periods, days off etc. In figure 14 we see an example of a split-shift work roster that may be drawn up for five kitchen assistants working in a seasonal hotel carrying out preparation for breakfasts and evening meals.

This work roster incorporates a flexible system of days off and also involves a simple job rotation. The two kitchen assistants who begin working at 6.30 will be responsible for the breakfast preparation, ensuring that the required amount of food is retrieved from the store, that an adequate supply of boiling water for teas, coffees etc. is available and that all the food for the breakfast menu is prepared and ready for service when the restaurant opens. The two kitchen assistants who begin working at 7.30 will assist in the preparation and service of breakfast. After breakfast service, all four kitchen assistants may have

Fig. 14  *An example of a Split-Shift'Work Roster*

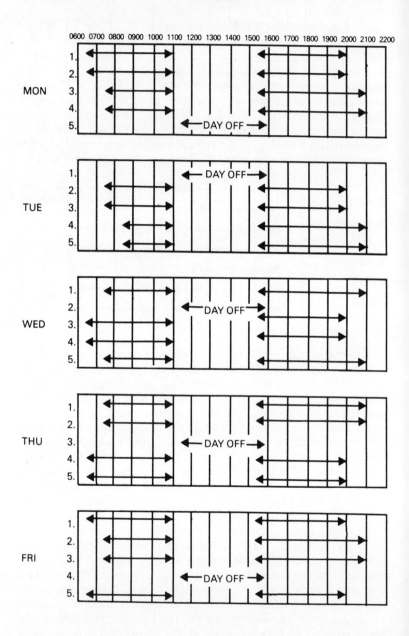

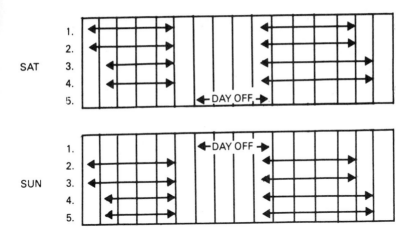

SAT

SUN

MEMBER OF STAFF:
1. J. COTTON
2. S. HORTON
3. S. TERRY
4. L. WALTER
5. C. DAVIES

their breakfasts and begin food preparation for the evening menu. The two kitchen assistants who work until 21.00 will be involved in cleaning down working surfaces and carrying out the pot wash. This simple job rotation, provides a variety of work tasks, offers some responsibility to the early breakfast shift and enables staff to work together in different working combinations. It should be noted that the split shift working arrangement is not one that is always popular with staff as it tends to lengthen the working day. Supervisors and managers for this reason sometimes try to avoid the split shift working arrangement. However, in the present example, where seasonal hotel work is being considered, the opportunity of free time during a summer afternoon at a popular resort is often a convenient arrangement for staff.

All work rosters should be drawn up during the planning stage and should be displayed to staff well in advance of their implementation. This allows staff to plan their private life in advance, as well as giving their work a structure and a planned coherence. The examples of work rosters shown in figures 13 and 14 are not the only type that may be used; it is important to emphasise that, whatever form of display is used, maximum clarity should be aimed for. The rosters should not appear complicated or in anyway confusing and, in drawing them up, supervisors should employ communication skills in assessing the most effective means of putting the intended message across, bearing in mind that visual representations such as bar charts or graphs can be more effective than words.

**Student Activity   No. 3.16**

(i)   Go to the catering section of your college library and find examples of work or duty rosters for a number of different positions and of a variety of different types.

(ii)   Draw up a suitable work roster for chambermaids incorporating extra staffing or duties for weekend changeover.

Use a different method of visual presentation in each case and draw up your roster on an acetate sheet so that you can explain your roster with the use of the overhead projector to the rest of your group.

**Work Schedules**

Work schedules will be used in conjunction with work rosters, and can be defined in the following way: they are designed to list the work to be undertaken by each member of staff at a given time of the day. A work schedule provides information of what has to be done and when it has to be done. A work schedule is therefore not simply details which are taken from the job description, it is a detailed listing of all the tasks an individual employee has to carry out within a given period of time, with a clear specification of the order of tasks and the amount of time that should be allocated to each task.

A supervisor will need to ensure that the various work schedules that he designs will meet the following requirements:

(i)   They make the best implementation of staff resources.

(ii)   They do not create an overlap or clash of duties between staff.

(iii)   They ensure that all work is covered.

(iv)   The allocation of tasks is realistic in terms of the capabilities of that member of staff.

(v)   They clearly describe the work to be carried out.

In planning the work of this section a supervisor may draw up a *master schedule* designating the work of the whole section and from this will be drawn the work schedules for each member of staff within the section. Each member of staff will be given a copy of his work schedule, either in notice or work card form, so that he may use it for reference at any time during the working day to establish what he should be doing at a certain time. Work cards are often designed to be carried by the member of staff so that an occasional check on what work is to be done can be carried out. Figure 15 is an example of a work schedule for morning duties that a floor supervisor might give to a part-time chambermaid working in her section in a large hotel.

The example given shows a work schedule for what is part of a daily routine. Similar work schedules would exist for other parts of the daily routine through the section and throughout the organisation as a whole. In addition to work schedules covering daily routine tasks, other schedules would exist for periodic tasks which have to be carried out on a monthly, quarterly, six-monthly or annual basis. An example of such a periodic schedule would be a maintenance schedule covering such tasks as carpet shampooing, wall washing etc. The way in which the schedule is drawn up would be similar.

## NORTHUMBERLAND HOTEL
### Housekeeping Department, Work Schedule

Section/Floor...................

Floor Supervisor...................

Staff Member...................

| Work Location (specified by supervisor) | Tasks | Time |
|---|---|---|
| ROOM 1 | Strip Beds, Remove Waste | 9.00 |
| | Make Beds, Renew Towels | 9.05 |
| | Damp Dust | 9.20 |
| | Vacuum Carpet | 9.25 |
| ROOM 2 | Strip Beds, Remove Waste | 9.30 |
| | Make Beds, Renew Towels | 9.35 |
| | Damp Dust | 9.50 |
| | Vacuum Carpet | 9.55 |
| ROOM 3 | Strip Beds, Remove Waste | 10.00 |
| | Make Beds, Renew Towels | 10.05 |
| | Damp Dust | 10.20 |
| | Vacuum Carpet | 10.25 |
| BREAK | | |
| ROOM 4 | Strip Beds, Remove Waste | 10.45 |
| | Make Beds, Renew Towels | 10.50 |
| | Damp Dust | 11.15 |
| | Vacuum Carpet | 11.10 |
| ROOM 5 | Strip Beds, Remove Waste | 11.15 |
| | Make Beds, Renew Towels | 11.20 |
| | Damp Dust | 11.35 |
| | Vacuum Carpet | 11.40 |
| BATHROOM/TOILET | Remove Waste | 11.45 |
| | Clean Bath/Toilet Basin and all surfaces, renew all towels | 11.50 |
| | Wet Mop Floor | 12.05 |
| STORE | Return Equipment | 12.15 |
| STAFF CHANGING ROOM | Wash/Change | 12.20 |
| OFF DUTY | Leave Premises | 12.30 |

Fig. 15  *Example of a Work Schedule for a part-time floor chambermaid*

**Student Activity   No. 3.17**
Prepare detailed work schedules for the following jobs, paying particular attention to the *content, order* and *timing* of tasks.
(i)   Coffee shop or restaurant waiter/waitress.
(ii)   Commis chef.
(iii)   A part-time job that you do or have done outside of college.

**Techniques of Control**
The exercise of control over his area of responsibility is a key element of the supervisor's role; without control the most well-conceived plans can be wasted. We need to consider how control is actually exercised and examine the practical aspects of this controlling function.

The use of work rosters and work schedules represents an important aspects of control because these provide the supervisor with a basis for testing whether or not the work has been carried out. The work roster enables him to oversee and therefore control staffing, by telling him who is working where and for what period of time. The work schedule specifies clearly who should  be doing what task and at what time; this enables the supervisor to check that the task has actually been done, within the allocated time and in the correct order.

Control techniques should therefore be employed to establish the following regarding the completion of tasks:
(i)   The name of the person who is doing a given task.
(ii)   If the task is being done in conjunction with other tasks.
(iii)   If the task is being done within the specified time.
(iv)   If the task is being done to the required standard.
(v)   If the task is being done according to health, welfare and safety requirements.

If the supervisor establishes that one of the above is not being carried out according to plan, he will be required to instigate remedial action of some kind. We will first of all examine the techniques that a supervisor might employ in carrying out his controlling function. These controlling techniques usually take the form of *inspections* or *checks.* Large firms employ inspectors in an official capacity to scrutinise the work but the function of inspection and checking in most organisations will be carried out by the supervisors. It may be done in an informal manner, by walking around the section and keeping an eye on such things as the work progress, the amount of waste or the level of stock. A more thorough and therefore more formal approach is to adopt a series of time and quality control check-lists.

We will consider the way in which these may be drawn up and used. The floor supervisor, in our earlier example, may wish to carry out a periodic check of the work of the chambermaids on her floor. In order to formalise and standardise this procedure she may use a standard form for the purpose, an example of which is shown in figure 16. This form enables her to classify the quality of housekeeping in each room on her floor and also to maintain a check on the quality of her staff.

## NOTHUMBERLAND HOTEL
Housekeeping Department Work Check List

Floor..........Room No.............

Floor Supervisor..................

Staff Involved...................

| ITEMS | Good | STANDARD Satisfactory | Poor | ACTION TAKEN |
|---|---|---|---|---|
| CARPETS<br>   Vacuum Cleaned | | | | |
| FURNITURE & FITTINGS<br>   Damp Dusted<br>   Polished | | | | |
| BEDS<br>   Blankets<br>   Sheets<br>   Pillowcases<br>   Mattress | | | | |
| HIGH CLEANING<br>   Curtain Rails<br>   Door Ledges<br>   Cupboards<br>   Ledges | | | | |
| LOW CLEANING<br>   Beneath Furniture<br>   Corners<br>   Radiators<br>   Skirting Boards | | | | |

Fig. 16 *An example of a Housekeeping Item Check-List*

## Student Activity No. 3.18
Using the same type of standard form that is used in figure 16 draw up an item check list the same floor supervisor might use for inspecting:
  (i)   The bathrooms and toilets on her floor.
  (ii)  The hallways.
Supervisory control techniques should influence the efficiency of the working environment that any given supervisor is responsible for. Not only will he need to be in control of the labour force in his section but also the equipment and the materials that they use. A good supervisor will carry out regular *maintenance checks* on all equipment in his section, ensuring that it is operating in a safe and efficient condition. Any faults in the equipment that might be observed should be reported to the maintenance staff for checking and repair and where a piece of

equipment is seriously affecting the efficiency of the section's work, because of continual breakdown, he may recommend to management that this piece of equipment be replaced. Management will then have to balance the costs of capital investment into new equipment against a potential gain in productivity as a consequence of replacing the defecting equipment.

The supervisor will also carry out regular *material control checks;* these might take the form of stock control checking, as in the case of the school meals, catering supervisor checking and recording levels of stock in the food store, or they might take the form of the floor supervisor checking that adequate supplies of cleaning fluids, soaps etc. are available in the housekeeping store.

The checks that the supervisor might make may be done on a *routine* basis ie. weekly, monthly, annually etc., depending upon the size of the section, the number of staff involved and so on. Routine checks, because of their regularity, are predictable and staff can often prepare in advance for them, creating an appearance of the quality of work, that may not fairly represent standards that are normally kept. To prevent against such an eventuality, a diligent supervisor will, in addition to making routine checks, carry out *spot-checks,* to ensure that his staff are maintaining standards at all times and not simply preparing for the routine checks. The *frequency* that checks occur is something that it is important to consider; normally routine checks should take place on an employee's work at least twice during the working day or working shift. The first of these will be at the beginning of the work period: this will ensure that the member of staff has everything he requires to start the work, that he has started correctly and on time. The second check will take place before the work of the member of staff, or the whole section, has been completed: this will ensure that the work is being completed correctly, to the required quality and within the time required.

A supervisor who is seen to be constantly checking on staff, noting their performance and scrutinising the quality of their products may be viewed with some distrust by his staff. The frequency with which a supervisor makes his checks must not therefore impinge upon the responsibility that an individual staff member feels he may hold. In contrast, if a new trainee has just begun working within the section, the supervisor may check his work more regularly not only from the point of view of quality control but also to deal with any of the trainee's problems, to build up his confidence and generally help him through the introductory phase of the work experience.

Controlling techniques should therefore be applied by supervisors carefully and sensitively, they need to be able, in carrying out their checks, to be seen to be in control and aware of all the daily work activities but at the same time they should avoid being viewed with suspicion or mistrust by the members of staff in their section. To facilitate this we will consider the various supervisory styles that may be employed.

**Student Activity    No. 3.19**
Draw up the following for use by the supervisor in your college training restaurant or coffee shop.
  (i)   An item check list for checking laying up procedures, including reference to cleanliness of cruets, correct placing of cutlery, availability of napkins, menus etc.
  (ii)  A control timetable, bearing in mind timing of first and last checks, time for spot-checks etc.
  (iii) Write a brief assessment of other controlling techniques that it may be necessary to apply eg. staff dress, continuity of service, furniture/fittings check list. Discuss the provision of such controlling techniques with other members of your group.

**Supervisory Styles**
In assessing the various styles that a supervisor might adopt we should refer to section C of the previous study book, where we considered the various leadership styles that a supervisor or manager might use. Although the correlation between style of leadership and style of supervision is not a strict or rigid one it is argued by most that the supervisor's role is essentially one of leadership. As we have seen throughout this and the previous study, the supervisor as a 'link man', as 'liaison' or as a 'front-line manager' will also play a part in a working relationship with management and superiors in which he will not be playing a strictly leadership type role.

The leadership styles classified in the previous study guides, authoritarian, democratic and laissez faire, represent the pure or theoretical forms and in reality do not exist in these pure forms. It could be argued, furthermore, that a good supervisor will adapt to the needs of the organisation and the needs of the individuals within his section, using different supervisory styles according to what he feels is appropriate in a given situation and at a given time. For example, he may be required to use a strict authoritarian approach, where the application of health and safety regulations, or fire drill precautions are concerned. In contrast, he may adopt a laissez faire approach where his section is seen to be diligently and responsibly carrying out their assigned task and do not require the advice or involvement of supervisors or management. Alternatively, he may apply a democratic or consultative approach in a situation where his staff have worked and been involved before eg. banquet planning. This would enable him to lean on the experience of his staff, to introduce ideas proposed by his staff and to delegate some responsibility for completing the task to them.

## Student Activity No. 3.20

Refer back to study book II, section C, activity 12, and assess the decisions and conclusions you reached in this activity, discuss them within your group and assess whether through experience your views as to the most appropriate styles have altered at all.

Any assessment of supervisory styles that we make will need to take into consideration the following points:

(i)   The choice of supervisory style will depend upon the situation in which it is going to be applied.

(ii)  The supervisor will need to be able to adapt to different situational and individual requirements.

(iii) The health, welfare and safety of staff must be a primary concern.

(iv)  The nature of work environments places emphasis upon achieving results through people, therefore the motivation and co-ordination of staff will be an important activity.

(v)   The experience, skills and general ability of the work force.

(vi)  A review of existing rules and guidelines and the ability to innovate should these prove to be outmoded or restrictive.

(vii) Recent research has shown that supervisors who are more employee centred than task-centred are more successful in getting the job done.

(viii) Delegation, if carefully and strategically carried out, will free the supervisor from routine tasks and enable him to concentrate upon conceiving new approaches to the work or setting targets for the work force.

(ix)  The personal qualities of the supervisor; the qualities of honesty, integrity, directness, reliability, consistency, good humour, respect for others and so on, will help to engender good working relationships.

(x)   The need for appropriate and carefully conceived communication skills.

(xi)  An understanding of the working group and the individuals who comprise it.

## Student Activity No. 3.21

In your practical supervisory sessions, in the training restaurant, the coffee shop, the reception area etc, adopt different supervisory styles in different situations. Make notes on the different responses of subordinates to the different supervisory styles you have adopted in these different situations. Use your notes as the basis of your contribution to a classroom discussion on the value and usefulness of different supervisory styles.

## THE SUPERVISOR AND THE LAW

Supervisors work within restraints. These may be imposed by the organisation or they may be imposed by the external environment in which the business organisation operates. All organisations operate within a legal framework and we saw in the previous study book the importance of legislation in relation to planning the work of an organisation. No work can be planned without careful consideration of the laws which affect the work environment and working relationships that operate within it.

The supervisor will be directly influenced by this legal framework and in many instances will be responsible for ensuring that his section of the work force is fully aware of this legal framework and is seen to be working within it. The supervisor, as the link man, has to ensure that organisational and individual staff needs are satisfied within the requirements of the law. The supervisor's knowledge of the relevant legislation will therefore have to be a *working* knowledge; he will have to be able to *apply* his knowledge of legislation to the work environment for which he is responsible. We will examine some of the more important pieces of legislation and consider the supervisory application of them.

### The Health and Safety at Work Act 1974

The importance of the Health and Safety at Work Act was stressed in the last study book; all industry is now affected by the rules and guidelines that the act lays down. The Offices, Shops and Railway Premises Act 1963 still has a considerable influence over the operation of hotel and catering establishments but, because of its general applicability, we will consider the influence of the Health and Safety at Work Act.

The act requires that all working organisations formulate a health and safety policy and makes clear the position of employers and employees in terms of matters of health and safety. Adequate health and safety training must be provided for all staff and a Health and Safety Committee may also be set up to scrutinise the necessary health and safety provisions. Different companies may approach these matters in different ways providing that the legal requirements are satisfied. The Health and Safety Executive exists, with inspectorate powers to ensure that this is occurring.

The supervisor's role is to follow the health and safety requirements of the organisation and to ensure that staff in his section are trained and made familiar with all health and safety requirements. The supervisor will carry out the initial health and safety training.

(i)   As part of the on job training programme   *and*
(ii)  As part of the on job induction programme.

In the first case the supervisor will ensure that the trainee is familiar with all health and safety requirements in relation to the job he is doing and the equipment and materials he is using. This will include ensuring that all equipment is adequately guarded, that the trainee is aware of the location of the on/off switch in cases of emergency, that protective clothing is worn and so on. Many firms employ an equipment training record for this purpose, which will be signed by the trainee and counter-signed by the supervisor. This record will be designed to confirm that the trainee has had the equipment demonstrated to him, that he is aware that it is a disciplinary offence to operate the equipment without the necessary guards, that any faulty equipment will be reported to the supervisor and so on.

In the second case the supervisor will ensure that the newcomer to the firm is familiar with all health and safety procedures relating to the total work environment. This may include a description of accident reporting procedure, the location of the first aid box and identification of the official first aid officer. In addition all aspects of fire safety and fire drill procedures will be covered by the supervisor in this period of induction; this might include a 'dress rehearsal' of the procedures to be followed in the event of a fire.

Supervisors will be required to maintain health and safety standards after these initial training and induction periods are successfully completed. This will occur in an informal manner, as the supervisor observes the work of his section on a day to day basis and in a formal manner, in the form of periodic fire-drills or equipment maintenance checks. The supervisor's role in implementing the Health and Safety at Work Act is particularly important and represents a crucial aspect of his position within the organisation.

**Student Activity   No. 3.22**
  (i)   Draw up an equipment training form that might be used by supervisors to ensure that all staff are fully trained in the operation of equipment in the work place. Discuss with your tutor and other group members what you are going to include on the form.
 (ii)   Explain how the following might be used in health and safety training:
     (a) Competitions.
     (b) Role playing exercises.
     (c) Committees.
     (d) Films/Slides/Videos.
     (e) Visits.
     (f) Visiting speakers.

**The Race Relations Act 1976**
Under the Race Relations Act it is unlawful for any employer to discriminate against any potential employee or job applicant on the grounds of his race, colour, ethnic or national origins. In addition,

discrimination is unlawful if it occurs to an employee in such areas as conditions of employment, promotion opportunities, provision of training facilities, transfer to another department or in relation to any of the benefits, facilities or services that are normally available to employees. Discrimination can be defined as the unfavourable treatment of one person in relation to another. It includes the imposition of terms or conditions which, because of racial or ethnic factors, an individual cannot comply with.

Supervisors should ensure, therefore, that when they are involved with management in the recruitment and selection of new staff and also in their general treatment of staff that they do not violate the regulations of the Race Relations Act. Great care should be exercised in this area, particularly as catering staff are traditionally employed from a wide range of racial and ethnic origins. Section 5 of the Act does make an exception, where a member of a particular ethnic group has a 'genuine occupational qualification'. The exclusive employment of Indian waiters in Indian restaurants, for example, would be acceptable on the grounds of 'genuine occupational qualification' because of the need to retain the authentic ethnic flavour of the restaurant. In contrast the case of the Race Relations Board v Mecca (1976) was upheld when it was proven that a catering manager of the Mecca company discriminated against an applicant for the post of buffet assistant on the grounds of 'colour'.

### The Sex Discrimination Act 1975
The principle underlying the Act is essentially similar to that underlying the Race Relations Act. Discrimination against individuals on the grounds of sexual identity is unlawful in the areas of recruitment, terms of service or dismissal. So, for example, job advertisements must not specify vacancies for 'waiters', 'barmen' or 'chambermaids' unless the establishment employs less than six people. Within the catering industry there are certain exceptions. For example, an employer may discriminate in the provision of accommodation for 'live-in' staff because he may have 'men only' or 'women only' staff accommodation.

Supervisors must exercise extreme care in relation to the act because numerous cases have shown that false assumptions about the jobs that women (or men) can or cannot do can often be made. Job transfers, promotions, access to training facilities and holiday entitlements are all areas where the supervisor must ensure that his treatment of staff is not discriminatory on sex grounds.

### Student Activity   No. 3.23
Research D. Fields, Case Studies in Hotel and Catering Law and use the cases under the Race Relations Act and the Sex Descrimination Act as the basis for a carefully prepared classroom discussion.

## The Employment Protection (Consolidation) Act 1978

This act provides the most comprehensive legislation in terms of employment protection and represents the culmination of a considerable amount of employment legislation that has taken place in the last 25 years. The Act embraces a wide range of areas concerned with the employment situation and we will briefly consider those areas that have a direct bearing on the supervisor's role.

### Written Terms of Contract

We pointed out in the previous study book that The Employment Protection (Consolidation) Act (which we will now refer to as EPCA) requires that an employee must be provided with a written contract, or a written statement of the terms of the contract. The terms will include the names of the parties ie. the employer and the employee, the date of commencement of the contract and so on (for full details see Section B, Supervisory Studies I). Supervisors should help in the completion of this contract, ensuring that the terms are both realistic and correct and that the employee receives his copy within 13 weeks of beginning employment. To avoid confusion or ill-feeling at a later stage supervisors can assist by offering information to employees regarding details of payment during sickness, length of notice, holiday payment or any other matter over which confusion might arise.

### Dismissal

Section 54 of the EPCA gives most employees the right not to be 'unfairly' dismissed. The unfairness of this dismissal might refer to the *method* of dismissal or the *reasons* for dismissal. Industrial tribunals exist for the purpose of testing cases of unfair dismissal and these are normally involved in examining whether or not dismissal falls in to one of the following six categories:

(i) Cases where there are reasons relating to the *conduct of employees,* eg. drunkenness on duty.

(ii) Cases where there are reasons relating to the *capabilities of employees* eg. employee with deteriorating faculties.

(iii) Cases where it would be *illegal* to continue the employment, eg. the continued employment of a delivery driver who has been disqualified from driving.

(iv) Cases where the employee is not *qualified* to do the job, eg. an apprentice who fails to qualify after the apprenticeship period.

(v) Cases where genuine *redundancy* can be proved and proved to be fair, eg. where it can be proved that an individual was not 'singled out' for redundancy, for other reasons such as trade union activities.

(vi) Cases where other substantial reasons exist outside of categories (i) to (v) above.

The supervisor plays a critical role in relation to dismissal, he will act as the formal communicant between the employer and the employee and will be able to provide information and advice to both, should the question if dismissal procedure arise. If an industrial tribunal takes place to consider a case of unfair dismissal, it may well be that the evidence of the supervisor is critical in enabling the tribunal to reach its decision.

## Maternity Rights
The EPCA in conjunction with the Sex Discrimination Act and the Employment Act 1980 set out to ensure that the employment rights of a woman who becomes pregnant are not jeopardised. These maternity rights extend to being able to take antenatal visits during working hours, to receiving maternity payments from employers, to the right of not being dismissed because of pregnancy and the right to reinstatement after the confinement period.

Supervisors should, first of all, be aware of these maternity rights and ensure that employers exercise these rights. Similarly, supervisors should be able to provide staff in their section with this information and to ensure that their rights are fulfilled.

## Time Off for Public or Trade Union Duties
In the case of public duties, such as magistrates, membership of tribunals, local councils etc., employees have a right to time off from work, although employers are not obliged to offer payment. In the case of trade union duties, such as industrial relations procedures or attendance on recognised trade union training courses, employees are entitled to time off with pay during normal working hours.

In each case supervisors should make employees aware of their rights and be able to re-organise staff to cover for those involved.

The EPCA contains a wide range of details which the supervisor may or may not have to deal with, those dealt with above represent the areas most relevant to his role.

## The Employment Acts 1980 and 1982
Many elements of the Employment Acts cover areas dealt with by the Employment Protection (Consolidation) Act, differing in the specific details that they cover. The Employment Acts are noted for the influence they have had upon the balance of industrial relations. In simple terms they designate the 'do's' and 'don'ts' of industrial relations practice. In practice a trade union can lawfully call upon its members to:
(i)    Take industrial action with employers in a dispute which is 'wholly or mainly' about wages and conditions.
(ii)   Picket peacefully at their own place of work.
(iii)  Take industrial action at other firms, only if they are the direct customers or suppliers of the firm involved in the dispute.

Trade unions can no longer lawfully call on their members to:
  (i)   Take industrial action for primarily political purposes.
  (ii)  Picket a place of work other than their own.
  (iii) Strike in sympathy with workers at another firm or place of work.
  (iv)  Take industrial action in order to force an employer to grant a closed shop or recognise the union.

Much of the above will have little bearing upon workers in the hotel and catering industry as trade union membership within the industry is low. In a case where the Employment Acts might influence the activities of a union based work force, the supervisor can only offer advice as to the contents of the legislation. Supervisors would normally help to deal with industrial relations situations in the hope that any form of industrial action might be averted. The supervisor along with the shop steward can play an important role here, because at the level they work ie. in close contact with the labour force, they are able to carry out informal negotiations, defuse potentially explosive situations and work to prevent a large scale dispute developing.

### The Wages Council Act 1979

This act supersedes the Catering Wages Act of 1943 and the Wages Council Act of 1959 and is designed to control the minimum wages paid to employees. This is achieved by the setting up of wages councils for sectors of the industry. Wages councils make proposals to the Government regarding wage and overtime rates, hours of working, holiday periods etc. When these have been accepted they become Wages Council Orders and have to be adhered to by law. Details of these orders have to be displayed in the appropriate premises so that they are visible to all staff.

  Wages councils exist for the following sectors of the hotel and catering industry:
  (i)   Licensed residential establishments and restaurants.
  (ii)  Licensed non-residential establishments and restaurants.
  (iii) Unlicensed places for refreshment.

It is generally regarded that the wage rates that are set by the wages councils are low and that in reality wage levels rarely fall as low as that stipulated by the wages council in question. As in the case of the previous legislation we have considered, the supervisor's main role is an advisory one, pointing out to employees in their section their rights under the Wages Council Act and representing their case to management should any problems arise.

  We should briefly consider the Truck Acts of the nineteenth century which stipulated that workers should be paid in wages for their efforts and not in kind, in the form of tokens or tickets. Certain agreed deductions from wages can be made for such things as board and lodgings, meals, tools etc. but only if they are realistic in terms of their value.

We have considered some forms of legislation, the knowledge of which is crucial to the supervisor's role. The good supervisor will ensure that he is not only familiar with current legislation but also with changes to existing legislation and new legislation as it is enacted.

## Student Activity No. 3.24

Go to your college library and obtain a copy of the HCITB training video, entitled 'Reasonable in all the Circumstances' and view the video, either in a library viewing booth, or as a group in your class. Use the video as the basis for a classroom discussion on 'unfair dismissal'. How would knowledge of Section 54 of the Employment Protection (Consolidation) Act 1978 have affected the outcome of the tribunal?

## INTERVIEW TECHNIQUES

We examined in some detail in section A the techniques and procedures involved in conducting a successful selection interview. Many of these apply to other types of interview that the supervisor might be involved in. The interviewer will need to plan the interview in advance; he will need to ensure that all the information necessary to conduct the interview is available to him. From this bank of information the interviewer will be able to plan his questions in advance of the interview; organising in his mind also the information that he hopes to obtain from the interviewee as a result of asking the questions. He will need to ensure that his questions are worded in such a way that they do not simply result in the interviewee replying in 'yes' or 'no' answers. In other words the interviewer and the interviewee must interact; the interview must be a two-way communication experience. The questions that the interviewer wishes to ask must also be placed into a certain order, they must not appear at random so that the interviewee cannot follow the logical sequence of the interview. In other words the interview must have a structure.

We will consider the way in which the supervisor might apply these various techniques in a range of different interviewing situations.

## The Problem Solving Interview

The supervisor plays an important part within the organisation, in his role as 'trouble-shooter'. As a 'front-line' manager, he is likely to be the first person in a position of authority who becomes aware of a problem in his section of the organisation. The recognition of a problem provides the stimulus for an immediate, or fairly speedy, response; some form of action, normally in the form of a decision, will be taken to alleviate the effects of the problem. A good supervisor will make routine decisions to solve problems without consultation with management but at the same time will know when to refer more serious non-routine problems to management for their consideration.

Before we examine the conduct of the problem solving interview we will briefly consider the way in which the supervisor will carry out problem solving in his section, this will also place the problem solving interview within a context.

## The Stages of Problem Solving

The way in which a supervisor solves a problem can be broken down into a number of stages. It will not always be the case that the problem will be severe enough to require such a detailed breakdown, but it is as well that supervisors are familiar with the stages involved so that they can always apply themselves logically and systematically to any problem which they have to deal with. The stages of problem-solving are as follows:

(i) *The identification of the problem* needs to be achieved before any remedial steps can be taken eg. the malfunctioning of a machine may not be due to faulty machinery but to operator error.

(ii) *A fact-finding exercise* should be carried out to ensure that all the information relating to the problem is available.

(iii) A problem is always the effect of something else occurring, in other words it is important to *establish the cause* of the problem eg. the cause of operator error in (i) above may lie in the fact the operator has been inadequately or poorly trained, or that his level of motivation has declined, or that he has personal problems.

(iv) Once the cause of the problem has been established the supervisor can begin to work out the most suitable *solution* to the problem eg. in this case a staff re-training programme, a wages review, or a few days staff leave.

(v) The supervisor, having chosen what he considers to be the most suitable solution, must then *decide upon appropriate action*. It may be the case that one of the solutions the supervisor has worked out may require the sanction of management eg. granting a short period of staff leave, in which case action may be in the form of a memorandum recommending such action to the departmental manager.

(vi) A *review* of the complete problem solving procedure should always be carried out, this enables the supervisor to evaluate if his approach was practical, methodical and effective in the circumstances. It also allows him to judge whether he would act in the same way should a similar problem arise in the future.

## The Interview

The supervisor will carry out the problem solving interview only when he has identified the exact nature of the problem and has carried out a fact-finding exercise which has provided him with a thoroughly researched and comprehensive set of information, which is relevant to the problem. Therefore, the problem solving interview will be conducted to deal with stages (iii) and (iv) above; to establish the cause of the problem and to find a solution to the problem.

We will consider a problem that is common to the majority of hotel and catering establishments, that of high levels of labour turnover.

The problem has first of all to be identified as such: many managers and supervisors view this phenomenon as one of the 'facts of life' in the hotel and catering industry and therefore a cost that has to be offset against customers, others may not be aware that the extent of labour turnover has reached high or problematical levels.

Fact finding can take a number of forms. It can take the form of a *cost analysis,* showing how expensive labour turnover can be in terms of recruitment, induction and training. It can take the form of a *survival analysis;* obtaining statistics which demonstrate when staff are most likely to leave, after a certain period of service. It can take the form of a *staff analysis,* showing what type of staff are more likely to leave and so on. The type of problem will determine which fact-finding procedure will be adopted by the supervisor carrying out the research.

The facts found in the preceding analysis will enable the supervisor to prepare for the interview. He will first of all draw up his list of questions ensuring that they require more than a 'yes' or 'no' response. He must ensure that he adopts a manner in the interview that allows interaction to take place; interviewing can represent a traumatic or unsettling experience for some interviewees even though, as far as they are concerned, nothing is at stake. He must structure the interview so that it appears to have shape and order to the interviewee and he should build into this structure the opportunity for the interviewee to propose his own ideas regarding the problem. For example, the supervisor's questions might have been directed toward solving the problem in terms of asking questions about the training programme, rates of pay, working conditions etc. and he may find that in fact the problem lies in an uncaring and insensitive management attitude toward staff. The successful interviewer by incorporating the right manner and by encouraging the person being interviewed to communicate in a positive way, may begin to find the solution to the problem. In the case of high levels of turnover a number of problem solving interviews may reveal the same explanation for its occurrence and a solution may become evident during the course of the interview.

The successful conduct of the problem solving interview, in this case, will enable supervisors to recommend a solution to management which will provide the basis for remedial action, the success of which may be periodically reviewed.

### Student Activity   No. 3.25
With the help of your lecturer and after discussions with other members of your group, identify a problem which exists within your

department eg. slow service at peak times in the student refectory, poor student attendance during practical restaurant sessions, lack of college student union activity etc. When a range of problems have been identified allocate these amongst members of your group; once again your lecturer will need to help you in this task. Now follow the procedures outlined in the preceding section, finding facts, preparing questions, structuring the interview etc. The next stage will be to actually conduct the interview; the arrangements involved here may have to be done in conjunction with your lecturer eg. obtaining permission, setting up video-recording equiment etc. After your interview has been conducted propose what you consider to be the solution to your chosen problem and recommend this solution to the rest of your group. Each student's solution to their own problem solving interview may be discussed in turn to evaluate the most expedient course of action that needs to be taken.

## The Counselling Interview

Counselling may be defined as talking over problems with staff and trying to resolve or find remedies for these problems. Counselling represents a form of communication; the successful counsellor will be able to gain the confidence of the person for whom he is providing counsel and help that person deal with the problem which he feels he has. Counselling is therefore an important element of the supervisor's personnel function. His success in this function will depend upon his ability to communicate with his subordinates, to show genuine concern for the problems they are expressing, to offer sound advice and to act to solve the problems in question.

The supervisor in this counselling role should be able to distinguish between those areas of counselling need related to the work and those areas of counselling need related to the personal life of the employee. As a general rule, the supervisor should be concerned with the work related problems rather than those of a personal nature. The objective of counselling is to improve the overall efficiency of the organisation and it may be argued that problems relating to the personal life of employees are not relevant. However, the employee whose work performance declines because of a drastic upheaval such as a family bereavement or an unfaithful spouse, may well be helped considerably by the counsel of the sympathetic supervisor. The successful supervisor will need to carefully distinguish between the two types of problem, bearing in mind that his primary concern, as an employee of the organisation, is to maintain the efficiency of his section. Therefore, serious and time consuming personal problems of staff may need to be referred to the personnel manager of the organisation, the employee's own doctor or perhaps to a quiet chat in a local pub after work.

In maintaining efficiency in the work place the supervisor should make himself *available for consultation,* he should be willing to *discuss decisions* with his staff, he should show *interest* and *concern* for his subordinate's welfare and above all *set a good example* himself in the work place. The supervisor is a 'front-line' manager, he operates at, or close to, the point of production or the point of sale, he should therefore be able to deal with problems as they arise. He should be capable of carrying out a counselling interview almost spontaneously and should work to ensure that the problems that may arise at the point of production or the point of sale do not escalate to a serious level.

*The Approach to Counselling*
The counselling interview may therefore take a number of forms; it may be a brief discussion between the coffee shop supervisor and the trainee during food service which offers information or advice about a certain activity. It may be, in contrast, a more formal interview, where the member of staff visits the supervisor's office to discuss a particular problem which may have arisen. Whatever form the interview takes a number of basic approaches can be identified.

(i) The supervisor should initiate the discussion, to help the subordinate relax and feel confident enough to explain the nature of the problem as he sees it.

(ii) With a rather informal atmosphere having been created the supervisor should ensure that the interview is not simply an idle chat, he should ask questions which sensitively and carefully direct the interview toward solving the problem in question.

(iii) The interview may appear unstructured to the interviewee but the supervisor should ensure that his questions are sufficiently open ended to allow the interviewee to explain his position and that these questions are arranged in some order.

(iv) From time to time the interviewer should establish or confirm the points that have been made so far, this enables both to keep track of the interview, so that it does not appear to ramble without consequence.

(v) Above all, throughout the interview, the supervisor must adopt an interactive approach and employ all his skills of communication. He must explain himself clearly at all times, allowing for no ambiguity of meaning and, of equal importance, he must listen to the comments of the interviewee and note down any important points that arise during the interview.

(vi) Finally, the supervisor must close the interview; it must be seen to have a definite ending which, preferably, will conclude with an intention to act in a certain way to remedy a problem, or which leaves the interviewee with a feeling that his problem has been solved or that action is being taken to solve the problem.

Successful counselling will benefit all concerned: the employee because his problems have been dealt with, the employer because work efficiency can now be maintained and the supervisor himself who can feel satisfied that he has successfully carried out an element of his role.

## Student Activity No. 3.26

(i) Draw up the details of a work-related case that may be dealt with by a supervisor in a counselling interview.

(ii) With the help of your lecturer, simulate in class a number of counselling interviews which may be conducted to deal with the various cases developed in (i) above. Ensure that all members of the group have the opportunity to be interviewed and to be the interviewer.

(iii) Monitor each interview that takes place, noting the various good and bad points that it contains and discussing these with the other members of your group.

## An Exit Interview

Exit interviews are invaluable in an industry where a high rate of labour turnover exists. The exit interview may, in an establishment where a high rate of labour turnover exists, provide the means of lowering the rate, because it should enable the interviewer to establish why the employee is leaving. In this sense, exit interviews should not be conducted in an attempt to encourage someone not to leave the organisation but, simply to find out the reasons for the employeer's intended departure.

The techniques and procedures of interviewing already described will also apply to the exit interview, with slight modifications in certain areas. We may classify the procedure involved in the following manner:

(i) A fact-finding appraisal should take place prior to the interview to establish, if possible, the reason why the employee is leaving. It is important at this stage to establish whether the reason for leaving is 'avoidable' or 'unavoidable'. Avoidable reasons may be based upon a dissatisfaction with wages or working conditions, an inability to co-operate with other staff, lack of job enrichment, poor welfare conditions and so on. Unavoidable reasons may be based upon retirement, pregnancy or leaving the area and may make the exit interview a pleasant formality.

(ii) The supervisor should initiate the interview by perhaps expressing regret at the person's intended departure or by stating that the purpose of the interview is not to try to persuade him to stay. He should make it clear to the interviewee, therefore, that the purpose of the interview is to establish the reasons for the interviewee's intended departure from the company.

(iii) He should ask a number of prepared questions based upon the facts found in (i) and upon the employee's personnel record card. The questions should be worded in an open-ended way to allow the interviewee to respond to the questions and explain his reasons for leaving the firm more clearly.

(iv) The interviewer should pay careful attention to the manner adopted during the interview. A friendly approach would normally be recommended even if the reasons for leaving were the source of disagreement between those concerned. It should be remembered that those individuals who leave a firm will represent an image of a firm to other potential employees, in which case the best impression should be left at this final contact with the firm.

(v) When all the avenues of investigation and discussion have been pursued and the interviewer has established that there is no more to be discussed the interview should be brought to a polite and friendly close. It is at this point that company property may be returned eg. uniforms and that thanks for good service, if appropriate, be given.

The exit interview should be conducted whenever staff are leaving and for whatever reasons. They provide managers and supervisor alike with valuable information about the firm and the attitudes of staff within it, as well as providing a polite gesture at the end of a period of service.

## Student Activity   No. 3.27

(i) Draw up the details of a work-related case that may be dealt with by a supervisor in an exit interview, eg. concerning a disagreement with an employer or to seek better prospects with another firm.

(ii) With the help of your lecturer, simulate in class a number of exit interviews which may be conducted with staff who are leaving an establishment for various reasons, developed in (i) above. Ensure that all members of the group have the opportunity to be interviewed and to be the interviewer.

(iii) Monitor each interview that takes place, noting the various good and bad points that it contains and discussing these with other members of your group.

In all of the interviews we have considered in this section, the emphasis is placed upon the supervisor's ability to be able to communicate with the staff concerned, so that the ends of the interview are most successfully achieved. Whether the interview is formal and lengthy or informal and short, the guidelines described must be adhered to if the supervisor is to be effective in his role. In the next section we will further consider the supervisor's staff relations role.

# ASSESSMENT QUESTIONS

1.  Prepare a work roster that may be used by a supervisor as part of his control function, indicating dates, times, shifts, different employees etc.
2.  Prepare a work schedule for a specific job, showing details of the location of work, the tasks involved, the time taken etc.
3.  Critically assess the various techniques of control that a supervisor might use.
4.  Explain the various techniques of control that a supervisor might use and the advantages and disadvantages of each.
5.  Explain the various supervisory styles.
6.  Critically assess the advantages and disadvantages of each supervisory style as it may be applied in different situations.
7.  Explain the provisions of the following legislation as it relates to the supervisor's role:
    (a) Health and Safety at Work Act 1974.
    (b) Race Relations Act 1976.
    (c) Employment Protection (Consolidation) Act 1978.
    (d) Employment Acts 1980 and 1982.
    (e) Sex Discrimination Act 1975.
    (f) Wages Councils Acts 1979 (inc. Trucks Acts).
8.  Compile a list of basic techniques that should be used in all types of interview.
9.  Identify the various stages of problem solving.
10. Explain the important points to consider when conducting a problem solving interview.
11. Explain the important points to consider when conducting a counselling interview.
12. Explain the important points to consider when conducting an exit interview.

# Formal Staff Relations

The importance of staff relations has been stressed on many occasions throughout this and other study books; the success of the supervisor hinges upon his ability to influence staff relations in such a way that both the staff and the organisation as a whole benefits. When a particular supervisory approach to staff relations has been shown to be successful then it becomes a part of the procedure of the organisation, in other words the approach becomes formalised. It is in this way that the personnel policy of the organisation develops. Any analysis of the formal aspects of staff relations and personnel policies will, as we have previously established, take into account informal practices and procedures. An effective personnel policy will therefore not only be well conceived and carefully thought out in advance, but also flexible enough to meet the changing demands of informal groups and those of the wider oganisation.

In this section we will consider the various policies and procedures that evolve to embrace staff relations in the work place, the various formal relationships that exist and the methods of representation used in these relationships and finally the negotiation and consultation procedures that are employed in reaching agreements in the various relationships involved.

## POLICIES AND PROCEDURES

We have demonstrated that varying degrees of informality exist in working relationships; informal groups and practices can influence working arrangements quite considerably. However, the effectiveness and success of industrial relations has been largely based upon the setting up of policies and procedures which govern the way in which employers and employees communicate with each other. The various policies and procedures that industrial relations are based upon, derive from traditional or customary practices within the firm itself and from government legislation. In recent years the latter has become more important in the formulation of industrial relations policy and pro-cedures.

The case for the adoption of formal policies and procedures is a strong one, despite recognition of the fact that it might be desirable to solve all industrial relations problems between employers and employees on an informal basis. Formal policies and procedures bring with them many advantages, the more obvious of these are as follows:

(i) They ensure a consistency of approach.
(ii) They clearly state the position of all involved.
(iii) Documents can be referred to at any time and are more likely to reduce the level of misunderstanding.
(iv) If earlier discussions have taken place and agreements have been made, formal policies and procedures represent evidence of this.
(v) New staff can be given a copy of the document so that continuity is maintained.
(vi) If tribunal proceedings should come about, agreed policies and procedures may provide the basis of certain cases.

The role of management and supervisors, in implementing these procedures, is a crucial one. If procedures are implemented in an atmosphere of goodwill, agreement and mutual acceptance then they are more likely to function effectively than if they are the result of an employment policy which is imposed from above with little or no discussion, consultation or agreement. Managers and supervisors in their capacity of employer representatives, should make this clear to employers before any industrial relations policy is formulated, so that the procedures that result from the policy are considered practical and sensible by all concerned. The solution to any industrial relations problem will be found in the context of the procedures that are being used, therefore, if these procedures have been mutually agreed upon by employer and employee representatives alike, both have a responsiblity to make these procedures work and find a solution to the problem. In contrast, if procedures emanate from an employer policy which has been imposed without discussion or consultation, then the emphasis of responsibility lies with the employer and his representatives.

The existence of agreed formal written procedures means that the nature of the relations between employers and employees in the future is to a degree predetermined. Therefore, managers and supervisors, on the one hand, and trade unions, or other worker representatives, on the other, must be constrained to work within the guidelines of the agreed procedures. Freedom of movement and action is, therefore, in the context of industrial relations, restricted by the procedural agreements that have been made.

In order to demonstrate this we will consider the various provisions of procedural agreements as they relate to discipline, grievance and the negotiation of wages. We will examine the role of the supervisor in the context of each.

*Disciplinary Procedure*

The Employment Protection (Consolidation) Act 1978 stipulates the need for companies to have a disciplinary procedure. The guidelines for this can be found in the Advisory, Conciliation and Arbitration Service

(ACAS) Codes of Practice. ACAS was set up by the Employment Protection Act 1975 as an independent, statutory body, for the purpose of helping to mediate, conciliate and arbitrate in the negotiations between employers and employees. The codes of practice which are laid down are not legally binding, so that although an employer could not be prosecuted for not following them, an industrial tribunal might take this into consideration when dealing with a particular case. Whilst the ACAS Codes of Practice cannot be expected to cover every case they do provide a framework for dealing with cases in a fair and consistent manner.

*The Characteristics of a Disciplinary Procedure*
All disciplinary procedures should display, in some form, the following characteristics:
- (i) They should be detailed in writing.
- (ii) To whom they apply should be clearly specified.
- (iii) Disciplinary action that might be taken.
- (iv) Management or supervisory levels that have the right to take disciplinary action and of what kind.
- (v) Communication between management and supervisors should disputes occur.
- (vi) No disciplinary action should be taken until the case has been fully investigated.
- (vii) Provision should be made for informing employees of complaints that have been made against them.
- (viii) Provision should be made for employees to state their case before any action is taken.
- (ix) Provision should be made for the employee to be accompanied if required (eg. by a trade union representative) when presenting his case.
- (x) Penalties should be clearly stated.
- (xi) Appeals procedures should be clearly stated.
- (xii) The mechanism of the procedure should allow for a quick and effective treatment of the case.

*The Contents of a Disciplinary Code*
We indicated previously that no code of practice will be totally comprehensive in its coverage of disciplinary action; the contents of the disciplinary code should therefore include reference to those areas that cause genuine disruption to the smooth running of the firm. The following are examples of the contents that a disciplinary code might include reference to:
- (i) Persistent lateness.
- (ii) Absenteeism.
- (iii) Violations of health, safety and welfare regulations.
- (iv) Theft.

(v)   Smoking in prohibited areas.

(vi)   Drunk on duty.

(vii)   Fighting or abusive behaviour.

Each of the above will vary in seriousness in terms of the number of times the action is committed and also in relation to the situation in which it was committed. For example, being drunk on duty might be viewed far more seriously if the welfare of other staff members or guests was endangered. Various penalities will therefore be attached to the actions outlined above, the nature of which will depend upon their seriousness and the circumstances in which they occur.

## The Stages of Disciplinary Procedure

The supervisor plays an important role in setting off the disciplinary procedure. The need for disciplinary action occurs normally as a consequence of something that happens in the work place; the supervisor should be the first person in a position of authority to be made aware of the action that has occurred. He has to make the *decision to act* and this normally represents the first stage in any disciplinary action.

Having made this decision he must then obtain information relevant to the case before he takes any further steps. In the case of persistent lateness, for example, the evidence might be in the form of clocking-in cards or statements from witnesses.

> Athena Hotel,
> 17-19, Gloucester Way,
> Sheffield 7,
> Yorkshire
>
> 8th April 198—

Dear Mr Belton,

    I am writing to confirm that on the above date you were given a formal oral warning regarding your persistent lateness.

    If no immediate improvement of your punctuality occurs and if this is not maintained you will receive an official written warning in line with the firm's disciplinary procedures.

       Yours sincerely

       Linda Robinson
       Reception Shift Supervisor

I acknowledge receipt of this official warning

Signature:..................... Date:.....................

Fig. 17   *An example of letter confirming official oral warning*

The supervisor should then issue the employee in question an *informal, oral warning,* pointing out the facts of the case and giving the employee the opportunity to improve upon his record of lateness. The relationship that the supervisor has with his staff is crucial at this stage; a supervisor who is liked and respected by employees in his section might be supported in his action and informal group pressures might function to pressurise the employee in question to improve his punctuality record.

If this step is not successful the supervisor will next issue a *formal, oral warning* the contents of which will also be contained in a letter confirming the facts of the formal warning, see figure 17.

If the contents of the official oral warning were ignored the next stage in the disciplinary procedure would be for the supervisor to issue a *final*

> Athena Hotel,
> 17-19, Gloucester Way,
> Sheffield 7,
> Yorkshire
>
> 11th May 198__

Dear Mr Belton,

You received from me on the 8th April 198__ a formal oral warning regarding your persistent lateness, which was confirmed in writing.

This following evidence indicates to me that you have apparently ignored this warning. You were late for work on 4 occasions in the last month, the dates of which are as follows:

15th April 18 minutes late
19th April 30 minutes late
26th April 15 minutes late
7th May 35 minutes late

If you are late for work on any occasions in the next 3 months, without adequate written explanation, you will be liable for dismissal from this company.

> Yours sincerely
>
> Linda Robinson
> Reception Shift Supervisor

I acknowledge receipt of this final warning

Signature: .................... Date: .....................

A copy of this warning is placed on your personal file

Fig. 18 *An example of a final official warning*

196

*official warning.* This would include evidence of continued misconduct, in this case lateness, after the receipt of the previous warning and also a specific time limit, representing the period in which the misconduct could be rectified before dismissal proceedings are enacted. Figure 18 is an example of a final official warning.

The supervisor would also be working in close liaison with management, informing them of the progress of the case, obtaining advice from them if necessary and discussing the next step in the disciplinary procedure. If the final official warning was ignored by the employee then the next stage in the disciplinary procedure would be for the supervisor to enforce *suspension without pay* or *dismissal* according to the nature of the misconduct. In the example explained above, on the final occasion of lateness the employee would be suspended, the supervisor would consult with management, the

Athena Hotel,
17-19, Gloucester Way,
Sheffield 7,
Yorkshire

15th August 198__

Dear Mr Belton,

### NOTICE OF DISMISSAL

Following your suspension from employment on the 15th August, the details of your case have been examined and it can be shown conclusively that despite a number of warnings your lateness for work has persisted for a considerable period.

You were given a formal oral warning on the 8th April 198__, which was confirmed in writing, and a final official warning on the 11th May 198__. It would appear that these warnings have been ignored by you, as your lateness has persisted.

Your employment with this company is therefore terminated, with effect from the 22nd August 198__, this incorporates the statutory week's notice that is due to you in these circumstances.

This letter is given to you at your request, under the Employment Protection Act in accordance with your rights.

Please find enclosed a copy of the company's appeal procedure should you wish to appeal against this dismissal.

Yours sincerely

Linda Robinson
Reception Shift Supervisor

*Fig. 19   An example of an official notice of dismissal*

personnel officer or the employer and an *official notice of dismissal* would be written and given to the employee. Figure 19 is an example of an *official notice of dismissal.*

*Appeals Procedure*
The appeals procedure that a firm implements will be drawn up and made available to all staff. Many organisations have their own appeals procedure where dismissal is concerned, particularly where dismissal is made by supervisors or management. Employees have the right to have their appeal heard at an industrial tribunal. In some cases appeals are heard as part of a grievance procedure although it is generally advisable to keep appeals and grievance procedures separate.

It is important to stress that whether an appeal is dealt with within the organisation or by means of an industrial tribunal it should be done quickly. Employees are normally given a time limit eg. 1 week, within which to lodge their appeal.

## Grievance Procedure
The Employment Protection (Consolidation) Act 1978 places a legal obligation on all employers to include in their written contract of employment with employees, details of how they might take up a grievance procedure within the company. A grievance procedure can be pursued by an employee if he feels that he has been unfairly or unjustly treated by the organisation, in respect of such things as working conditions, promotion, pay etc.

A grievance procedure will follow a number of stages, each stage involving higher management levels within the organisation. The importance of the supervisor in grievance procedures lies in his ability to deal with grievances at the point of origin ie. in the immediate work environment. A sensitive supervisor may detect the possible source of grievance and be able to deal with it before the problem escalates. The Commission on Industrial Relations Report on the Hotels and Restaurants Sector noted that many staff in this sector of the industry were 'unaware' of grievance procedures and many gave up their job without taking up a grievance with supervisors or managers, 'thus leaving the cause of it (the grievance) behind him unremedied and perpetuated'. As the report further indicates 'this happening on any scale could be a factor in high labour turnover figures'. For this latter reason alone, therefore, the supervisor has an important role to play in informing staff of the firm's grievance procedures.

*The Stages of a Grievance Procedure*
A firm may set up a grievance procedure to operate in the following way:
*Stage 1:* Discussion of the grievances should take place with the supervisor. If the employee receives no satisfaction at this stage he should be informed of, and proceed to, stage 2.

*Stage 2:* Discussion of the grievance should take place with management at an intermediary level. If the employee gains no satisfaction at this stage he should take his grievance to the next stage.

*Stage 3:* In many firms this may represent the final stage of the grievance procedure; it is the stage at which the employee discusses his case with senior management.

*Stage 4:* It is at this stage that the employee's grievance may be heard by the company director or employer.

As the grievance procedure develops from one stage to the next, clear written details of the case should be passed from the supervisor to middle management and so on. This will help to avoid confusion, it will clearly describe the details of the case and, finally, will allow for a clear statement of the outcome of the grievance proceedings to be made.

Finally, it should be pointed out to staff that not only are they allowed to be accompanied during any grievance procedure meetings but also that grievance procedures can be made by staff without retribution.

**Wage Negotiation**
In most industries wages are negotiated between employers and employees; collective agreements are made and wages are set at a level which is more or less acceptable to both parties. Negotiations do not always proceed amicably and, from time to time, industrial disputes occur, in which action is taken by both sides in order to bring about a pay settlement that is acceptable to them. The hotel and catering industry does not normally follow this procedure, mainly because trade union representation of the work force is at such a low level, in comparison with other industries. This means that wages are not negotiated collectively but individually; the system of 'individual contracts' represents a practice that is common throughout the industry.

The Wages Council Act 1979 is applied when collective agreements between employers and employees have not be achieved. A Wages Council will set minimum standards in relation to basic levels of pay, holiday pay, overtime rates etc., for its area of industry. Wages Council Orders lay down minimum gross wages which the employer is legally obliged to pay employees in cash, if so required.

The systems of payment in the hotel and catering industry are many and are often negotiated, not only between employees and employers, but also between employees and customers, as in the example of gratuities. The relationship that an employee develops with a customer is often a determinant of his level of income.

The supervisor has a difficult role to play in terms of wage negotiation. His first duty is to ensure that the employee is familiar with his rights and under the relevant leglisation, such as the Wages Council

Act, the Equal Pay Act etc. He should keep up to date information of this legislation and in the case of Wages Council awards, display the information in the work place. He should keep up to date records of staff wages, length of employment, holiday periods etc., so that he has a source of reference, should he be asked for advice regarding the wage structure by management. He should be familiar with the different sources of remuneration that catering workers rely upon, such as tips, gratuities, service charges, knock-offs, fiddles etc. In this way he will be fully informed of the employee's wage structure and will be able to offer detailed information which can be used by employers and employees as wage negotiation takes place.

## Student Activity   No. 3.28

(i)  Carry out research in your college library to find the different pro-
     cedural arrangements that firms adopt in relation to discipline,
     grievance and wage negotiation. Make notes on these different
     procedures and the various sources of information.
(ii) Write a short report to management recommending a particular
     system of:
     (a)  Disciplinary.
     (b)  Grievance  and
     (c)  Wage negotiation procedure that they might adopt.
In your report make reference to the advantages and disadvantages of the different procedures you discovered in your research.

## Company Policy Constraints

Supervisors, throughout the industry, will be constrained to implement company policy. We have already examined their role in relation to the setting up and implementation of various procedures. The supervisor will also be obliged, as part of his role, to enact company policy in relation to such areas as training, welfare and industrial relations. Any attempts he wishes to make, in terms of innovation or the introduction of different procedures, will have to be carried out within the constraints of the company policy. As a general rule, policy decisions will be made by management and decisions regarding the actual operation of sections of the work force will be made by supervisors. A progressive and forward thinking supervisor will pass on his innovations and suggestions to management, in an attempt to bring about changes of policy. The policy of a company must be flexible and adaptable to change and new ideas, from any source.

It will be in this way that supervisors will influence management decisions regarding policy. It is important to stress that, whilst pro-gressive supervisors are working to influence changes in company policy, they will at the same time be constrained to maintain the existing policy, even though they may feel that it is out-moded and in need of modification. The supervisor is entrusted with putting company policy into action and, conversely, it should be him who can best judge if that policy is bringing about the best results for the company. A number of examples might illustrate this point. Training needs in a particular establishment may not be satisfactorily met by the company's traditional training policy. It may be found, for example, that employees who attend a day release cookery course at a local college are being trained in outmoded techniques, inappropriate to the needs of the particular firm. It will be the supervisor of the employee in question to whom this deficiency will become apparent. It will be his responsibility to recommend to management that a more suitable course be sought and that the company policy toward training be changed to prevent something similar occurring in the future.

Welfare in its practical, applied sense refers to the provision of recreational and social facilities for the staff of an establishment. It may be found that the attitude of management toward welfare is outmoded or old-fashioned and that this is reflected in their welfare policy. Supervisors work in close contact with the work force and may well be able to present to management the best appraisal of the welfare needs of the work force. If the company's welfare policy is to reflect changing needs and the demands that employees bring from their wider social environment, then management must be prepared to listen to and implement the supervisor's point of view and recommendations on these matters.

It is in the field of industrial relations that the constraints of company policy may be felt most seriously. A supervisor might, for example, be expected to maintain the company's industrial relations policy in the context of increasing worker dissatisfaction, in relation to wages, conditions of service, working conditions etc. Policy decisions can sometimes take a considerable length of time to change and this presents the supervisor with serious problems in maintaining the good-will of the work force. He may find himself defending a policy decision to his subordinates which he does not personally agree with but finds he is relatively powerless to change.

Good working relationships between supervisors and management should prevent the situation from becoming intolerable for the supervisor but in the field of industrial relations the supervisor often finds himself in an invidious position. His 'middle man' or 'link man' role within the organisation can place him in a 'no-mans-land' in relation to the divide that can exist between management and the work force, if an industrial dispute occurs. We will consider this in more detail in the next section.

### Student Activity   No. 3.29
With specific reference to the areas of training, welfare and industrial relations, explain the most effective means by which the supervisor might:

(i)  Work with management to put into operation an element of company policy which they did not necessarily agree with  *and*
(ii)  Represent to management the views of the work force with regard to changing the existing company policy.

## REPRESENTATION, CONSULTATION AND NEGOTIATION

We have seen throughout these study books the way in which managers and supervisors alike represent their employers and the various policies and objectives which they put forward. The preceding discussion of disciplinary and grievance procedure indicated the employee's right to be accompanied by 'friend's' during the progress of disciplinary or grievance procedures. In industry, in general, the role of worker representation is carried out by trade unions of a variety of different types, who represent different crafts, industries and groups of workers. However, where the national average trade union membership is currently 52%, the figure for the hotel and catering industry is 5%. There are a variety of reasons why trade union membership is generally low within the industry, some of these are: the system of individual contracts, the high level of staff fragmentation, the large number of casual staff employed and so on. If a trade union is going to represent a sector of the work force then it has to obtain recognition by the employers in the industry concerned. When a union has obtained recognition it then becomes the official representative of the work force and is able to negotiate and enter into consultation with employers regarding matters of pay, working conditions etc. Without this official recognition no formal framework for discussion, negotiation and consultation exists. This factor tends to encourage employees to rely on the system of private negotiation between themselves and management, leading to the formation of individual contracts, which has the effect of further fragmenting the work force because of secrecy and suspicion about the privately negotiated contracts.

Against this background it is difficult for trade unions to establish any meaningful working relationships within the catering industry. This generalisation is not completely accurate because in sectors of the industry such as the industrial and welfare sectors, some degree of unionisation has taken place, allowing for a negotiating structure to develop. However, in the vast majority of catering units where the numbers employed are small, the informal structure and close working relationship between employers and employees tends to reduce the likelihood of any trade union structure developing.

### Industrial Democracy

We have examined the way in which some managers and supervisors adopt a democratic style of leadership, allowing the workforce in their department or section to participate in the running of that department or section. Where the work of the organisation is concerned this approach can have many advantages, it allows supervisors to use the experience that might exist in their sector to gain advice regarding the most sensible way of going about a particular job. Since the Bullock Report of 1975, various forms of worker participation, involvement and representation have been recommended to increase industrial democracy. Where many industries and firms have welcomed and implemented job centred participation, as described above, they are reluctant to implement any other forms of participation at management or board level. The main reasons for this are as follows:

(i)   Worker representatives may be seen as lacking sufficient knowledge of the decision making process.

(ii)  Worker representation is sometimes viewed as undermining the power of managers and proprietors alike.

(iii) Worker representatives are sometimes regarded as being obstructive, only having other worker's interests at heart.

(iv)  Worker representatives may not be fully committed to the company objectives therefore may not make a constructive contribution.

(v)   Worker representation may be seen as a threat to secrecy and the possible leakage of commercially sensitive information.

(vi)  The election of work place representatives can often have a divisive effect amongst the work force, particularly if a trade union exists within the firm and is not officially recognised by the firm. In this situation the trade union might feel by-passed.

(vii) Large work councils or consultative committees tend to be cumbersome and rather slow-moving.

So, although worker participation and industrial democracy may be regarded, in principle, as being something which is beneficial to industry as a whole, there is a reluctance, in practice, in many industries to set up a framework for its development.

It is possible within the hotel and catering industry particularly, because of the low level of unionisation, that industrial democracy may be achieved and operated with some success. If forms of worker participation are achieved at all levels of the organisation ie. job centred, management centred and board centred, then this can lead to the organisation becoming an integrated and cohesive whole. Through the structure of consultative committees and involvement in the negotiating and decision making procedures, the work force can feel that they are participating in, and making a contribution to, the running of the firm.

## Consultation
Although the value of integration is obvious, the way in which it might be achieved is more difficult; we have already considered the problems

involved with introducing forms of worker participation. We will now examine the practical aspects of achieving integration by means of worker consultation.

It should be pointed out, first of all, that consultation is a mode of communication, it will therefore be two way and interactive. If consultation is viewed in this way it is likely that decisions that are made will have gained from the contribution of the staff and that 'a higher degree of worker/management participation will develop in the future. It is also essential, therefore, that the elected representative *is* representative of the work force and is recognised by them as being such.

Formal consultation can take place at a number of levels, this is largely determined by the size of the organisation. It is possible in a large organisation for a kind of formal consultative hierarachy to exist, where consultative committees exist at job, management and board levels. To enable us to fully appreciate and understand the nature of consultation we will examine the nature of consultative committees, bearing in mind that more than one may be structured into the organisation.

*Consultative Committees*
Consultation will take place in meetings which are usually known as consultative committees. These committees will meet periodically, on at least a two-monthly basis, and will represent a formal group within the organisation. The group will be *structured* and will be made up of *official positions* such as chairman, secretary and so on. The business of the consultative committee will follow an *agenda,* which will have been distributed by the secretary, well in advance of the next meeting to all members of the committees. Items on the agenda might include: safety matters, customer complaints procedure, duty rosters, uniform etc. All members of the committee will have a role to play, will represent an area of the organisation, either a department or a section of the work force and will be restrained to work within the framework of the committee.

Consultative committees are likely to be set up initially by pro-gressive and forward thinking management but, in order to obtain the most benefit from them, participation and involvement of all kinds should be encouraged. This may be achieved by following these guidelines:

(i)   The aims of the committee should be clearly stated at the outset and from then on defined by the agenda ie. the committee will have specific terms of reference.

(ii)  Specific rules should exist covering areas such as the election and co-option of members, taking of minutes, providing information to the work force, the role of the chairperson and so on.

(iii)   If trade union membership exists within the organisation but is not formally represented on the consultative committee it should be ensured that all decisions made are communicated to the officials of the trade union in the organisation. They may be requested to attend when certain issues are discussed.

(iv)   The chairperson should employ communication skills to ensure that all members of the committee have the opportunity to air their points of view, that a reasonable amount of time is allocated to discussion topics and most importantly, to ensure that some decision has been taken and a recommendation for action has been made. This will ensure that the committee is seen to have a meaningful purpose and is not simply part of a cumbersome bureaucratic procedure.

(v)   The secretary should always distribute the minutes of the meeting to all members of the committee so that they can be considered well in advance of the next meeting (they are sometimes sent with the agenda for the next meeting).

Carefully conceived and well ordered consultative committees can prove very beneficial to the organisation: they help to integrate the work force with management, they draw on a wider range of resources than an authoritarian or monopolistic approach, and they establish a formal communication structure which can improve the overall efficiency of the organisation.

### Student Activity   No. 3.30

You are an employee/staff representative on the consultative committee of a large hotel, you have received your agenda which contains the following topics:

(i)   Attracting new business.
(ii)   Induction of new staff.
(iii)   New equipment.

Explain in detail how you would go about your preparation for these topics prior to the meeting and write down some of the points that you might feel it is important to raise in the committee meeting.

### Negotiation

The fundamental difference between consultation and negotiation is that, where the former is essentially a problem solving and investigative activity, the latter is a bargaining exercise, designed to secure a 'deal' for the participants in the negotiating process. The two processes should not be seen to overlap. Problems often arise if, for example, the trade union shop steward who acts as the worker's representative on the consultative committee, is then expected to negotiate a better wage deal for the work force. The dual nature of this role can cause considerable strain upon him.

Negotiation takes place within a recognised 'bargaining unit' which will normally be made up of representatives of both parties in the negotiations; this might be managers and supervisors representing the company, on the one hand and trade union or worker representatives on the other.

The process of negotiating is not unlike a game of chess, where opening gambits are employed, strategies are used, certain calculated sacrifices are made and bluff is an accepted part of the game. Quite often, as in chess, no apparent 'victory' is achieved and the sides tame their aggressive stance and settle for an 'honourable draw'. The opening of negotiation is therefore quite crucial, both sides often present a negotiating position which they may well recede from at a latter stage of the negotiation. Quite often the opening demands are intentionally rather general so that more specific details can be negotiated during the course of the meeting. Negotiation, if successful will strike an acceptable balance between the 'demand' of one group and the 'offer' of another. In striking this balance many points will be exchanged by the negotiators, 'clarification' will be requested, adjournments will be required, consultation with other parties will be needed and a great deal of time and patience will need to be available. Essentially, the success of the negotiator will depend upon his ability to successfully employ strategies and tactics, his ability to exercise inter-personal communication skills and his ability to exercise self control when he might feel exasperated and frustrated with the slow progress that is being made.

Negotiation represents a communication process and all those involved in it should be aware of this. Therefore negotiators should attempt to state their position clearly and concisely, they should make efforts to understand the other side's point of view, they should be well informed about *both* sides of the argument and they should use all their communication skills to ensure that an agreement is reached, which is acceptable to all involved in the negotiations.

### Student Activity   No. 3.31
Go to your college library and research 'negotiation' and 'collective bargaining'; in particular you will need to refer to the guidelines offered by the HCITB, ACAS and the Industrial Relations Code of Practice, paragraphs 71-95. When you have done this draw up a check list of practical points to bear in mind when negotiations are entered into, the points you make should be applicable to both sides of the negotiating table.

### Further Reading
Staff Management in the Hotel and Catering Industry: J.L. Magurn
The Supervisory Hand Book: J. Reay
Personnel Management in the Hotel and Catering Industry: M.J. Boella

Hotel and Catering Supervision: K.J. Gale and P. Odgers  *MacDonald & Evans*
Manpower Management in the Hotel and Catering Industry: T. Hornsey and D. Dann

## ASSESSMENT QUESTIONS

1. Explain in detail the characteristics of a disciplinary procedure.
2. Explain in detail the characteristics of a grievance procedure.
3. Explain in detail the characteristics of wage negotiation.
4. Explain the way in which procedural agreements may affect the supervisor in terms of:
   (a) Discipline.
   (b) Grievance.
   (c) Wage negotiation.
5. Explain the advantages and disadvantages of formal policies and procedures.
6. Describe the constraints that a company policy might have upon the supervisor in relation to:
   (a) Training.
   (b) Welfare.
   (c) Industrial relations.
7. Explain with the use of examples the way in which a supervisor maintains company policy.
8. Explain in detail the role of the supervisor in:
   (a) Disciplinary proceedings.
   (b) Grievance proceedings.
   (c) Wage negotiations.
9. Describe the importance of welfare in maintaining staff relations.
10. Explain the role of trade unions in relation to wage negotiation.
11. Describe the way in which a trade union may contribute to sound relationships within an organisation.
12. Distinguish clearly between consultation and negotiation.
13. Explain the role of the work place representatives in the context of industrial democracy.
14. Explain the arguments for and against worker participation and representation at different levels of the industry.
15. Analyse the contribution of consultation and negotiation to integration within industry.
16. Explain clearly the role of consultative committees.
17. Describe the way in which negotiation may be structured to bring about the most beneficial results.
18. Explain the nature of formal consultation, in terms of its process and the effects that it might have.

# CONCLUSION

In this study book we have placed the emphasis upon the practical aspects of the supervisor's role. The practice of supervision is, in fact, the test of supervision; until the supervisor applies what he has learned about supervision he will not be able to assess his abilities in this field. It has been argued that the qualities of good supervision cannot be taught, they can only be learned by experience. However, experience takes a long time to accumulate and, in the course of gaining experience, mistakes are invariably made on the way. This and the preceding study books are designed to help the potential supervisor, or manager, to avoid some of the pitfalls that he may encounter on the way to learning his trade. Wherever possible therefore, it is intended, by using these study books, that the potential supervisor will have learned something about supervision and can then test out his or her learning by applying it in different situations.

Finally it should be emphasised that the supervisor's role should not be seen as unchanging. Not only will the supervisor be ready to react and adapt to the changes that are occurring in the work environment, he should also be aware of the significance and importance of his position in the organisation and be ready to develop himself and instigate changes that may be beneficial to working conditions in general. Good supervisory practices are often the lynch-pin of successful organisations, they should therefore be given thorough care and attention so that this success is maintained.

# Index

achievement of results, 82, 83
advertisements, 142, 143, 144, 145
Advisory, Conciliation and Arbitration Service (ACAS), 134, 193, 194, 206
alienation, 22
appearance, 43
appraisal, 91
Argyris, G. 43
assessment, 129, 130
attitudes, 8-10, 36, 48

Beynon, H. 112
Blauner, R. 22
Boella, M. J. 164
business climate, 72
business organisation, 71, 73-75

Catering Wages Act 1943, 183
check-lists, 173, 174
collective bargaining, 206
college environment, 16
communication, a definition, 25, 30
communication and the individual, 28, 29, 30
communication and the organisation, 75
communication and tone, 44, 45
communication, formal, 107, 108
communication, forms of, 27, 28, 30
communication, informal, 39, 107
communication, non-verbal, 47, 48
communication, the process of, 26, 27, 30, 107
communication, verbal, 46, 47
company policy constraints, 200
consultation, 110, 202-205
consultative committees, 204, 205
contract of employment, 18, 91
control, 59, 97, 98, 122, 123, 128, 167, 173, 174, 175
controlling, a supervisory function, 81
Cooley, C. 31
costs, 140
counselling, 187, 188
customer complaints, 64, 65
customer environment, 50, 51
customer relations, 45, 46, 61

decision-making, 83, 84
delegation, 59, 75, 80
democratic approach, 105, 106
de-skilling, 89
directing, a supervisory function, 80, 96, 97

disciplinary procedures, 133, 134, 193, 198, 200, 202, 205
duty rotas, 16, 80, 87

economy (state, laissez-faire, mixed), 72
Employment Protection (Consolidation) Act 1978, 91, 99, 163, 182, 193
Employment Acts, 1980, 1982, 182
employment records, 162
environment, 3
ergonomics, 88

family and attitudes, 9
feedback, 75, 97, 117
forecasting, demand, 121
forecasting, supply, 121, 122
fringe benefits, 132

goals, 90
gratitudes, 132, 200
grievance procedure, 110, 133, 134, 198, 199, 202, 207
group attitudes, 36
group cohesiveness, 36, 37
group influences, 21, 22, 41, 99
group norms, 35
groups formal, 33, 34
groups, informal, 34-36
group types, formal, 33, 34
group types, informal, 34-36
group types, primary, 31, 32
group types, secondary, 31, 32

Hawthorne Experiments, 40, 41, 101, 110
Hotel and Catering Industrial Training Board (HC1TB), 19, 115, 206
Health and Safety at Work Act 1974, 92, 93, 99, 101, 112, 113, 178, 179
Health and Safety Committee, 178
Health and Safety Executive, 93, 178
heredity, 3
Herzberg, F. 101, 112
home environment, 16
hygiene factors, 101

image of the firm, 61, 62
incentives, 132
induction, 98-100, 126, 151-153, 178
induction check-list, 164
induction programme, 152, 153
industrial democracy, 202, 203
Industrial Relations Act 1971, 99
industrial relations, 192
information provision, 99, 100
inspections, 173
intelligence, 8

intelligence quotient, 8
interactive selling skills, 62, 63
interviews, 126, 146, 147-151, 189
interview grading form, 148
interview planning, 147
interview structure, 149, 150
interviews, counselling, 187, 188
interviews, exit, 189, 190
interviews, problem-solving, 185, 186

job analysis, 84, 124, 125, 126, 146
job chart, 158
job content, 156, 158
job descriptions, 123, 124, 126, 142, 143, 145, 146, 158
job design, 84
job enlargement, 161
job influence, 22
job rotation, 160, 161
job satisfaction, 158, 160
job security, 117
job specifications, 125, 126, 143, 144, 145, 146
job title, 145
job training, 151

labour market, 140
labour sources, 141, 142
labour turnover, 135, 143, 159
laissez faire approach, 106
leadership styles, 104-106, 176, 177, 202
line organisation, 21
line management, 75

Magurn, J. D. 164
maintenance factors, 101, 112
manpower needs, 120
manpower plan development, 120-122
manpower planning, 141
Maslow, A. 49, 50, 104, 164
mass media and attitude, 10
maternity rights, 182
Mayo, E. 40, 41, 101, 110
McGregor, D. 109, 161
memoranda, 108
menu planning, 93-95
method study, 157
Moreno, J.L. 37, 38, 110
motivation and needs, 11, 49, 50, 109
motivation to work, 11, 101, 104
multi-skilling, 127, 135, 160

needs, 11, 49, 50, 109
negotiation, 201, 202, 205, 206
numerical ability, 7

Office, Shops and Railway Premises Act 1963, 92, 93, 178
open ended reports, 128
operation, a supervisory function, 80
oral ability, 7
organisation, 20, 21, 33, 73, 74, 156
organisation, a supervisory function, 79
organisational evaluation, 156
organisational influences, 19
organisation needs, 140, 158, 159
organisational objectives, 89, 93, 96, 103, 104, 112, 128
over skilling, 122, 143

Payment of Wages Act 1960, 164
payment, systems of, 164
perception, 13, 14
peer group and attitude, 9
performance appraisal, 159, 160
performance appraisal form, 126
performance analysis, 100, 101
performance assessment, 128, 129
performance, influences on, 133
performance levels, 127
performance needs, 162
personal record files, 162, 163
personality, 3, 4, 60
personality and staff interactions, 24, 25, 30
personality types, 24, 25
personnel functions, 83-85
personnel policy, 192
planning, a supervisory function, 77, 78
planning production and service, 88, 89
planning, the legal aspects, 91-93
planning, the process, 89-91, 111
planning the work, 87, 88
policies, 192-194
problem solving, 185
profitability, 77

quality control, 84, 85

Race Relations Act 1976, 91, 125, 179, 180
records, 162
recruitment, 91, 110, 123, 125, 146
representation, 202
roles, 17, 59
role-set, 17
routines, 101

Saab experiments, 161
Schein, 73
school and attitudes, 9
school environment, 16
selection, 126, 146
selection forms, 146
selection procedure, 126, 127
Shops Act 1950, 92, 93
situational demands, 57-59, 61
situational skill
social animal, 1
social contacts, 63
social environment, 16
social skills and appearance, 43
social skills and the work situation, 43
social skills and communication, 44, 45
social skills defined, 42, 43
social skills in sectors of the industry, 51-53
social skills, the development of,
sociograms, 37, 38
spatial ability, 7
split-shifts, 170
staff development, 159
staff position, 49, 50, 55-57, 60, 80
staff records, 162
staff relations, 55-57, 60, 192
staff turnover records, 162
staffing evaluation, 140, 141
staffing levels, 103
staffing needs, 139-141
standards, 81, 95, 96, 110
supervision and leadership, 106
supervision and motivation, 109-111
supervisors and the law, 178
supervisor's position, 75, 77 81
supervisory control, 97, 98
supervisory functions, 76-81
supervisory responsibilities, 81, 82
supervisory styles, 176, 177

targets, 90, 93, 94, 112
tasks, 95, 96
task training record, 154
Taylor, F. W. 157
trade unions, 117, 164, 182, 183
training, 153, 154, 155, 178
training, benefits to employees, 113
training, benefits to employers, 114
training methods, 114-117
training needs, 114

training, off the job, 115
training, on the job, 115
training policy, 121
training programme, 153, 154
training record, 162
training timetable, 155
Truck Acts, 183

verbal ability, 7
Volvo experiments, 161

wage negotiation, 199, 207
wages, 132
Wages Council Acts 1959 and 1979, 183, 207
Wages Council Order, 183, 201
welfare, 117
Western Electric Co. 40
work conditions, 92, 93, 131
work design, 90, 111
work environment, 112
work environment and attitude, 9
work environment, influences of, 18
work experience, 143
work measurement, 157
work rosters, 167, 168, 170, 173
work schedules, 90, 91, 111, 171
work specification, 111
work study, 157, 158
worker representation, 203

# Purchasing Costing and Control for Hotel and Catering Operations

**Peter Odgers FHCIMA., Cert. Ed.**

Any study of hotel and catering operations must, inevitably, include the elements of purchasing, costing and financial control involved in those operations. The financial investment involved in setting up and running such an operation will demand optimum profitability from any such investment and, therefore, be blended with an approach that satisfies customer demands for the product or service offered for sale. The materials used in hotel and catering operations are either of an essential or attractive nature to both staff and customers alike. These reasons therefore emphasise the need for control of materials used, in both their standard and their quality. A hotel and catering operation will also need to ascertain its financial efficiency at any given time, in order to monitor its progress towards achieving targets it has been set.

The material in this book covers these aspects of purchasing, costing and control with a supervisory and managerial approach, it is intended to provide students at all levels with an understanding of all that is involved in dealing with these aspects of hotel and catering operations. The study book covers aspects of Purchasing, Storage, Stores Procedures, Basic Costing, Portion Control, Pricing, VAT and Cash Control at a basic level. Expanding these aspects at level two to include Costing Concepts, Departmental Costing and Pricing Methods and including an expanded section on the preparation of accounts through to a Balance Sheet. Level three covers aspects of Forecasting, Budgeting, Variance Analysis, Operating Statements, Costing of Labour and Overheads, Cost Behaviour, Marginal Costing, Computerisation and Case Study Applications. The study book not only provides students with a relevant and comprehensive set of texts but also with a wide range of learning aids. These take the form of student activities, assessment questions and suggestions for further reading and research. The book covers specific aspects of 1985 BTEC course submissions for BTEC Certificate and Diploma courses and for BTEC Higher Diploma Bridging Units, in addition to HCIMA Part A Food, Liquor and Business Studies and Part B Financial Management (B205) and Food and Beverage Management (B204) Studies.

Peter Odgers has a broad experience of the hotel and catering industry in both commercial and institutional operations, has been employed by Trust House Forte and Holiday Inns in aspects of Food, Beverage and Financial Control, as well as a variety of positions in smaller and seasonal type operations. He is currently Senior Lecturer in Financial and Food and Beverage Management at Westminster College and a visiting lecturer at Middlesex Polytechnic.

Copies available from:
Stanley Thornes (Publishers) Ltd
Old Station Drive, Leckhampton, Cheltenham GL53 0DN